CONTENTS

PREFACE

This book is intended for the non-specialist but educated reader who wants to have a comprehensive but succinct view of language characteristic of West Indian speakers. The reader I have in mind is either the literate adult reading for pleasure and enlightenment, or the student at the beginning stages of serious language study either at secondary level or at university level. The intended readership specifically includes teachers who are preparing secondary school pupils for CXC (Caribbean Examinations Council) English, students at the University of the West Indies who are required to sit the first-year university course, or courses in linguistics and West Indian literature.

This book must be treated as an introductory text in that I have attempted to present language data as simply as it is possible to do so objectively, thus avoiding the highly technical presentations and arguments which characterise the field of linguistics and Creole linguistics specifically. At the same time, however, there is a constant attempt to preserve scholarly objectivity, thereby presenting West Indian language within a framework of the known principles and procedures of linguistics. There is no consistent attempt made to document and explain away folksy and received beliefs about language in the West Indies, for such an attempt might do no more than perpetuate or promote such beliefs, given the extreme degree of conviction, fondness and colour inherent in such beliefs. Whereas it is extremely difficult for linguistically untrained readers to approach their own and related language with openness, it is hoped that an objective-type presentation will help to promote reflection and analysis and suppress unsubstantiated prejudice and emotion.

This book is divided into seven chapters which cover a broad area of interest. The first chapter looks at and tries to resolve problems involved in the common use of terms such as dialect, language, slang, etc. in the context of the West Indies. In chapter 2 the different varieties of language to be found in everyday West Indian society are dealt with, showing how West Indian society is similar to or different from other societies.

Although chapter 3 is the most technical chapter in the book and as such the most difficult, it is indispensable because it is the very core of the subject matter. The most difficult part of this chapter is the orthography used to represent spoken language, an orthography which is new to the non-linguist but which helps to give a more precise and unemotional representation to West Indian speech sounds. This chapter requires careful and repeated reading to be fully understood. In cases where the reader is not intensely interested in language details the general intention in this chapter is to show that West Indian language is normal language but differs in details, not principles, from language elsewhere.

Chapters 4 and 5 should be of special interest to most West Indians, who in their everyday activities are acutely aware of differences among themselves in 'accent' and history. However, the very differences among themselves in 'accent' which West Indians identify and mimic lose their very being when represented on a written page. I have therefore tried to capture differences in exclamations, words whose meanings would be misunderstood and a few other outstanding features of individual territories. Chapter 4 is not meant in any way to be a small dictionary. Chapter 5 is especially important because it contains information about the historical sources of West Indian English which is not generally well known and which should at least begin to dispel some of the myths about West Indian language.

Chapter 6, on language and culture, looks at the difficulties of representing a predominantly oral culture in writing and also gives an indication of the way in which language is used in the different cultural genres. One of the main purposes of this chapter is to explain the blending of a variety of linguistic sources in a single recognisable culture.

The book ends with an overview of language policy and practice in teaching and learning in school. The whole question of the relationship between standard and non-standard English is discussed and also the role of language in development in the context of changing values in society in the face of modern technology.

In a book of this length and type many interesting and even important features will not be included. I hope that these omissions will serve as a challenge especially to the West Indian reader, to provoke discussion, to supplement examples, to seek out further explanation and to develop more precise ideas about West Indian language. If this is done, this book will then have served a better purpose than if it were to be regarded as a reference book or an arbiter of disputes.

Peter A. Roberts

NOTATIONAL CONVENTIONS

Presentation of West Indian speech in writing is problematical for the normal reader of English because West Indian speech differs in sound and words from other varieties of English. For ease of reading I have used essentially two different systems of spelling: one, normal English orthography; the other, technical (phonetic). At the peril of being deemed inconsistent and not satisfying either linguists on the one hand or laymen on the other, what I have tried to do is to represent as many of the examples as possible in normal English orthography. Normal English orthography has the advantage that it allows for variety in pronunciation and this is especially helpful in a situation where one is giving examples of phrases and sentences which are common to the various territories but which are pronounced differently in each case.

Where I have not used normal English orthography, it is for the following reasons:

– the word does not have a well-known spelling;
– differences in sound are being highlighted;
– English spelling may be misleading.

The current spelling of English words is the result of a long developmental process and the result of general acceptance of English spelling conventions by people over the English-speaking world. Current spelling of English words does not constitute a consistent, simple and worldwide system of representing sound – this is painfully clear from the earliest years of primary education when one has to learn to spell. The objective of a technical orthography is to represent in a consistent manner each sound by one symbol and conversely to have each symbol represent only one sound. Although this may seem logical and simple, it is not simple for the layman primarily because the system is unfamiliar. Unfortunately, there is no other way of identifying accurately and efficiently to natives of different countries the sounds of the predominantly oral languages of the West Indies.

Where a technical (phonetic) representation is deemed necessary, I have chosen the following symbols to represent sounds:

Symbol	Examples

Vowels:

i	as in	sh*e*, t*ea*, m*e*, h*ea*p, b*ea*t
ɪ		h*i*t, l*i*t
e		p*ay*, h*ea*r, s*a*le, b*ai*t
ɛ		l*e*t, m*e*t
a		b*a*t, m*a*n
ʌ		b*i*rd, g*i*rl, th*i*rty (stressed vowel)
ə		*a*bout, pyjam*a* (unstressed vowel)
ɔ		h*o*t, p*o*t, b*o*ttle, c*au*ght
o		c*oa*t, n*o*te, gh*o*st, b*ow*l
ʊ		p*u*ll, f*u*ll, f*oo*t, b*oo*k
u		b*oo*t, ch*oo*se, fr*ui*t, n*ew*s
ai		b*i*te, n*i*ght
oi		b*oi*l, sp*oi*l
au		b*ou*t, sh*ou*t, h*ou*r

Consonants:

z	as in	*z*oo, ho*s*e, bu*s*iness
s		a*ss*, *s*lack, *s*o, recei*v*e, *c*eiling
k		*c*all, *k*ill, la*ck*
s		*s*ugar, *sh*oe, ca*sh*
c		*ch*urch, lun*ch*, ha*tch*
j		*j*u*dg*e, ra*g*e, bri*dg*e
z		rou*g*e
ŋ		si*ng*, bri*ng*

p, t, k, b, d, g, m, n, r, l, h, f, v, w, y represent the same sounds as in English spelling.

The English consonant symbol *th* basically represents two different sounds, as in *thy* and *thigh* (the last part of both words is identical in sound). The standard English pronunciation of these two sounds is represented by [ð] and [θ] and the non-standard West Indian by [d] and [t] respectively.

The symbol [ʔ] indicates that the vocal cords in the throat came together momentarily to separate two vowel sounds rather than there being a full articulation of a consonant in the mouth as in ah-ah, oh-oh (i.e. where the hyphen occurs). The sound is called a glottal and the process glottalisation.

The symbol ˜ put over vowels means that in the pronunciation of the vowel there is some nasalisation (i.e. air coming through the nose).

A colon after a vowel, e.g. [a:] means that the vowel is long or drawn out.

Where technical representation is used in the text it is put within square brackets, or is written in italics.

Curved brackets are used for optional elements and comments.

Quotation marks enclose quotations and meanings.

1 · *Introduction*

The term 'West Indian'

The perception, by others, of the West Indian in terms of uniformity, especially as regards language, could be taken as justification for the use of the term in the title of this book. For just as a person from the USA, when abroad, as soon as he begins to speak is labelled (mentally) by hearers with the all-inclusive term 'American', and just as people from the British Isles are almost automatically labelled 'Englishmen' (much to the distress of the Scots and Irish), so too people from Jamaica, Trinidad, etc. are labelled 'West Indian' (or 'Jamaican'). Furthermore, to many the West Indies is a single nebulous area in the New World and so no possibility of difficulty in definition exists.

However, there has been a tendency among developing nations to discard names given to oneself by others and to use one's own name. In this case, there have been no serious attempts, if any at all, to reject the name 'West Indian' even though originally it was the result of a mistake. The problems with the term 'West Indian' are firstly that it confers on the people of many different islands an identity or homogeneity which all of them do not want to be associated with; secondly the term 'West Indies' does not always refer to the very same islands or territories whenever it is used and one is not too sure whether certain specific islands are ever included under the designation 'West Indies'. The term therefore is not clear and precise.

If one were to draw conclusions from the purpose of Columbus' quest and his initial belief on landing at San Salvador (Bahamas), one might say that the whole of the New World was the 'Indies'. However, the term has obviously narrowed as a result of the increase in geographical knowledge and development in political history. From a geographical point of view the term 'West Indies' refers to the islands as distinct from the South, Central and North American landmasses. There is no essentially geographical reason why the term refers to islands seeing that the 'Indies' (i.e. China, India, etc.) were not thought to be islands. The adjective 'West' was, of course, added to rectify Columbus' original mistake.

Geography also makes use of the term 'Antilles', dividing the islands into the 'Greater Antilles' to the north and the 'Lesser Antilles' to the east. This classification, which is based on the size of the islands and their closeness to each other, excludes the Bahamas, the Turks and Caicos Islands, Aruba, Curaçao, Bonaire and Margarita, because although they are small, they are not close to the Lesser Antilles. In spite of the fact that the two terms 'Greater Antilles' and 'Lesser

Antilles' are used, in English the term 'the Antilles' (to refer to all the islands) is rare; instead the term 'the West Indies' is used. Geographically the only other group distinction that is made is the subdivision of the Lesser Antilles into the Leeward Islands and the Windward Islands. This distinction which was originally made on geographical grounds is today more of a political one.

Politically the geographical West Indies is made up of numerous entities depending not only on present political status but also upon colonial associations. It is European colonial policy above all else which determined the entities in the Caribbean by creating great distances or close links between the islands regardless of their actual distance from each other. European rivalry and the spirit of domination were so intense during the colonial period that the British, French and Dutch not only established entities of geographically close but sometimes disparate territories, but also sought rigorously to eradicate cultural, linguistic and political influences of the previous colonial power when the territory changed hands. Nowhere is this better illustrated than in Grenada where successive British and French administrations in the period 1763–1810 decimated the free population in attempting in turn to remove influences from the previous administration. European colonial policy has been so successful that in spite of basically the same colonial experience, in spite of geographical closeness and in spite of constant migration, the former British territories, the French territories and the Dutch territories seem to be worlds apart. To aggravate this situation there is the more recent US influence which is not only official in Puerto Rico and the Virgin Islands, but is also attracting the Bahamas and Jamaica to such an extent that they are fast losing traces of their British orientations.

It is British colonial policy specifically which created the political 'West Indies' and this was done by subdivision of British possessions in the Caribbean for political and religious administrative purposes. This subdivision made a distinction between the Bahamas, the Virgin Islands and the West Indies with British Guiana (a part of South America) being associated with the West Indies. The political subdivision culminated in the federation of islands called 'the West Indies', which Guyana chose not to join.

As a result therefore of a combination of geographical, political, religious and historical factors, one can identify objectively a vague association of territories in the Caribbean as 'the West Indies'. This association is also maximally identifiable in sport in West Indies cricket, and in education in the University of the West Indies. It is more important, however, for our purposes to determine whether this association is identifiable from the point of view of language.

One of the major determining factors in the subdivisions of the geographical West Indies was quite clearly, and to a great extent still is, language. In spite of the fact that migration took place across linguistic barriers, there was much more migration within linguistic barriers as the fortunes and attractiveness of territories changed from the earliest days up to the present. This has established close and extensive family ties between Trinidad, Tobago, Guyana, Barbados, Grenada, St Lucia, St Vincent and Dominica and between Antigua, St Kitts, Nevis, Anguilla and Montserrat. Jamaica, because of its distance from the other territories, stands out in this respect, but this has become less so in the last two decades as a result of the presence of the University of the West Indies.

It is evident that in the Caribbean territories which have English as the official language the people from those territories just mentioned, even if they do not regard themselves as having the same speech, would not make a major dialectal distinction among themselves as they would on hearing a native of the Bahamas or the Virgin Islands, whom they would immediately regard as American. There is, therefore, a passive perception of sameness in language among those territories previously mentioned.

Another linguistic factor of interest is the very terms 'West Indies' and 'West Indian'. It is only the English language which has a preference for these terms. French, Spanish, Dutch and Portuguese all prefer a version of the word 'Antilles' and a direct equivalent of *West + Indies* is not common.

In conclusion, therefore, the terms 'West Indies' and 'West Indian' have a specific reference and viability as far as language is concerned in that the inhabitants of certain specific territories have had a close historical relationship with Britain, with the English language and among themselves to such an extent that while admitting to differences among themselves they perceive greater differences between themselves and others. For our present purpose therefore, 'the West Indies' coincides with the following territories of the Commonwealth Caribbean: Jamaica, Trinidad, Tobago, Guyana, Barbados, Grenada, St Lucia, St Vincent, Dominica, Antigua, St Kitts, Nevis, Anguilla, Montserrat.

The term 'language'

The second half of the title of this book, 'their language', is in a way like the first: initially it seems quite clear what is meant, but under closer scrutiny it becomes increasingly controversial. A brief analysis of the term, however, will help to reduce the controversy.

First of all a distinction must be made between *language* and *a language*. This distinction corresponds basically to the distinction between the *individual* and the *society*. Language is an ability which every normal human being has and it allows him not only to communicate with other human beings but also with himself. It facilitates the transmission of ideas, emotions and desires from individual to individual and the refinement of the same within the individual. It is therefore external in the form of sound and symbols and internal as mental activity. According to this first definition then, *West Indians and their language* means West Indians and their ability to communicate ideas, emotions and desires and their ability to think.

When one talks of *a language* it refers to one recognisable, identifiable or accepted entity used by one or more communities of speakers. One is dealing with the production of language (in the first sense) by speakers in one or more communities and the recognition by the same communities and others that a single entity is being produced. In fact, recognition is much more important in the identification of a language than is identity or commonality in the production of speakers. In other words, it is not impossible or contrary to the definition of *a language* for a speaker of language X not to understand or produce the same speech as another speaker of the same language X. This is so in the case of the Chinese language, for example. Recognition in some cases is dependent to an extent on linguistic similarities in production, but in other cases it is dependent on cultural and historical identity, especially if it is within one political entity or country.

According to this second definition, therefore, when one talks of *West Indians and their language*, one is talking about production which has a measure of similarity and which is also recognised (passively or actively) by West Indians and others as the same, based on shared cultural, historical and political experience.

The distinction between *language* and *a language* can be looked at as two faces of the same coin: the two are mutually dependent and determine each other. This is best illustrated in what is called linguistic *competence*. Competence in a language (i.e. the linguistic ability every normal human being has) is a result of the fusion of an innate capacity or predisposition every normal human being is born with and the actual input from the society. In other words, in the acquisition of a language, the child, unlike a cow, horse, ape or bee, is pre-programmed to learn a language but the actual language (sounds, words, phrases, meanings, conventions) comes from the society in which the child is raised.

The two-sided nature of competence is also seen in the distinction between active competence and passive competence. Active competence is that part of the language each individual produces and controls (the idiolect). Passive competence is that part of the language, over and above active competence, which each individual has internalised from his own experience in society and makes use of to understand all the other people in society. For example, an upper-class speaker in a society does not produce the same speech as a lower-class speaker in the same society, but the passive competence of each one facilitates the understanding of the speech of the other.

The relationship between active competence and passive competence is normally subsumed under the terms *production* and *comprehension*. These two are said to have an asymmetrical relationship; that is, the latter is bigger than the former, because whereas production is simply active competence, comprehension is active competence plus passive competence. The significance of this relationship cannot be overstressed in an understanding of the linguistic competence of the West Indian. Comprehension in the West Indian extends to varying degrees over most if not all forms of standard English (directly and through radio, television, newspapers, etc.) and many forms of non-standard English. His production, on the other hand, is restricted and controlled by social and historical factors within the society.

Language and social history in the West Indies

The development of language in the West Indies has been completely dominated by the structure of the society, which in turn has been dominated by slavery, the plantation system and more recently by political independence. The plantation economy of the territories during the slavery period depended for its success upon a pyramid-structured society with sharp stratification (Fig. 1).

Owners and administrators

Poor whites

House slaves and artisans

Field slaves

Fig. 1.1   The society of the slavery period.

The structure may be considered the only constant in a society in which the people were always changing. A high mortality rate in all sectors of the population, a preference for imported replacement and increase (natural increase meant a loss of women from the labour force), changes in colonial administration in most territories and the consequent change in personnel, attempts at revolt and escape and the subsequent dislocation, post-emancipation increase in migration between territories, the post-emancipation influx of new arrivals from Asia – all these factors militated against stability and relatively homogeneous language development. Instability continues today with inter-territory migration, migration to and from metropolitan centres and general tourism. The combination of constantly changing participants within a rigid structure has resulted in societies in which there is a high degree of linguistic variation within a broadly specifiable linguistic spectrum. The rigid social structure has produced language differences between all the West Indian territories.

A comparison of Barbados and Jamaica, both of which were under British colonial rule and the influence of the English language for over 300 years, shows that there are clear differences in language between the two countries. These differences result principally from two factors: a much greater dependence in Jamaica on the importation of new Africans, especially in the late slave period, and a greater degree and amount of physical remoteness from the English language in Jamaica. In effect it has meant that whereas in both countries there is a spectrum of language varieties related to the English language, in Jamaica there are not simply more varieties but more varieties more distant from English.

A comparison of the length of British rule (approximately 160 years) and the ethnic composition of the populations in Trinidad and Guyana (a little less than half East Indian, a little less than half black and mixed, the rest white and other) would suggest a great similarity in language. It is clear, however, that whereas the East Indian presence in both countries is considerable and has influenced the language to some extent in both cases, the crystallisation of the language took place before the massive influx of East Indians. In other words, it was the early 19th century which was the critical period of formation of language in both countries and it was during the early 19th century that there were significant demographic differences between the two countries. Strategically and economically both Trinidad and Guyana were unimportant to the colonial powers before the 19th century and had small populations. In fact, Guyana did not become a single country until 1831, three years before the abolition of slavery.

Significant increase in the population in Trinidad came about as a result of turmoil in the French world and more specifically the French Caribbean (the French Revolution and the Haitian Revolution). An open-door policy in Trinidad allowed the immigration of thousands of French and French Creole-speaking refugees so that by the middle of the 19th century Trinidad was linguistically and culturally more French than English, although it was British and had never been officially a French colony. As the natural resources of Trinidad became economically and strategically more important, the British and American presence grew and was accompanied by many migrants from English-speaking Caribbean territories. The net result was that a French and French Creole-speaking territory became an English and English Creole-speaking territory.

In Guyana, on the other hand, there was no sudden and massive increase in the population before the East Indians came in the late 19th and 20th centuries. Before that the population, the majority of which lives along the coast and in towns, grew gradually by natural increase and by migration from Barbados and other Caribbean territories, principally English Creole-speaking areas. Linguistically, therefore, Guyana is English-dominated, with all the other influences being minimal. In fact, it is more difficult to differentiate a Guyanese speaker from a Barbadian speaker than from a Trinidadian, whose language has been significantly affected in its pronunciation by French Creole.

St Lucia, Dominica and Grenada in their political history have a lot in common – they all changed hands between the French and the British before finally becoming British at about the beginning of the 19th century. But whereas St Lucia and Dominica are and have always been in a chain of French influence (the four islands, Guadeloupe, Dominica, Martinique and St Lucia are next to each other and for a significant part of their history were French), Grenada is a little removed from these and historically has stronger ties with Trinidad. In fact, there is more similarity in linguistic development between Trinidad and Grenada than between Grenada and the other two. The decline in French Creole with the corresponding increase in English was similar in Trinidad and Grenada. This situation, together with other dominant cultural factors like Roman Catholicism and Carnival, and the constant traffic between the two islands, has produced more similarities in language between these two than between either one and any other territory.

St Lucia and Dominica are similar in their language situation today in that French Creole has remained strong in both countries and is the native*   language of the majority of the population. This strength is remarkable when one takes into consideration that (a) the same French Creole declined sharply in Trinidad and Grenada where it was once the native language of the majority of the people, (b) concerted attempts were made by administrative and educational policymakers and by foreign schoolteachers (a lot of them Barbadians) to eradicate French Creole, and (c) English as a world language has had so much power that it has invaded even those countries not under direct British or American control. The strong presence of French Creole in St Lucia and Dominica is reflected in all facets of the English produced by natives of these countries. However, in spite of the distinguishing speech characteristics of St Lucians and Dominicans, the generally common features of Caribbean Creole languages and the constant and widespread communication in English in and between the islands make for general similarity in English and Creole English between St Lucia and Dominica and the other West Indian territories.

The political history of Dominica runs parallel to that of St Vincent,

---

* The term *native* used here and elsewhere has no pejorative connotations. It simply refers to the first language learnt as a child.

yet the two countries have different language situations today.
Officially both islands were supposed to be under the control of the
Caribs up to as late as 1763, with both becoming British around the
beginning of the 19th century and staying so until the late 1970s. In
actual fact, however, St Vincent was under English influence from very
early times. This was facilitated by the closeness of Barbados, the early
radiator of English influence in the region, whereas Dominica,
bounded on one side by Guadeloupe and on the other by Martinique,
was very much under French influence. However, Dominica was part
of the Leeward Islands group between 1871 and 1939 and had been
politically administered from as early as 1833 from Antigua. This
however seems to have had little effect on the strong French influence
on the language.

The island of St Kitts in its early history (1623–1712) was divided into
three parts with French colonists controlling the two ends and British
the middle. Today French influence in the language of St Kitts is
practically non-existent principally because, like Barbados, St Kitts was
under constant British rule and was used by the British as a
stepping-stone for colonising neighbouring territories. It was from
St Kitts that Nevis was colonised and also Antigua. In fact, St Kitts,
Nevis, Antigua and Montserrat could be said to have had the same
kind of linguistic development creating a linguistic situation today
which is part way between that of Jamaica and that of Barbados.

The social stratification of the plantation system created in each
territory a spectrum of language varieties. The European language was
the target language and acquisition and mastery of the target was in
direct relation to social position and degree of social contact with
speakers of the target. The pyramid structure of the society was
therefore the same as the linguistic structure of the society, with those
at the top socially speaking the European language, those at the
bottom furthest away from it and those in between gradually
approximating it. Significant differences between territories are related
not only to differences in method of increase of population – that is,
dependence on importation as was the case in Jamaica and in St Kitts,
Nevis and Antigua as opposed to Barbados – but also to ratios and
social relationships between the component groups in the society. For
example in Barbados the percentage of whites was always significant
and a comparison of domestic slaves to field slaves at the time of
emancipation is also significant: Barbados 18.5 percent, St Kitts
16.5 percent, Jamaica 12.5 percent and Antigua 9.5 percent.

Another factor which affected all the West Indian territories except
Barbados was the wave of Indian, Chinese and Portuguese
immigration between 1838 and 1924. The languages of these migrants
did not have as great a structural effect on the languages in the
territories as those of the Africans before them had done, because there

were enough speakers in each territory to absorb the newcomers into the already existing language. The real effect was that since these newcomers came to act as a racial and cultural zone between the blacks and the whites and since the newcomers themselves had to learn the language of the territory, progress of the blacks and general progress towards mastery of the European language slowed appreciably. The result of this is that today there are fewer Creole features in the most non-standard speech of Barbadians than in the most non-standard speech of other West Indians.

The linguistic spectrum which exists in all the territories narrows (has fewer varieties) moving from Jamaica to Guyana to Antigua, Montserrat, St Kitts, Nevis to Barbados. In the case of Trinidad, Grenada, St Lucia, Dominica and to a small extent St Vincent, the spectrum in each case has an additional element of complexity; that is, the historical effect of French Creole.

Varieties of language

English

The wide spectrum in Jamaica challenges the definition of a language in that it calls into question the extent to which two speech varieties in a society can differ and still be treated as belonging to the same language. In St Lucia and Dominica there are clearly two different languages in operation not only because they are mutually unintelligible but also because they are considered as different by the society. In Jamaica there is some degree of mutual unintelligibility between extreme varieties, but they are not thought to be different languages by the people mainly because of the existence of intermediate varieties or, in other words, the spectrum as a whole. Viewed from a wider perspective, however, Jamaica is just a small part of the English-speaking world and the most non-standard varieties in Jamaica are not readily understood by most of the English-speaking world. Therefore it could not be the best solution to treat the whole spectrum in Jamaica and the other West Indian territories as English.

The nature of this situation is clear to all West Indians, who in spite of the many intermediate varieties in the spectrum resolve the situation into two parts: English and the rest. The term 'English' in this context is usually preceded by the adjective 'good' or 'proper'; that which is not 'good' or 'proper' English has been given many derogatory names, but the one which is least provocative as a term is 'dialect'. The term 'dialect' used with this specific reference in this context becomes increasingly problematical the closer one examines it and especially so when the term is otherwise defined in its general use as a *component of a language*. Other one-word 'respectable' terms that are substituted for 'dialect' by West Indians are 'Creole', 'slang' and 'patois'. At this point it is appropriate, in order to avoid confusion and frustration, to make some distinction between these terms.

There are three areas of difficulty in the definition of these terms: firstly there is a difference between the linguist's use of the terms and the layman's; secondly people very often believe that meanings must be fixed, permanent, clear and distinct; thirdly language is a very emotional subject and one in which everybody considers himself an expert.

Normally, correct usage is understood to be educated usage. In the case of language terms, however, educated usage must refer to usage by both linguists and educated non-linguists, for one cannot restrict the meaning of common words to the way they are used in specialised disciplines, because the precision that is required in these disciplines is not always necessary in everyday communication by laymen. Yet in the present case, as a result of the amount of vagueness which attends the use of these terms by educated non-linguists, it is better to rely more heavily on the linguistic definition of the terms.

In general, linguistic definition is based on the realisation that a language is a living thing which changes in response to social and other pressures. The meaning of a word not only changes over time but is not separable and distinct in an absolute sense from meanings of other words. In fact, one school of thought is that all meanings are basically relational; that is, a meaning becomes real when there is a context and because similarity with and difference from other entities are perceived. For example, *cat* and *dog* are similar in that they are both animals, but obviously different. In addition, the specific reference of *cat* or *dog* can only become clear in an utterance, e.g.

Terrence, the cat, is curled up on the TV
(specific household pet)

The cat has four legs
(generic animal including many types)

So the relational nature of meaning is layered and interwoven.

The foregoing does not mean to suggest however that precision in definition is valueless or not desirable; in fact one can say that a better appreciation of the history and current usage of certain linguistic terms may prevent useless arguments and show a clearer path to arguments of substance. For example, an argument about 'Creole' may founder because the participants may have vague and different ideas about the definition of the term or it may be fruitful because the participants have a good and common definition of the term. Precision in definition, therefore, must go hand in hand with context of usage, evolution of meaning and ambiguity.

Dialect

The linguist's definition of 'dialect' initially appears contradictory and nonsensical to the non-linguist when, for example, the linguist says 'British English is a dialect of English' or 'Standard English is only one dialect of English'. The reason for this is that the term 'dialect' either may carry with it a social value judgement or it may be used as an objective term. Usually the linguist uses the term without social value judgement and the non-linguist uses the term with social value judgement. As a result the non-linguist gives the term a restricted meaning, whereas the linguist gives it a general meaning.

For the linguist 'dialect' refers to a variety of a language – any variety. If one takes as an example English in the USA (a big country is here used as an example because differences are more numerous and more easily noticed than in a small country), one can identify persons from the southern states, from the northeastern states, and from the central area with very little difficulty, and further subdivisions can be made depending on the keenness of the hearer. Each one of these identifiable differences the linguist labels as a dialect of American English. The linguist makes no claim that one sounds better or is better (a social-value judgement) than another. So that when one speaks of the dialects of American English one is dealing with geographical varieties of English across America and this includes everything that can be identified as English in America. One can then go one stage further and talk about the dialects of English generally, in which case one would be dealing with the different varieties of English across the world. One would therefore get American English, British English, Canadian English, Australian English, Indian English, New Zealand English, West Indian English, etc. and each one of these is identified as a dialect of English. British English is not judged as better than all the rest, and set up in a parent relationship with the others. (This would only be done to some extent if one were looking at the history of the English language.)

So far the term 'dialect' has been used to refer only to geographical varieties of the language, but an equally important kind of variety of language is the social kind. For every language one can make distinctions between the speech produced by upper-class people and the speech produced by lower-class people. In many situations one can make further distinctions in between upper and lower, so that in every case one is identifying a variety of speech with a certain class. In short, one can talk about social class dialects. The term 'dialect' therefore refers to both geographical varieties and social class varieties and these two kinds are intertwined in an integral manner. The simple chart in Fig. 1.2 gives an idea of the relationship between the two varieties. In this figure the terms 'urban' and 'rural' are used for convenience to represent geographical varieties, but one can also think in terms of

	Urban	Rural
Upper class		
Middle class		
Lower class		

Fig. 1.2   Geographical and social class varieties of dialect.

different parishes, counties, states, or any such geographical division. In no case, however, will geographical distinctions (i.e. as represented on maps) correspond neatly to geographical varieties of speech – when one crosses a parish boundary the speech variety does not suddenly stop being one thing and become another. The same is true for social class distinctions.

A complicating factor not represented on Fig. 1.2 is education. There is a tendency for education to reduce geographical difference – the more educated a person becomes the more characteristic geographical differences in his or her speech tend to disappear. In the West Indies this goes so far that it is sometimes difficult to identify the native island of a person. On the other hand, there are sometimes marked differences between the educated speech of one geographical area and that of another. For example, educated speech of the southern part of the USA differs markedly from educated speech of the northeast of the USA.

An assessment of the social value or prestige given to geographical and social dialects in a country shows that in most cases the upper-class urban variety is given highest prestige and the lower-class rural the lowest prestige, with the others falling in between these two. In addition, the upper-class urban speaker is usually identified as educated and enlightened, whereas the lower-class rural speaker is regarded as the opposite. Even more important is the fact that the term 'dialect' is associated with the lower-class rural speaker and the speech of the urban upper class is regarded as the desired form of speech of the country – the standard – and in fact opposite to 'dialect'. So for the non-linguist, 'dialect' refers to a non-standard form of speech that has the lowest prestige in the country. Furthermore, it is associated with the non-serious or comic, and if it is used in serious situations it is most likely to be for relaying information about farming, health or welfare. Assignment of low or high prestige to a language variety is a straightforward reflection of the values and aspirations of a society and also a reflection of the economic and political power of the speakers of the variety. It has little to do with the communicative power of a language form. In many countries over the centuries low prestige varieties have changed to become the standard of the society.

Creole

The term 'Creole' is a good example of a word whose meaning has changed considerably in a relatively short time. Dell Hymes' book *Pidginization and Creolization of Languages* gives the following historical explanation of the term:

> 'The term "creole" (from Portuguese *crioulo*, via Spanish and French) originally meant a white man of European descent born and raised in a tropical colony. Only later was the meaning extended to include the indigenous natives and others of non-European origin e.g. African slaves ... The term was then applied to certain languages spoken by creoles in and around the Caribbean and in West Africa, and was later extended to other languages of similar types. Most creoles ... are European based, i.e. each has derived most of its vocabulary from one or more European languages. Creole French (also called patois) and Creole English are the most frequent in West Africa and the New World, but Spanish, Dutch and Portuguese Creoles are common in other parts of the world ... A creole which shares most of its vocabulary with English is traditionally called an English-based creole or creolized English.'

As a result of the changing meaning of the word, 'Creole' is a very fuzzy word to some people, especially since it is not restricted in its reference today to language and may still be used to refer to people and even horses. However, to those who are serious about language study the term has a fairly precise meaning. It is normally used to refer to a dialect or language which is the result of contact between the language of a colonising people and the languages of a colonised people. The language itself is characterised by many reductions in the word forms of the language of the colonisers with many sound, phrase and sentence patterns which are typical of the original language(s) of the colonised people.

A Creole represents a stage in a developmental process which started as an unstable, structurally restricted, non-native form of communication between peoples of different cultures. This communication has become stable, and more expanded in roles, functions and structures and represents the native language of the descendants of those originally involved in the contact situation. The subsequent evolution of a Creole is neither predictable nor uniform in all cases of Creoles across the world, but in the case of the West Indies a paradox has developed. On the one hand as a result of the constant presence of English accompanied by more social intercourse, economic betterment and greater educational opportunities for many, the linguistic spectrum seems to be losing its extreme Creole varieties; on the other hand these same factors are creating less insecure and more nationalistic peoples who believe that the extreme Creole varieties preserve their historical and cultural experience and allow for more genuine expression of things West Indian.

In the Caribbean as a whole, Creole languages are the result of contact between English, French, Spanish, Portuguese, Dutch ('languages of colonising people') and West African languages ('languages of a colonised people'). It is quite easy to identify the European element in Caribbean Creoles because the words sound like or look like the words of the European language. It is not so easy for the cursory observer to identify the West African elements or even think in terms of West African elements, because not only does he not know any West African languages, but even if he did, his tendency to think of a language in terms of words and combinations of words would not allow him to determine common pronunciation, word, sentence and meaning patterns in Creoles and West African languages. The value system of colonial slave society created the belief that the Africans had no language. This belief, with its total vacuum of knowledge on the African side, left the West Indian with no alternative but to think of his language negatively in terms of English; hence the terms 'broken English', 'bad English', etc.

Such terms are equated with the notion of 'bad grammar' and are based on the belief that only certain languages have grammar. This results from the fact that just a few of all the thousands of languages of man have had their rules or structures and social conventions set out in written form within an educational framework, which has created the impression that those which are not set out in this way are grammarless. It is quite easy to show that as long as a variety of speech is used and understood by people every day in normal circumstances it must have rules, which means therefore that every normal form of speech has rules or, in other words, a grammar. The term 'bad grammar' may then be properly applied to unsuccessful attempts to conform to the rules of the standard language when the speaker is trying to conform. It should not be applied indiscriminately to all non-standard forms of speech. The terms 'broken English' and 'bad English' are prejudiced terms, without foundation or support in historical linguistics generally, and they have no place in serious and objective considerations about West Indian language.

Patois

The word 'patois' is a French word which is also used in the English language. In French and also in English generally it is used to refer to a geographical dialect which differs from the standard language of the country. As such it carries the usual associations and (lack of) prestige which characterise non-standard rural or regional dialects. In some cases in the West Indies, in Jamaica for example, the word 'patois' is used with precisely the meaning outlined above; that is, to refer to Creole English. In other cases, especially in the Eastern Caribbean, the word is used with a more restricted or precise meaning. It is used to refer to the language spoken by the majority of people in Dominica, St Lucia, Martinique and Guadeloupe; that is, French Creole. The obvious explanation for the latter restricted meaning is that a French word is being used to describe a situation in which the French language is historically involved. So in the former usage the term refers to any geographical dialect and in the latter it refers to a specific geographical dialect or language, but both within the context of the Caribbean.

Slang

Many West Indians use the word 'slang' interchangeably with 'dialect' to refer to non-standard language of the region. This is not what 'slang' means in standard English generally. 'Slang' in standard English does indeed refer to the language characteristic of a group within the society but does not refer to the total language of the group. In fact it is normally restricted to words, phrases or expressions which are novel and initially have a dramatic effect, but because they are fashionable and consequently over-used, either they are soon forgotten or they pass into the general vocabulary of the language. Slang expressions are basically of two types: they are either normal English words which are suddenly used with an unusual meaning, or quite normal and everyday meanings or concepts that are captured in a new or concocted word. Slang expressions are characteristic of teenagers more than of any other single group. The current use of Rasta words and expressions by the general public throughout the West Indies is a good example of slang use.

West Indian English

In discussing 'dialect' earlier, attention was drawn to the fact that several dialects of English can be identified; for example, Australian English, American English, British English, West Indian English, among others. In each case there is the common factor 'English' and a distinguishing factor 'Australian/American/British/West Indian'. This relationship is symbolised in Fig. 1.3. If each circle in the figure is understood to represent a variety of English (West Indian, American, British, etc.), it will be seen that the shaded area is common to all the circles and this may be regarded as common or basic English. It will be seen also that there are parts outside the shaded area shared by two or more dialects, and that each circle has a part not shared by any other circle, thus representing features that are characteristically British

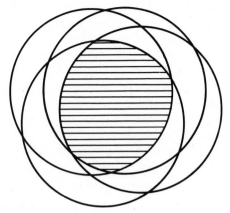

Fig. 1.3   The relationships between different dialects of English.

or Indian or Canadian or West Indian. This, roughly, is the interrelationship between the dialects of the English language.

West Indian English, therefore, shares features with all other dialects of English but at the same time has features found only in the West Indies. West Indian English, however, unlike other dialects of English (perhaps excepting Indian English), has features which are significantly different in nature, features which have resulted from the nature of the contact between Africans and Europeans and from the circumstances of development of language in the West Indies. As was pointed out earlier, West Indian English varies from territory to territory as a result of different historical influences. The relationship between the West Indian territories can be symbolised in exactly the same way as that between varieties of English across the world; that is, as in Fig. 1.3.

2 · *Language varieties in the West Indies*

In all societies of man the spoken language has always been more used and more powerful than the written language. On the other hand, the written language, in societies where it exists, has a higher prestige than the spoken language and is often perceived by the general public to be a 'higher' version of the spoken. The greater prestige of the written language is gained from its being 'learnt' language – an indication that 'one went to school' – as opposed to basic spoken language which is normally acquired by all human beings. This dichotomy has been heightened in the West Indies by the history of social development and by a much less considerable (than British which served as the source) history of written literature. In other words, since basic literacy is not enjoyed by all or the vast majority of West Indians, being literate to the extent of being proficient in English is seen as having a very high value for personal and social betterment. At the same time, however, as a result of general technological advancement in communications and a history of 'talking sweet' in the West Indies, it seems much easier and more appropriate to talk your way to the top than to write your way to the top.

The two channels, the written and the spoken, influence each other, but vary in significance depending on the variety of the language. In the West Indies the language is divided into a number of perceived or identifiable varieties or types. The dichotomous relationship between the written and the spoken, the fact that all types can be written and spoken, and a general ambivalence in sentiment about types, do not belie completely the vertically descending status of the following types of English found in the West Indies:

Foreign English
Radio and television English
Erudite English
Colloquial English
Creole English
Rasta English
Profane English

These types have not been set out by linguists to correspond to measurable objective variants in the society. They are the powerful stereotypes operating in the minds of people that correspond to the characteristic behaviour of the following (respectively):

A foreigner
A radio or television announcer
A good speaker
An educated person
An uneducated person
A Rasta
General usage

Although these stereotypes are not objectively separable at all times, they operate very strongly as norms in the society and dictate or motivate certain linguistic behaviour. The obvious complicating factor is that the linguistic competence of each individual varies according to his personal experience and the requirements of his social situation. No individual is limited to any one of these stereotypes. In fact one can say that there are three realities of each one of these stereotypes: objective reality, perceived reality and produced reality. For example, with regard to foreign English, a linguist can identify the differences between West Indian English and non-West Indian English (objective reality); any West Indian individual can recognise non-West Indian English and has his own idea of what the differences are (perceived reality); and any West Indian can give his own imitation of a British, American, Canadian or Indian speaker (produced reality). Although there is no documented proof that these realities are of greater import in the West Indies than anywhere else in the world, there is no question that they are powerful in societies in which slavery, rigid social stratification and inequality of opportunity made language a powerful instrument and measure of achievement. An outline is given below of all these types of West Indian English except for Creole English which is dealt with in the next chapter.

Foreign English

From the visiting absentee landlord in colonial days to the tourist today, foreign English has always been a significant factor in the West Indies. In addition today, the inescapable presence of radio and television makes the foreign English voice a part of the everyday life of all West Indians. The small size of the territories and the long years of closeness to the 'mother country' have made the West Indies linguistically outward-looking so that English is a means of being in closer communication with the powerful countries of the world, whose language it is.

Foreign English is by and large British, American and Canadian English, although Australian and Indian English (through cricket) are not uncommon. This is in cases where the English is actually produced by the foreigner, but foreign English is also produced by the West Indian. It may be produced by a West Indian speaking to a foreigner, e.g. a taxi-driver to a tourist, or by a West Indian to a West Indian, e.g. a returning resident to a resident. It is not the specific reasons why West Indians produce foreign English that are being considered here; rather the fact that West Indians are able consciously to produce a different form of speech, the nature of which and the extent of use of which vary from individual to individual.

Changes in speech to correspond to formality or otherwise are normal in all languages; there is no doubt that all societies have 'sophisticated' forms of speech. The 'sophisticated' form of speech is usually one of the dialects of the country, probably modified or homogenised, or it is a 'koine' type; that is, one with all the regionalisms removed. The use of a non-national form of speech as a 'sophisticated' form of speech is common only in colonial and post-colonial situations. For example, it is not normal for an American to imitate a British accent when talking to an Englishman or any other speaker of English. In contrast, many West Indians not only produce foreign English as 'sophisticated' English, but even try (according to their own perception) to vary the foreign English according to that of the interlocutor; that is, if one is speaking to an American, produce American speech, etc. It is not necessary here to examine the linguistic differences between West Indian English and other varieties, but it is necessary to look at the nature of foreign English produced by the West Indian as well as the linguistic and psychological effect of it.

Foreign English produced by the West Indian is not uniform in structure, but there is uniformity in the strategy used to produce it. The strategy is a combination of elements:

i   Use the 'best' form of English.
ii   Change the quality of certain vowels (and occasionally consonants).
iii Change the intonation pattern.
iv   Change the word stress pattern.
v   Insert certain characteristic words and phrases.

The extent to which each one of these is done varies from individual to individual, but as is the case with most individuals producing a non-native dialect, especially if the intention is to impress, performance will be inconsistent and exaggerated. In other words, the individual's perception of a foreigner's dialect or language is usually limited to a few salient items, generally pronunciation and words. The individual's production is further limited by his own ability to produce the foreigner's dialect or language and his own ability to produce the perceived differences. In addition, the individual's production is distorted by the overuse of the few perceived differences.

To illustrate this first of all in the reverse, an Englishman or an American imitating West Indian speech will do three things: insert the word *man* before and after almost every clause; change every 'th' to *t* or *d*; and use a 'sing-song' or a 'Jamaican' accent. The result sounds quite unusual to the West Indian. The second illustration is the case of an 'educated' West Indian, producing for artistic or other purposes 'genuine' written or spoken non-standard West Indian English. His success is greater than that of the Englishman or American, but still distorted because the desire to pack as many of the perceived differences into as short a space as possible is still there. Although it may be claimed that West Indians have been trying to produce foreign English for 200 years and more, over-compensation and the long-acquired habits of pronunciation of the native language limit success. In addition, monitoring of speech (the extent to which one consciously concentrates on forms and structures while speaking) varies inversely in relation to expressiveness, colour and genuine feeling. Accordingly, as these three increase in intensity, the speaker increasingly reverts to spontaneous native language.

As a result of unlimited variation it is not possible to give an outline of what is produced by West Indians as foreign English. A few of the perceived differences are as follows:

vowel [a] becomes [æ]   e.g. [man] > [mæn] 'man'

vowel [ɔ] becomes [a/æ]   e.g. [prɔbəbli] > [prabəbli] 'probably'

vowel [i] becomes [ɪ]   e.g. [hapi] > [hapɪ] 'happy'

t/n + y + u > t/n + u   e.g. the word *tune* is pronounced [tun]
the word *news* is pronounced [nuz]

Insertion of characteristic clause endings
e.g. *oh, ain't it, I say, do (let us . .)*

Substitution of characteristic words
e.g. *chaps, guys*

Use of characteristic phrases and greetings
e.g. *how ya doing, brother*

Another perceived difference is referred to in a comment by Richard Allsopp (1972a) in an article on Caribbean English:

> '. . . one hears
> The matter was DIS-cussed . . .
> The PO-lice gave a DIS-play . . .
> – nonsense displayed as good public speech, which may go back to a false notion of correctness in the Anglicised orientation of classroom speech.'

In these examples the speaker moves the word-stress from the second syllable to the first because of the mistaken idea that this is how Englishmen and Americans pronounce words of this type.

Foreign English produced by the West Indian may vary from a very good and extensive representation to a very poor one or to a very slight one. However, since the West Indian generally is very sensitive to shifts in language, the slightest injection of foreign English will not pass unnoticed when one West Indian is speaking to or is overheard by another (especially if they are both from the same territory). General conclusions about an individual's speech in the West Indies are reached as a result of the salient features used, irrespective of the actual frequency with which they are used. In fact, perception of non-standard or foreign features is much higher than actual occurrence. A person, then, may be judged to be using a 'twang' after using only one or two foreign features. This is the most crucial point in the present identification of foreign English as produced by a West Indian.

In all the territories there are a significant number of people in prominent positions who use foreign English. These people may be foreigners working in the management of the private sector (banks, industries, etc.) and in the public sector as advisers to the government or in a role like that of the Peace Corps worker; British- and American-born children of West Indian emigrants; West Indians who have spent a long time overseas; or West Indians educated in foreign institutions. Except for those who work in private enterprise, many of these foreign English speakers work in educational institutions and in their role as teachers serve as a model for students. Even though in private and informal contexts there is ambivalence towards and even distrust of those who use foreign English, especially in the case of West Indians who were once poor, or whose parents were once poor, there is no question that a significant percentage, probably even the majority, of people in the West Indies have a great admiration for foreign English in the public formal context. The principal reason for this is that English is seen as a window to the world and the user of foreign English thus transcends the local and small and takes a place in the international and worldwide community. This is negatively supported by the fact that by and large politicians, whose task is seen as dealing with local issues, do not rise in the esteem of West Indians if they use foreign English.

The effect of foreign English on native English in the speech of West Indians is difficult to calculate. There is a contrast between a hotel worker who switches back and forth between foreign and native English and a teacher who cultivates foreign English in everyday speech over a period of years. Cases of the latter are few and declining and over the past twenty years have hardly produced many carbon copies among the students. Since speech is controlled by group expectation and social position, the major considerations in this case are the extent of changes in social intercourse in the West Indies and the effect of bidialectalism (using or hearing two dialects) on speakers generally.

Although radio and television serve unconsciously as sources of training in foreign English, it is tourism more than any other factor which causes the production of foreign English. Differences between the West Indian territories in this respect are directly related to differences in tourism. Guyana, for example, has had little or no increase in foreign tourists over the past twenty years and a declining number of Guyanese returning home from metropolitan centres. There is therefore little change in the linguistic situation. There has been a gradual increase in tourism in Trinidad but the Trinidad economy has not been dependent on tourism as a main contributor. Without tourism as a major factor, however, there is in the oral and written literature of Trinidad (e.g. Naipaul's *The Mimic Men* and a number of calypsos) the recurring theme of the West Indian aping the manners and speech of the English and Americans. On the other hand, Trinidad was the only island to have Black Power demonstrations in the early 1970s; it seems as if counterbalancing forces have prevented any major change in the linguistic situation and the production of foreign English.

Jamaica exhibits a great deal of complexity in this area with several contending forces: there has been and still is a considerable and increasing movement of Jamaicans of all types in and out of the USA; there are traditional and strong links with Britain and the English language; there is a very strong love and promotion of things Jamaican and Jamaican Creole, but there is also a very vocal anti-Creole element in the society; there has always been a significant amount of foreign tourism on the north coast of the island. The net result of all this is that, leaving aside the polarised types, a great percentage of Jamaicans have developed an acute facility in moving from one type of English to another depending on where they are and whom they are talking to.

Barbados is dominated by tourism and this has caused Barbadians generally to develop habits to deal with tourists. One of these habits is foreign English, which is spontaneously perceived as a way of making communication and life in general easier for the tourist in order to make greater gains for oneself. For many Barbadians who work directly with tourists, therefore, foreign English is not occasional and inconsistent, but is a practised and everyday form of speech, although it is restricted to interests common to the tourist and the worker. However, the crucial distinction between tourist and resident which has developed is paralleled by a distinction in behaviour towards tourist and towards resident. Part of this distinction is in language use. Foreign English then is felt to be functionally separable from 'normal' speech.

The other islands in the West Indies are increasingly depending on tourism, but are not yet as dominated by tourism as is Barbados. The amount of foreign English produced therefore varies in relation to the extent of tourism. In St Lucia and Dominica the fact that French Creole is the native language of the majority of the people, especially in the rural areas, means that foreign English is more restricted. The spectrum of English in these two islands is narrower and there is a greater concern to produce English well than to produce foreign English.

Overall the effect of foreign English on West Indian English is perceptible more in vocabulary and idiom than in pronunciation, but even this claim is not easy to prove conclusively. In the case of pronunciation, since the native language is used overwhelmingly and is perceived as distinct from foreign English, it can be claimed that the repertoire of the individual is simply added to and not altered. In the case of vocabulary and idiom, even if in their normal speech West Indians employ foreign words and phrases, there is nothing unusual in this, because not only is borrowing of words across dialects normal, but also across languages. It may be that in the West Indies when words and phrases are borrowed they retain more of their original pronunciation for a longer time than is normal, especially when they belong to the world of entertainment (particularly music).

The majority of studies of the effects of bilingualism on the individual deal with its effects on intelligence and there is no consensus on these effects. Studies in the earlier part of this century gave the impression that bilingualism led to a lower level of intelligence, but more recent studies give a positive view, suggesting that there is more flexibility and creativity in the intelligence of bilinguals. The positive view however relates to situations where both languages have high social value and respect (as for example in parts of Europe where both French and German are used). In the case of languages/dialects which are functioning in an unequal way (as in the West Indies), it is often assumed that the social situation itself creates psychological pressure or anxiety and that this negatively affects understanding. There is no study indicating possible positive effects resulting from the kind of shifting back and forth which is characteristic of many West Indians.

The fact that in the West Indies there is foreign English, and a great deal of variation and inconsistency in the production of that foreign English, and much switching backwards and forwards, creates a picture of instability and a lack of homogeneity, with the overall effect that there is nothing uniform and characteristic enough to be called West Indian English. The effect, then, of foreign English is not so much on the intelligence or the language ability or the language development of the individual, as on the way West Indian language is classified, according to the perception of both West Indians and non-West Indians. In fact the majority of books dealing with varieties of English identify British, American, Canadian, Australian, New Zealand and Indian varieties, but not a West Indian variety.

There is no objective way of identifying a variety of English or any other language. It is a matter of general consensus, based to some extent on perceived common characteristics. For example, American English is identified as such because there are a significant number of people in America speaking recognisable forms of English with characteristically American elements and also because America is strong enough to establish a consensus that there is a variety called American English. The West Indies apparently has not established a consensus that there is a variety called West Indian English and part of the reason for this lies in the widespread and dominant presence of foreign English in the West Indies.

Radio and television English

There are two major aspects of radio and television English in the West Indies. The first, which is really worldwide, is the assumption or fact that radio and television speech differs from normal speech. The second, which is peculiar to the West Indies, is that what is produced as radio and television speech is not necessarily in the same relationship to normal speech as is the case in other countries.

There are a number of factors which have to be taken into consideration in deciding what kind of speech to use on radio and television, both of which are mass media catering to the general public. In countries like Uganda and India the problem is even greater because a decision has to be made first of all about what language(s) to use, since many different languages are being used by the people in these countries. In countries like Britain and the USA the decision is less difficult in that there is one general language and it is then only a matter of deciding what dialect to use. Once the decision is taken or the conventions understood, the radio and television person is trained to speak or practises speaking in a specific manner. Such decisions or conventions are serious and an integral part of presentation, which is one of the most important elements of radio and especially television.

Radio and television differ from the other mass media in that they involve sound and the human voice. The quality of sounds and of the human voice produces many different reactions in listeners, consciously or unconsciously springing from all types of prejudices and beliefs. The intention of radio and television stations is to increase positive response and minimise negative response. Judgements about the human voice are essentially aesthetic and subjective, but within a society over a period of time there develops a fair amount of agreement in these judgements and this usually results in conventions. Judgements about language reflect social values, and conventions that have developed in radio and television certainly do.

The language of radio and television can be divided into four categories: newscasts, music programmes, advertisements and general public features. The category 'general public features' embraces a wide area, e.g. interviews, soap operas, public participation programmes, community programmes, regional programmes, etc. However, it is the first three which are important in the context of conventions.

Newscasts require speech that is intelligible and authoritative by being standard and general. The main convention here is that newscasts should not be delivered in a regional variety because regional varieties provoke strong negative reaction in other regions, and distract listeners. This means not only that the newscaster has to suppress his own regional characteristics but also that he has to use the standard form of the language. In the case of Britain the term 'BBC English' is used to identify this form of the language and in the USA the term 'network English' is used. Such terms are important in that they create the impression that a positive, homogeneous, unifying entity exists, although in reality the convention itself is negatively stated and in actual practice there is a lot of variation. In the West Indies the same convention exists, but historical factors and differences in perception have created a greater amount of variation.

Radio especially and television newscasts in the West Indies from their very beginning up to now have had a considerable percentage of foreign English, both in the form of extracts from overseas international news and in the voices presenting them locally. These voices belong either to foreigners residing in the West Indies, West Indians returning home after a number of years in a metropolitan area or West Indians who have spent little or no time away from their native homes. In general, newscasters come to enjoy a lot of respect from the public, but in the West Indies there is no doubt that a lot of admiration is gained not from delivery, correctness or ability to read well, but from the amount of foreignness in the voice. This is of course related to the fact that the complexity of social and ethnic compositions of the populations in the West Indies ensures that the newscaster's voice will offend some segment of the population. Newscasters therefore adopt a personal solution to the problem, which means that overall there is no perceptible homogeneity in policy or practice other than that structurally standard English should be used.

Music programmes, with their host – the disc jockey – have been a major influence in the spread of a certain jargon across the Western world. Unlike the newscaster, the disc jockey does not have the convention which restricts him to non-regional, standard English. In fact, the disc jockey's task is to establish a rapport between the music being played and the audience, and most music programmes are geared to specific audiences, the biggest of which is young people's pop music. In short, then, the language of pop music spreads from country to country very quickly, with its primary source being the USA. Within the West Indies other sources of disc jockey language are Jamaica and Trinidad.

Language associated with music – the lyrics of songs, descriptive terms, etc. – relayed through or enhanced by the disc jockey, passes into the fashionable language of the people and quite often settles into normal usage. For example, words like 'jam' and 'dub' have expanded meanings for the West Indian, whilst 'dig' and 'get down' are known by almost all English speakers. The language of music varies considerably, from songs with well-structured English sentences to compositions of sounds, totally or partially produced by electronic equipment. There is no question that the language of music is reflected in the behaviour of the whole of society in the West Indies, but it is difficult to separate out music from general cultural changes and expressions of independence and nationalism. In short, the concept of freedom as it applies to politics and economics is not clearly separable in the minds of many younger West Indians from freedom in communication. The influence of the language of music is to be understood as applying not only to words and phrases and pronunciation, but also, more importantly, to the freedom to express oneself according to one's own feeling and according to one's own preferred form of language. It is heightening of emotion caused by music which causes the language of music and disc jockeys to have such widespread and powerful influence.

The language of advertisements is not as much a powerful influence as it is a mirror of current social values. Advertisements make use of all the forms of language in the society because they have to appeal to all the people in varying ways. Whereas major producing countries like the USA and Britain have almost complete control over advertisements and thus the language in them, in the West Indies, for economic or other reasons, this is not so. There are foreign advertisements, foreign advertisements with local voices totally or partially replacing foreign ones, and local advertisements. Another point of contrast between the metropolitan areas and the West Indies is the amount of research that goes into the advertising and marketing of goods and services. Such research dictates the form, images, language and locations of advertisements. In the West Indies advertising firms are usually privately owned, relatively small and depend more on the judgements and belief of managers than on extensive, documented research in their specific market. The advertisement is of course dependent on the budget constraints of the advertiser.

From the point of view of language, the safest, cheapest advertisement is seen as one with a single individual producing standard English. The more realistic the advertisement becomes, with scenes and people speaking 'normally', the more costly it is to produce, especially if (semi-) professional actors or celebrities are used. The advertising firm often chooses to use in-house people or non-professional acquaintances in order to cut costs. Paradoxically, then, in the West Indies where most of the speech produced is non-standard it requires more expertise, it is generally more expensive and is considered more risky to produce an advertisement in which the actors are attempting to represent typical speech. Overall, standard English, native or foreign, is over-represented in advertisements in the West Indies primarily because of the source and cost of advertisements and secondly because most advertisements use an appeal to sophistication or to greater intelligence, which in the West Indies is associated with standard English.

The major areas of radio and television (newcasts, music programmes, advertisements together with general public programmes) provide the listener with a variety of language types. However, whereas the economic worth of non-standard English in music programmes and advertising is significant and has been rising over the last twenty years, there is no question that for the presentation of the serious and the sophisticated, standard English is unrivalled as the preferred form of language. At this time in the West Indies it is difficult to determine the extent to which, and the direction in which, the development of language is being pushed by the ratio of native to foreign English and by the economic, cultural and emotional value of non-standard English used on radio and television. There is some indication however that the traditional attitude of regarding one form of a language as a threat to another is being replaced – happily for some, unhappily for others – by greater tolerance and appreciation of the function of the differing forms of a language.

Erudite English

Erudite English in this context is not simply standard English; in fact, it is not necessarily standard English. Nor is it just English which reveals erudition on the part of the speaker. Erudite English is English which contains features which clearly indicate to the hearer that the speaker is quite conversant with words, phrases and idioms, especially older ones and foreign ones and those considered perceptually difficult. Erudite English embraces performance English, biblical and proverbial English, and 'schoolmarm' English. These three areas, which fuel the desire to demonstrate linguistic facility, are really related to two traditions, the one West African and the other a factor of colonial education.

One of the notable cultural features in the history of Afro-American culture is the competitive and performative use of words. One of the salient factors in 'talking sweet' is that the communicative function of language is not paramount. In fact it is very often absent and the sole intention of the speaker is to impress by sound, length or unusual combinations of words. The hearer most often does not seek to interpret any great meaning or philosophical content, but reacts as one normally does to poetry and music. Abrahams (1970) cites the following from St Vincent:

> '... that song reminded me of Moses standing on the banks of the Red Sea. It fills my heart with phil-long-losophy, entrong-losophy, joken and conomaltus. Impro, imperium, pompry, comilatus, allus comigotus, which is to say I come here today without any study. Dia Gratia, by the grace of God, I have tried my best. Time is tempus fugit. The same. I will say a few words about Moses...'

Performance English in the West Indies is in this tradition; it is pompous and sonorous with a very involved or unorthodox sentence structure.

The situational contexts for extreme forms of performance English have almost all disappeared in the West Indies today. Such contexts were tea meetings, service of songs or equivalent social functions, at which principal speakers, driven by a need to outdo rivals absent or present, would produce speeches made up of long sentences with many Latin and Greek (sounding) words and phrases accompanied by some of the longest words in the English language (e.g. 'phantasmagorical valetudinarianism'). The performer was serious and thought of himself as providing uplift and the highest quality of oratory and English to his less fortunate listeners. The main elements in the sentences were explanation, contrast and impressive sound. For example, the Latin and Greek phrases, which were at best only partially correct, were often followed or preceded by English phrases, the one meant to be an explanation or amplification of the other, but both having some alliterative, repeated, rhyming, or otherwise significant sound feature. The following example, taken from Louis Lynch's *The Barbados Book* (1964), illustrates this:

> 'Ek-keehomo, behold the man.
> Ek-keehomo, here I stand:
> I will now rise from my esteemed seat
> and I will say Bon Swar or Good Evening
> to the ladies and gentlemen of this nocturnal congregation.'

The performer in earlier days was usually self-taught, respected and one of a few. In those days the arts and the classical languages specifically were the prominent subjects in formal education and indirectly provided the material for the performer. Today, the influence of the classical languages has declined to be replaced by the language of technology, which is not readily understood by the general public and is non-emotional in nature. The level of intelligibility in performance English has increased and the presence of Latin and

Greek words has decreased. However, the desire of principal speakers at weddings and in eulogies to perform well is still there and the comedy sections of calypso and other shows still retain the desire on the part of performers to outdo rivals. Although performance English may have changed substantially, it is still maintained in the general admiration of flowery phrases, classical references, long words and the use of the less-used and older English composite adverbs and conjunctions (*wheretofore*, *herein*, *hereunder*, *inasmuchas*, etc.). In fact, the best current example of it is the public orator's speech in graduation ceremonies at the University of the West Indies. The University is the highest educational institution, the graduation ceremony is the biggest occasion in the University and the public orator introduces the highest 'graduates' – those who are being honoured for outstanding service. The public orator's speech is therefore at the very pinnacle and the tradition of this speech has invariably been an exhibition of verbosity.

The public speaker, whether in earlier times or today, punctuates his speech with biblical references and proverbs. Part of the definition of a proverb is that it encapsulates wisdom, so it is quite normal for erudition to be characterised by the use of proverbs. Religion has always been one of the most influential instruments of colonisation and crusades. In the West Indies the Bible was introduced at the very beginning of European colonisation and has continued strong up to now. The Bible was the instrument of the Church and it was the Church that was at the root of general education and uplift. Prowess in education meant mastery of theology and philosophy and this in the West Indies was often interpreted to mean extensive knowledge of the Bible. From the lowest to the highest levels, Church-controlled education involved rote learning, especially of the Bible.

The effect of this was the belief that demonstration of knowledge of the Bible was a clear indication of higher learning. Even now knowledge in this area is not judged by one's understanding of philosophical and theological concepts but by the ability to recite biblical passages and identify where they occur in the Bible. As a result of the major role played by the Church and the Bible in general education in the West Indies, together with continued love of the Church and church-going, the language of the Bible is widespread. For example, in the West Indies where illiteracy is still a problem and where standard English, written or spoken, is not always completely understood by everyone, there are a significant number of people who have such a strong attachment to specific older versions of the Bible (even though they often do not understand a form of language that is difficult even for educated standard speakers) that they go so far as to regard the specific version as sacred and reject versions which are easier to understand.

Whereas it is clear that such preferences are not restricted to the

West Indies, there is no question that the removal of the distance and foreignness of the older version destroys a traditional yardstick of achievement and narrows the distance between learned and unlearned, much to the chagrin of many. For these people the removal of the old pronouns and adverbs of English (*thee, thou, ye, yonder, thither*), the old negative structure (*thou shalt not, know thee not*), the old verb endings (*dost, doest*), the old meanings (*even, without, prevent*), symbolise the disappearance of the mystique of the Bible. It also clearly indicates the extent to which the West Indian is fascinated by the English language and especially that version of it dear to his spiritual history.

 The term 'schoolmarm English' is American in origin and pointedly reflects colonial and social class experience in the acquisition of standard English in the formal school setting. The notion of being old-fashioned and punctilious which is part of the definition of 'schoolmarm', as is to be expected, is in keeping with the beliefs of the older and more influential people as far as the mastery of standard English is concerned. Much of schoolmarm English concerns itself with acquisition of standard English features which are either contrary to vernacular and lower social class use or are specialised and restricted in occurrence. The acquisition of such features has always been interpreted as a clear indication of formal schooling and a prerequisite for entrance to higher social circles.

 Schoolmarm English can be pinpointed in two areas – the difficult problems faced by teachers when teaching young children to read and write, and the type of comments one would find in the press that are critical of the press. The latter are seldom of any great consequence, will never disappear and may be regarded as part of every citizen's right to express an opinion. The former, however, are more important although as insoluble. For example, a good teacher faced with the inconsistencies of English spelling knows that no matter what method is tried, current vernacular pronunciation and standard English spelling are often strangers. Some teachers, believing that the written form of the language is the best form, try to make the pronunciation fit the spelling. In other cases where a more enlightened approach is adopted, the phonics of the author of texts may not correspond to the phonics of the teacher which in turn may not correspond to the phonics of the pupils, and so the teacher has to choose a uniform, 'dictatorial' method.

 The variations and contradictions which are a part of the difficulty of teaching the English language are reflected in schoolmarm English in the West Indies and accentuated by the general language situation of the West Indies. In terms of changing values, however, it is clear that diction and recitation, of the tutored and stilted type, which were once a measure of achievement for children at primary school and those performing at church functions, have now declined in importance, in spite of the fact that national cultural festivals in the West Indies always include this traditional category. This category is now seen by some to be competing with 'dialect' speaking, if not being replaced by it.

The three areas – performance English, biblical and proverbial English and schoolmarm English – demonstrate that erudite English in the West Indies is rooted in the past and is gradually declining in importance. This development is consonant with the perception that English is declining as a language of a specific culture as it becomes more powerful as a language of universal communication. In other words, it is tied less to the history of a specific people than it is a response to the practicalities of the modern world.

Colloquial English

Colloquial English in this context refers to English which is characteristically West Indian without being Creole English. Although from a linguistic point of view it is very difficult to draw a line through West Indian language and differentiate precisely between Creole English and colloquial English as defined here, it is necessary to do so because such a distinction exists in people's perception and is based on the notion of acceptability.

Acceptability itself in language is negatively determined in that there is a history and general practice of deeming things unacceptable, with the assumption that that which escapes stigmatisation is acceptable. Acceptability also varies in degree according to formality of context and of course according to groups and individuals. Acceptability may result from knowledge or from ignorance, but it is generally the case that people's beliefs prove more important than historical fact. For example, the word *tinnen* is generally dismissed as unacceptable because people believe it is a West Indian concoction based on *tin*. If they knew that it was an old form of English in the pattern of *earthen, golden, leaden, brazen, woollen, linen* (*lin* 'flax'; cf. *linseed* 'seed of lin'), as in *tinnen cup*, the reaction to it would be quite the opposite. Colloquial English rests on general acceptability as evidenced in the usage of educated people.

The most marked difference between West Indian colloquial English and other varieties of English (British, American, Canadian, etc.) is in pronunciation. There are of course differences between West Indian territories themselves, with Jamaica especially differing in many respects. Bearing in mind, however, that Jamaica is only one of several islands, it can be said that difference between West Indian speech generally and other varieties exists principally in four areas:

i   Dissimilarity in the quality and gliding of stressed middle and low vowels (see Fig. 3.1).
ii The relationship between stress and pitch.
iii Preference for syllable timing as opposed to stress timing.
iv Clause intonation.

It would be quite misleading in trying to make a comparison to give a list of vowels to represent British speech, for example, and a corresponding list to represent West Indian, because in both cases it would be a distortion of the social and geographical variation which exists. It is quite clear however that whereas in West Indian speech middle and low vowels tend to remain pure in stressed syllables, in other varieties of English they tend to glide. Examples of this difference are as follows:

British	West Indies	Examples
eɪ	e	space
ɛə	e	share, wear
əu	o	poor, tourist
ʊə	o	coke, goat

Other apparent correspondences in vowels and consonants between West Indian English and other varieties of English are not general, because of the great amount of geographical variation in the pronunciation of both British and American English.

The relationship between stress and pitch is the most clearly distinguishing mark of West Indian English. Although the difference between the two, stress and pitch, is not always easily differentiated in hearing, the two are given fairly clear definitions. *Stress* is the relative prominence given to a syllable in relation to neighbouring syllables according to the amount of force used to produce it. The three distinctions – primary stress (symbolised by ' before the syllable), secondary stress and tertiary stress, corresponding to a decrease in force – are not absolute values but relative ones; primary stress is not specified in terms of a specific number of decibels but in that one syllable is more prominent than neighbouring syllables. *Pitch* is a direct result of the speed of vibration of the vocal cords (in the voice-box in the throat) in the production of vowels, with increasing speed corresponding to increasing pitch height. Pitch in human speech is basically the same as and best understood in terms of musical or instrumental pitch. The separation of stress and pitch is quite clear in music in that a high-pitched note, for example, can be produced loudly or softly. Normal human speech does not employ as wide a range either of notes or of loudness as does music.

Non-West Indian varieties of English usually have an alliance of high pitch and primary stress in the production of words; i.e. the syllable with primary stress usually has the highest pitch (symbolised with the number 2 or 3). In West Indian English there is no necessary connection between the two. Take, for example the word *calypso*. Other varieties of English give the word the pattern *ca-'lýp-so*, with primary stress and high pitch on the second syllable. A typically West Indian pattern for the word is *'ca-lyp-sô*, with primary stress on the first syllable and high pitch on the last syllable. In other instances the West Indian pattern coincides with that of other varieties.

The freedom of relationship of stress and pitch in West Indian English is directly connected to the preference for syllable timing over stress timing. If in uttering the sentences of a language the time taken to move from the first primary stress to the second is approximately the same as that taken – irrespective of the number of intervening syllables – to move from the second to the third (and so on), then the language is said to be being produced with *stress timing*. If, on the other hand, each syllable lasts approximately the same length of time, then it is described as *syllable timing*. The term 'sing-song', used to describe West Indian speech, has derogatory connotations, but it is an overall impression provoked in the minds of hearers as a result of the separation of stress and pitch together with the use of syllable timing. West Indian colloquial English therefore has its own distinctiveness in pronunciation.

Clause intonation in West Indian colloquial English can be divided into pitch patterns in the clause itself and pitch patterns in tags (short words or phrases tacked on after the clause). Pitch patterns generally give one or two kinds of information: the type of sentence (statement, question, command) or the emotional reactions of the speaker (surprise, annoyance, satisfaction, etc.). With reference to the first kind, West Indian colloquial English employs rising intonation at the end of clauses to indicate yes–no questions more frequently than do other varieties of English, which tend to prefer sentence inversion, e.g.

You are going? in contrast to *Are you going?*

With reference to the second kind as used in the clause itself, every language and in fact every community has its characteristic way of expressing emotion by pitch pattern. So much so that a 'tone of voice' which one community may be regarded as 'businesslike', in another may be regarded as 'hostile' or 'unpleasant'. In other words, a lot of misunderstanding and distress can be caused as a result of difference in characteristic pitch patterns. Because of the highly specialised method of indicating intonation patterns and also because, for clarity, contrasts with other varieties of English would have to be given, the characteristic pitch patterns of West Indian English will not be illustrated.

Pitch patterns in the clause itself are also used by West Indians for the same reason that speakers of other varieties use psychological verbs (verbs that require a human subject) to introduce clauses. In other words, where a speaker of another variety uses a sentence of the type

I think/believe/feel that he is coming

in West Indian speech there is a lower incidence of sentences of this type. The modification is more often expressed by the West Indian in the intonation of the sentence and supported by a sentence tag.

Compare *He's coming*
and   *He's coming, ya*

In other words, the tag *ya* and the special intonation of the sentence are equivalent to the kind of uncertainty expressed in *think, feel, believe*. In West Indian speech there is also a series of other sentence tags used to express varying degrees of emotion. These are not words or residues of words but a variety of oral and nasal sounds which occur at the beginning, inside and at the end of clauses. They can be symbolised as

m , mmm , m$^{?}$m and ε , εεε , ε$^{?}$ε

The symbol [m] represents a nasal consonant, in the articulation of which the lips are kept closed; the sound seems to be produced in the nasal cavity and comes out through the nose. Allsopp (1972a) goes on to explain the [ε] group as follows:

> '. . . there is a parallel set in what may be called an /ε/ list, with open mouth and spread lips, containing items equivalent, as far as I am aware, to nearly all if not all those in the /m̃/ list . . . and performing the same function.

> The full range covers *varieties* of "yes" and "no", and varying intensities of concern, surprise, approval, disapproval, pleasure, regret, disgust, contempt, warning. Secondly, the items, though functioning mainly as response, are message-carrying in the recognized way, so that they are identifiable in isolation and can occasionally be the opening utterance in a conversation.'

West Indian colloquial English is unusual in its pronunciation in the sense that it differs quite markedly from all other varieties of English. The principal reason for this is that West Indian colloquial English gets most of its character, not from its consonants and vowels, but from its pitch, stress and overall intonation patterns, which have been shown to be strikingly different. In spite of this, however, specific claims have been variously made that, for example, Montserrat and Barbadian speech contain Irish or Scottish elements. It is always difficult to account for the characteristic elements of pronunciation in a variety and the more so in the case of the West Indies. Evidence connecting West Indian colloquial English with British varieties has not gone much further than being impressionistic and evidence connecting it with West African languages has principally been in the area of consonants and vowels. While such claims are of interest, it is the kinds of differences mentioned here which are more crucial.

West Indian colloquial English also differs from other varieties of English in vocabulary, idiom and minimally in sentence structure. The multitude of contributory factors in the history and culture of the West Indies, together with flora and fauna, have provided West Indian English with many characteristic, acceptable words, meanings and phrases. These range over a number of areas: there are irreplaceable words like *calypso, bush tea* and *ackee*; there are old words like *stupidness* and *cuffuffle* and new words like *shirtjac* and *ital*; there are words with West Indian meanings like *tea, lime, cool out* and (calypso)*tent* and usages like *stink* as an adjective; there are the many words of Carnival and other festivals, and words in several other categories. Over the years glossaries have appeared listing characteristically West Indian words, but in most cases these have been done for specific territories and have either concentrated on non-standard usage or have made no distinction between formally acceptable and unacceptable usage.

The understandable preference for the exotic and the exaggerated in print and in the electronic media has created the general impression that the specifically West Indian contribution to acceptable, literate English is minimal or non-existent. An examination of actual usage not only shows that the specifically West Indian contribution is significant but also illustrates the theoretical point familiar to anthropologists and translators – that a considerable amount of the significance or meaning of the language (formal and informal) of a community is specific to the community. In other words, it cannot be replaced without alteration or loss of expressiveness or meaning.

The characteristic sentence

She is to call him uncle

will not disturb most West Indians from the point of view of acceptability or meaning. On the other hand, most non-West Indian speakers of English will regard the structure as unusual if it has the meaning that West Indians give it:

She is his niece

or might suspect that the relationship between the two people is so-called rather than true, not realising that the words *niece* and *nephew* are far less frequently used in the West Indies than the other terms for blood relatives (*mother, father, son,* etc.). In other words, characteristic usage is not necessarily exclusive usage, but is in many cases preference for quite normal and 'innocent' words and phrases, which may or may not acquire special meanings. In fact, one of the claims about West Indian colloquial English is that the basic words of English are so heavily used (because of limitations of vocabulary of the people) that they come to acquire meanings which are acceptable to West Indians but unknown to speakers of other varieties of English.

Until studies of characteristic and acceptable West Indian colloquial English appear and become familiar, ignorance will continue to fuel negative beliefs about characteristically West Indian elements. Such negative beliefs are of course partly responsible for the use of foreign English and also for the notion that there is in existence an absolute entity called 'good English' into which all other forms of English can be translated.

Rasta English

The word *Rasta* is simply a shortened form of *Rastafarian*, which itself derives from *Ras Tafari*, of Ethiopian origin and specifically referring to Haile Selassie. No attempt will be made here to distinguish between 'true' and 'fraudulent' Rastas. No attempt will be made to distinguish between the terms *Rasta* and *Dread*. Such distinctions, which may be important elsewhere, are not germane to this presentation. The term *Rasta* has become a commonly used and general term covering certain facets of social behaviour and language. It will be used in this general sense in this presentation.

Rastafarianism has spread across the West Indies and affected all the people in a way unequalled by any other practice, belief or linguistic influence. Rastafarianism developed in Jamaica for more than twenty years before its sudden and quick spread across the West Indies. For example, when the most serious Rastafarian uprising took place in Jamaica in 1962, resulting in the leaders being tried for treason, Rastafarianism was unknown outside Jamaica and continued to be unknown in spite of the trial, except to a few people directly connected with Jamaica. When the unwilling god of Rastafarians, Haile Selassie, visited Jamaica in 1966, thus providing a spiritual peak for the brethren, Rastafarianism was still generally unknown as a practice outside Jamaica. In fact, it was only after the Black consciousness movement, heightened by events in North America, forcibly struck the West Indies around 1970 that Rastafarians were increasingly seen as less deviant and became more attractive symbolically. In addition, political leaders throughout the West Indies, probably in order to avoid the problems of Trinidad in 1970, unwittingly made the general population more aware of Rastafarians by passing laws against or imposing bans on people who looked like Rastas.

The anti-establishment, anti-war posture of movements like the hippies in the late 1960s affected the whole of the Western world and to some extent also facilitated the progress of Rastafarianism, which in itself was a way of life involving a religious belief, a social grouping, an economic method of self-employment and a non-partisan political stance. Movements like the hippies were associated with long hair and the use of drugs for the purpose of reaching an elevated state of mind. The same is the case with Rastafarianism. The effect of movements like the hippies is clear also from the fact that when Rastafarianism began to grow rapidly inside and outside Jamaica, it immediately became almost exclusively a young people's movement, which it was not necessarily in its early development in Jamaica. So what started off as a serious reaction against the status quo based on a philosophical rationale, became popular, fashionable and typical especially among the younger section of the population.

Unquestionably, however, the spread of Rastafarianism was stimulated by the boom of reggae music across the West Indies and far beyond. It is not simply that the language of the songs became the language of the people or that all reggae music was sung by Rastas, but that the most famous singers of reggae music were identified as Rastas and that the message of the music espoused or promoted a certain lifestyle involving the rejection of many traditional values and the promotion of other values, the best known of which are a certain hairstyle, a certain style of dress and a certain form of the language.

Since there is no essential or fully accepted link either objectively or in the early development of Rastafarianism between hair, dress and language, these three elements of Rastafarianism have had varying degrees of popularity. There is little doubt, however, that of the three, language is the most popular. The greater popularity of language over dress and hairstyle is clearly due to the fact that the last two are visible and concrete and require a much greater degree of courage and commitment especially in the face of hostile parents, relatives and administrators. Language behaviour, on the other hand, may be dismissed by the same people as the slang of youth, and adults themselves may use it in order to associate themselves with youthful things and not to appear old-fashioned, ignorant and inflexible.

Linguistically Rasta English is in some ways like cockney rhyming slang in that it is a transformation of a dialect of the language concentrating principally on sound correspondences. For Jamaicans Rasta English is substantially a matter of words; for non-Jamaicans it involves increasing familiarity with a non-native dialect together with word creation. In addition, the extent to which Rasta language is simple acquisition as distinct from creativity is related to the extent to which the person feels himself to be a Rasta and a speaker of an in-group language. Greater creativity is constantly required to preserve in-group status or in other words to remove the language from the clutches of those who are encroaching upon it.

Viewed from the point of view of the speaker of Jamaican creole English the vocabulary of Rasta speech can be divided into four parts:

- biblical and apocalyptic words;
- words related to Africa or things African;
- punning or playing on words;
- 'I' words.

Of these the only one that is truly novel is the last one. The other three are associated historically and currently with non-Rastafarian language inside and outside the West Indies. However, they do have specific and restricted reference within the context of Rastafarianism.

Violent biblical language, especially of the Old Testament, has been ever-present in the New World, especially in the lives of the slaves and their descendants, who were always the object of conversion. As was pointed out earlier, biblical language is near and dear to the hearts of many West Indians. Within recent times this same biblical language has become enmeshed with the language of harsh urban ghetto life, a context in which Rasta language flourished. Familiar biblical terms, which in their history had already been subject to re-interpretations and extensions in meaning, were again re-interpreted in the context of Jamaican ghetto life and the Jamaican society at large. For the Rastafarian, well-known proper names like *Babylon, Zion, Israelites,* and the title *Pharaoh* were given new meaning. In addition, as has always been the case, biblical events were related to current events and there seemed to be little distinction between predicted social revolution and divine intervention. Many words therefore took on double significance – e.g. *brethren, judgement day, captivity, redemption, freedom, war, darkness, enemy, paradise* – and words like *love, hate, burn, wail, dread, violence* came to characterise Rasta speech.

The fact that much of Rasta vocabulary deals with social protest is natural because Rastafarianism involves rejection of many traditional Western values and withdrawal from the mainstream of society. The connection between Rastafarianism and reggae music in this respect is also quite natural because both of the major streams of music in the West Indies (calypso and Jamaican music) have historically been tied to songs of social protest, the theme of emancipation and freedom, and the cultural practices of the black man. The biblical and apocalyptic nature of Rasta language is therefore the latest and most forceful manifestation of the fusion of two of the strongest themes and movements which have characterised the history of the West Indies: Christianity and the exploitation of the black man.

In the same way that in Haiti voodoo fuses European (Christian) and African religious beliefs and practices, Rastafarianism consciously did the same by pushing the prophecies of the Holy Scriptures southwards into Africa and adopting Selassie as 'lion of the tribe of Judah' and as lord and king. Rastafarianism flourished after 1970 because it provided a solution in a search for Black identity, an African god and a real or symbolic heaven, Ethiopia. That part of Rasta vocabulary which dealt with things African was therefore in union with the general promotion of Africa and things African. However, except for the word *Rasta*, some proper names and a few other words, the words used to symbolise African and Rastafarian features were not of African origin. Even the word *Jah*, the term for the Rasta deity, taken from Selassie's original name, Jah Ras Tafari, familiar to Barbadians specifically because there is an African King Jah Jah of Barbadian folklore fame, is intriguingly close to *Jehovah* (pronounced [Jahovah] by some) which is related to *yahweh*, a word used for God in early pre-English versions of the Bible. (The symbols j, y, i were used to refer to the same sound, so the first syllable in *yahweh* and *Jah* are similar in pronunciation.) In other words, the choice of the word *Jah* by Rastas to represent God fits perfectly into the tradition of ambivalence, ambiguity and religious syncretism, characteristic of word use in the West Indies and the wider Caribbean.

Many of the words used to refer to Rasta items are basically English words used with a new meaning, e.g. *sister, queen, reason, check, dreadlock, dub, weed, herb, chalice*. However, some of the words used in Rasta practices (smoking, drumming, chanting) are of direct Rasta creation; they may vary from community to community and are not always long-lasting. Much of this Rasta slang or in-group language depends on word-play, a combination of the visual, auditory and semantic features of words. Consider for example the title *Haile Selassie I. Haile* can give *hail*, the greeting of older English and now the Rasta greeting; it can give the Rasta name *Iley*; it can give *I* and coincide with the form following *Selassie*. *I* in the title means 'the first' and so is related to *one* (compare the concept of *number one* 'I' now fashionable in America). *I* in the title is pronounced [ai] (the same sound as English *eye*) by Rastas. [ai] can mean 'I' (first person singular) or 'eye' or 'high' (Jamaican pronunciation). [ai] is also the same as the last syllable in *Tafari*. *Tafari* combines [far] and [ai] into the meaning 'far-seeing', 'omniscient'. *I* is thus also related to *see, seen, sight*, favourite words of Rastas. The full title *Haile Selassie I, Ras Tafari, the Most High* is then not only an alliterative play on the sounds of the words, but a rich interplay of meanings also.

Such an interplay of sounds and meanings is not essentially different from the tradition of ambiguity and the risqué found in calypso where the artist subtly manipulates the sounds of the language in order to deal with taboo areas or political topics. It is also not far removed from the malapropism or inaccurate word structure common in performance English (see pp. 28–29). In addition, the kind of word-fracturing that occurs normally in the West Indies as in *op it in* < *open it* and *devel it up* < *develop it* indicates that syllables can have a greater degree of independence. The acute awareness of the sounds of the language and the fusion of sounds and meanings was superbly exemplified by a Jamaican cricket spectator who, enthralled by the unrivalled prowess of Sir Garfield Sobers, shouted from the stands:

'Garfield St Aubyn Sobers, G–S–A–S, Jesus, God sent *a* Saviour'

Playing with the sounds and structures of words has also been regarded by Rastas as an attempt to make the words more logical or more consistent with progressive thinking. The examples most often given to illustrate this are the words *oppress* and *forward*. The word *oppress* is changed to *downpress* because *op-* is phonetically the same as *up* and so inconsistent with the meaning of the word. The word *forward*, the meaning of which is clear, is used as a verb for almost all motions, i.e. 'going', 'coming', 'leaving', 'returning', by the Rasta. Such an intellectual approach to language change is rare and lends itself to inconsistency and individualism, because there can be very little consistency in the universal semantic interpretations of the sounds of English words and far less in subsequent changes attempting to 'rectify' the words or to select out only the 'forward' looking ones. As a result Rasta language is highly variable in this respect and differs from group to group. This in itself is regarded positively by Rastas for whom manipulating language is a primary, essential and constant element of Rastafarianism.

The really novel part of Rasta vocabulary, 'I' words, also varies in size from group to group, but there are certain basic 'I' words which characterise Rasta speech, giving it its special identity. These words are *I, I-man, I and I; I-rie* [airi], *I-tal, I-yah* [aiya], *I-tes* [aits]. Structurally these words are of two types – words used as pronouns (the first three) and words deriving from English words with their first syllable being (changed to) the sound [ai]. For example, *I-tal* derives from *vital*, and *I-yah* and *I-tes* are the non-standard Jamaican pronunciation of *higher* and *heights*. *I-rie*, which is regarded by many today as a Rasta word, has a long history in Jamaica. Note the following in Lewis (1834: 201):

'– "Massa, please, me want one little coat."
– "A little coat! For what?"
– "Massa, please, for wear when me go to the Bay?"
– "And why should you wear a little coat when you go to the bay?"
– "Massa, please, make me look *eerie* (buckish) when me go abroad."
So I assured him that he looked quite *eerie* enough already; . . .'

The connection in form and popular usage between *I-rie* and *eerie* seems quite clear. Another characteristic of these words is that they are not restricted to a specific sentence slot or part of speech as in English, but have freedom of occurrence. The words used as pronouns – *I,*

I-man, I and I – are used as subject, object or in any other position in the sentence.

Most other 'I' words are commonly used words in the wider society with their first syllable changed to [ai] or words with their first syllable as [ai] and the rest of the word constructed in accordance with English word structure. For example, *ailalu* comes from *callalu*, *I-niverse* from *universe*, but *creation* gives *I-ration*. It is this set of 'I' words which is limitless and highly variable. One of the overt marks of a Rasta is a Rasta name and in many cases in order to retain a link between past and new name the new convert changes his old name by replacing the first syllable with [ai], e.g. *David* becomes *I-vid* [aivid]; *Llewellyn* becomes I-lo [ailo]. On the whole today, 'I' words, which initially had a strong philosophical motivation, provide the easiest means of claiming to be a Rasta.

However, Rasta language is not simply a matter of changing words. In fact, just as a stream of speech may be identified as non-standard English even though it contains only a few non-standard features, so too speech may be identified as Rasta speech even though it contains only a few Rasta words. The reason for this is that Rasta speech contains very strong pronunciation, sentence and conversational features designed to create an unmistakable style of speaking. In fact, the overall effect so created disturbs many traditional-minded people to such an extent that it prevents them from following the content of what is being said and makes them come to the conclusion that the primary purpose of such speech is to shock and disturb rather than to communicate.

In Jamaican Creole English there is a tendency to change [ə] in an unstressed syllable and [ɔ] in certain contexts to [a]. This tendency is carried further in Rasta speech by 'drawing out' the vowel or making it long. For example, the words *Rasta* and *Ethiopia* are pronounced in standard English contexts with the same vowel at the end as that in the word *the*. The Rasta pronunciation of the words makes the final vowel the same as that in the musical note *la*. The same vowel is also used by Rastas in words that in English end in *-tion*. The same vowel also occurs in a word like *war*. This change to [a:] is strong in Jamaican Rastas even if it is not universally so in non-Jamaican Rastas.

There is also in Rasta speech a clear tendency to speak with a 'deep voice' rather than in the normal pattern of the rest of the society. Generally such a practice is associated with attempts at being macho or sexy, but in the case of Rasta speech this is not so. In fact, it is often interpreted as threatening. It may best be interpreted as a counter to the patterns of standard English used in polite circles. For instance, phrases like *please, do, I'm so sorry, excuse me, pardon me* most often require high-pitched and 'light' tones and are used because they are socially necessary rather than because the speaker means what he says.

It is one of the Rasta's intentions to reject the hypocrisy of socially polite English and so he employs a different kind of intonation with deeper tones, which seems to him more consistent with the image of the black man. Furthermore, the Rasta's non-use of the phrases themselves is a refusal to agree with the generally accepted notion that they are expressions of civility rather than of subservience.

The sentence and conversational features of Rasta speech combine to give it a special kind of effect. The two significant features of sentences are an involved sentence structure and repetitions; the significant conversational feature is interjections or what may be regarded as indentation in the sentence. Consider the following extracts from Pollard, 1983b (transcribed from recordings by Kathryn Shields):

'(a)   Listen me now, Miss, about this whole rule and thing them a talk bout. By them know say by by whereby Rastaman live, but, Miss, I a wonder, simple, the basic thing with them Rastaman things is love, seen, so that if you just live, Miss, with love as your guideline, I don't see how . . . you don't really need no really rule and thing . . . Take the simple concept of love, Miss, you really see how certain things must be wrong, like war, envious and them thing there must be wrong, yu no siit?

(b)   This price increase is for that reason . . . right . . . like take corned beef, dollar ninety three, bap, gone sky high. Man couldn't afford . . . aam . . . to buy rice and thing, yu no siit . . . and use his bread and corned beef, you see that gone out of his reach now.

(c)   Well, is what . . . you know is really bad, for as a black person now, you have certain people, not even as a black person, as a citizen of this world, for I know that them people here know a substantial amount about Haile Selassie first, yu no siit, just because them people see to it that them know what going on in Earth.'

Normal conversation is often elliptical because the interlocutors understand much of what is going to be said without it having to be expressly said. Normal conversation also contains repetition because speakers are interrupted or because they want to stress their point. In addition, the spoken language, in contrast to the written, is characterised by mazes of ill-formed sentences as the speaker stops. However, the thread of thought is easy to follow.

In the preceding passages the thread of thought is not so easy to follow. In the first passage, for example, the hearer's thought process is diverted first of all by the pronunciation and intonation, then by the playing with sounds (*by by whereby*), by the interjections and repetitions. Note that this is a case of a student speaking to a teacher where the teacher has to try to follow what is being said, in contrast to much of normal conversation in which the hearer does not have to and in most cases does not hear precisely what the speaker says.

In the case of the second passage, without the intonational pattern it does not seem different from normal Jamaican speech. However, the use of *man* ('poor people') quickly followed by *yu no siit* gives the whole passage the stamp of Rasta speech. In the case of the third passage the only indication structurally that the speaker is a Rasta is the interjection of *yu no siit* and the combination *in Earth* (compare older versions of the Lord's Prayer's *. . . in Earth as it is in heaven*). It is therefore the pronunciation of the spoken language principally which distinguishes the form of speech.

One of the requirements of conversation is that the hearer must acknowledge the speaker by giving some indication of comprehension, agreement or encouragement. This is done normally in English by the interjection of *yes, uh-huh, I see, I know*, etc. when the speaker pauses. Arguments have been put forward that this is very important in African and Afro-American cultures, as for example in audience reaction in story-telling, joke-telling, calypso singing, in the call and response structure of slave work songs and of African singing generally and also of Afro-American preaching. Whether or not this is stronger in African and Afro-American cultures than in other cultures, there is no doubt that indications of acknowledgement are a primary characteristic of Rasta speech. In fact, it is not only the listener who interjects expressions, but also the speaker himself. The salient feature of these expressions is that they differ from those of normal English so strikingly that they are attractive to the general population, they are filtering into the general language and they are the first features of acquisition either in becoming a Rasta, in appearing to be a Rasta, or in appeasing Rastas. Interjecting expressions such as *seen, sight* is fairly general whereas *love, I-rie* [airi], *yu no siit, Jah Rastafari* still appear to require some implication or indication of Rastafarianism.

Popular music in the form of reggae music, drumming and chanting, which all helped to popularise Rastafarianism, have also given rise to 'Dub Poetry', a popular form of entertainment in Jamaica which combines poetry and Rasta language and is set to the beat of reggae music. It is significant that Rastafarianism is able to make appealing the literary genre of poetry which traditionally in the West Indies was restricted to the formal domain of the academic.

The spread of Rastafarian language throughout the West Indies outside Jamaica illustrates again (see Foreign English, pp. 18–24) the great propensity and ability of West Indians to imitate non-native dialects. There is obviously no formal training and no mass migration of Rastas across the West Indies, so that Rasta speech was spread indirectly through music, by young Jamaicans residing in other West Indian islands, by those returning from Jamaica after living there some time, and also by those involved in the trafficking and use of marijuana. Rastafarianism has never had or required central leadership. It has always allowed groups and individuals the freedom of variation, which some have used as licence to do whatever they please. It is probably this aspect of freedom which has made it appealing to young people throughout the West Indies. For although much of Rasta speech outside Jamaica involves the imitation of Jamaican Creole patterns, which are the source of Rasta speech, there is no compulsion to use them. It is quite normal therefore for Rasta speech outside Jamaica to be produced with the patterns of the local non-standard dialect with only the basic and common Rasta words serving as an identifying mark of all Rasta speech. Linguistic creativity and freedom for Rastas is further illustrated by the fact that Rastas have devised their own patterns in St Lucia, where the language of the majority of the people is not immediately compatible with Jamaican Creole.

From its very beginnings Rasta language has supplied fuel to the argument whether the English language in its standard form in the West Indies is a deliberate tool of colonialism and oppression or whether it is the path to progress and an integral part of the West Indies. The fact that English is the official language in the West Indies and has never been seriously challenged as such means that it is generally accepted as the path to progress. At the same time it is generally realised that a great number – probably the majority of people in the West Indies – simply because of the circumstances of their birth and through no fault of their own are put at a serious disadvantage and discriminated against because of their ignorance of standard English. Rastafarianism may seem to some to be a means of escaping from these two realities and a way of establishing independence and self-confidence.

In other words, in order to avoid being looked down on for being able to use only Creole or non-standard English, and in order to avoid the humiliation of trying but failing to produce standard English or in order to avoid the pretensions and lack of camaraderie involved in the use of standard English, the person turns to Rasta language as a way of getting around the difficulty. The fact that there are many well-educated West Indians proficient in standard English who are Rastas and use Rasta language prevents Rasta language from having the stigma of being the language of the illiterate and the poor and makes it a viable alternative for some as a social language.

Profane English

The term 'profane English' is being used here to refer to impolite and shocking expressions and obscenities (used in cursing) involving God and religious things and also sex, sexual organs and practices. Profane English or 'bad language' is of course not restricted to the West Indies and generally can be looked at both as a type of behaviour and as an attempt to add to the colour and effectiveness of language. In the case of the West Indies, however, there is the question whether the frequency of profane English is higher as a result of social and economic frustration and of frustration with the English language itself. There is also the Afro-American tradition, a part of performance English, which features individuals trying to outcurse each other, and which may historically and 'culturally' help to account for the level of profanity in the West Indies. Without substantive proof many West Indians believe that the level of profanity is unusual and significant.

Profanity is used not only in serious contexts but also in comic ones. Profanity sometimes indicates a close and friendly relationship between males and it is quite clear that there is little equality between the sexes in this matter. Among young males it has always been, like smoking cigarettes and drinking alcohol, one of the ways to indicate manhood. Also among young people principally profanity is a source of great fun and laughter when it is used by or to persons who do not understand the meaning and correct context of it. Although such 'experimentation' with profanity is characteristic of many societies, it is known to be more characteristic of lower-class behaviour than of upper-class.

Arrests and convictions for the use of indecent language alone net governments in the West Indies a sizeable sum of money each year and indicate the extent of the occurrence and the seriousness with which it is treated. The public use of indecent language can be interpreted as the ultimate tool of the powerless and frustrated, and an immediate, spontaneous and satisfying way of humiliating the opponent, without having to resort to physical violence in some cases and as an accompaniment to violence in others. Of course in most cases the opponent reacts to profanity in similar vein and the ensuing 'bassa-bassa' may be won or lost according to one's proficiency in profanity. Profanity is also a part of the marketplace either between vendor and vendor or between vendor and unwilling customer – the customer who refuses to buy and indicates that the goods are defective or too expensive is just as likely to be followed by a stream of obscenity as a vendor who tries to gain advantage over his competitors. Even the beggar who does not receive according to his expectation will resort to obscenity to show his dissatisfaction. Profane language in public is therefore a significant feature of West Indian life.

Life in villages and tenantries, and in ghettos and tenements, has people existing together in such close quarters that friction becomes a constant element. This friction is most often manifested in verbal confrontation between mother and children, woman and man, and between neighbours, all of whom become accustomed to the use of obscenities. The use of profane English is therefore so real that it is referred to in many different ways. The basic words like *cuss < curse* and *buse < abuse* are expanded in many colourful ways with noun or prepositional phrases containing as many obscene words as the situation seems to demand. The same basic words are transformed into nouns (*cussing, busing*) and used in phrases like *give someone a good cussing, put a good cussing in his ass, bathe his ass in cuss* and many others. There are also words referring to confrontations, like *cuss out, cuss-cuss*.

The words used in profane English in the West Indies are for the most part the same as those used in most English-speaking communities and in sentence position they are used with the same freedom of occurrence. In other words, these words may be merely expletives or they may fit into sentences as nouns, verbs, adjectives or other parts of speech. In addition, words referring to God may be combined with words relating to sex, so that an original oath like *May God strike you dead* may be transformed in many ways usually leaving unchanged only the word *God*. Although there is a great deal of latitude in choice of words in profane English constructions, there must be conformity with the basic structures of the dialect. Thus profane English which is not expletive or oaths (alone or as part of sentences) is essentially either name-calling where the profane word is the noun, the adjective or both, or action words where the profane word is the verb or a modifier in the predicate or both.

In many cases where the profane word is a part of name-calling, it may simply be an accompaniment to excitement or used in awe or admiration. This is especially so at peak moments in games outdoors (e.g. cricket) or indoors (e.g. dominoes). In fact, if one were to consider the differences between the playing of bridge and dominoes in the West Indies, a major one would be the level and crucial role of obscenity in the latter in which it is used to enhance reputations, excuse defeat, intimidate opponents and humiliate partners.

There are of course specifically West Indian words used in profane English referring to male and female body parts, menstruation, homosexuality, sexual intercourse and other areas usually identified in profanity, but in most cases these words are territory-specific. The one word that is commonly used in all the territories is *rass* which is related to *ass < arse*. However, whereas in most of the territories it is a fairly strong word, it does not seem to have the same intensity for Trinidadians. Of all West Indians Jamaicans are the only ones who in using obscene language make constant reference to and have a number of words for women's sanitary pads and it is only in Jamaica that a word as innocent as *parts* can be used as an obscene word.

Profane English which characterises situations of stress, frustration and anger is understandable even if its use is generally regarded as coarse behaviour. So too is profane English used to show manhood or to provoke mirth. However, when obscenity is consistently used to add colour and effectiveness to language and when it seems to be an integral part of the language of a considerable number of individuals, it has to be examined as possibly symptomatic of a social, psychological or linguistic disorder.

Sex is undeniably one of the main preoccupations of human beings. However, it is much more so for poor people since in comparison with other pleasures it is not as costly. It is also revealed in its details more graphically at an earlier age and constantly to people living in close conditions caused by poverty. In addition, words associated with sex are mostly regarded as taboo or obscene. There is therefore a reasonable explanation for the prominence of sex and obscenity in the language of poor people who transfer the terms and images of sex to other contexts. The problem is that in contexts where profane English is not permitted or is not normal the speaker is not able to express himself effectively and seems deficient, and if there are a considerable number of speakers of this type, it is the language of the community as a whole that seems deficient and not providing enough flexibility and style to cope with all contexts.

Although it is dangerous to generalise about the number of major types of languages which are normal in most societies, one can safely say that few societies exhibit as many types as is the case in the West Indies. Educated, colloquial, network and slang types are common in most developed and developing societies with profane language present but not dominant. 'Foreign' versions of many languages exist (i.e. a language may be spoken in many different countries) and vary in degree of appeal to non-natives, but seldom assume the importance that they do in the West Indies. Speakers of regional dialects in most countries who are socially and geographically mobile face the pressures of having to adjust to some national standard, but are seldom confronted with the assumption or widespread belief that their native speech is not a language. And few societies are currently being confronted by a form of speech which is deliberately created as anti-standard or a-standard as is the case with Rasta language in the West Indies.

The individual's choice of types according to their appropriateness is not necessarily any more difficult in the West Indies than it is anywhere else, because each individual will already have developed his own idiosyncracies which limit his choices. The more important considerations are firstly whether all these types in the West Indies cohabit happily or whether they are like seven men going in different directions, and secondly whether the existence of so many types puts language in too prominent a place in the development of society, consuming energy that could be put to better use elsewhere.

Laws in all societies indicate quite clearly that the use of profanity is regarded as disruptive and undesirable behaviour. At the same time psychologists will say that it is necessary for people to 'let off steam'. Others will say that pent-up energy from frustration can be channelled into paths much more productive than profanity. Rastafarianism is regarded by some as an innocent (as opposed to society-threatening) energy-consuming form of escapism in which the very use of violent rhetoric and the preoccupation with language and music diffuse the energy and frustrations of the user. Profane English and Rasta English may then be of much greater importance than at first realised. Viewed from an economic point of view these two types can be judged as negative in that they use up human energy without producing anything useful. Viewed from a social point of view they can be judged as positive in that energy is being diverted and dissipated which without outlet would be destructive. Whether the economic is more important than the social is not easily resolved, but it should be noted that 100 percent useful use of energy in the production of anything is virtually impossible.

Foreign English presents itself as a paradox and a dilemma. It is the type that has been longest in existence – that is, from the days of the earliest settlers and absentee landlords – and it is still a major influence in West Indian English. There is widespread documentation of comments from the earliest days of colonisation by visiting Englishmen to the effect that the speech of the 'locals' was substandard in some way. 'Locals' in earlier days referred to white people, but the tenor of the comments has remained the same even if the colour of the 'locals' has changed. Nowadays the same attitude is maintained in the media and especially in the comic stereotyping of West Indian speech found in television programmes made in the USA. (Stereotyping is characteristic of US television and is not necessarily intentionally malicious; it is generally used as a quick and easy method of identification without having to spend time on explanation. The comic aspect of it is accepted as an added bonus.)

It is evident that although the element of racism cannot be completely ruled out, foreign English is principally related to the metropolitan, sophisticated, international and unrestricted as opposed to the local, stigmatised and restricted. This is not a situation that will change and it is not really unique. Speakers in the Southern States of the USA have always been the object of laughter because of their 'drawl' and even today are 'encouraged' to change or are schooled out of their 'accents' in order to be 'more intelligible' nationally. The response of Southerners, whatever the reason may be, has generally been one of acquiescence. In a country that is very sensitive to issues of equality and discrimination, there are no movements to have Southern speech accepted as being just as sophisticated as Northern speech;

there are no significant cases brought before the court for discrimination against Southern speakers, and many university departments of speech therapy and speech pathology still spend a lot of energy teaching specific 'acceptable' accents. Acquiescence suggests that learning of a non-native and less marked accent is reasonable and advantageous. It also suggests that language is not so important and productive an issue in itself as to consume the energy of the people. This does not mean however that Southerners like Northern accents or are increasingly losing their dislike for them. It may be just a matter of 'facing facts'.

The notion of cultural pluralism, which has been presented for the West Indies and which may be used to discredit the acceptance of a single (foreign-influenced) linguistic standard, is a much greater factor in the USA, but there it has not changed the quality of network standard – it is easier for an English-born, standard-speaking person to become a newsreader on national television than for a Southern-speaking American. The real dilemma for the West Indies results from the fact that the West Indies are small, fragile, developing new nations seeking identity and independence in a world in which characteristic identity and independence in such nations is progressively being undermined by technology, communications and power struggles. In short, marks of identity and independence in small, developing nations are merely symbolic, and the only way of preserving self-esteem and human dignity, whereas alignment with and acceptance of the foreign may be the easiest and most practical way to power. The other ongoing dilemma is that although West Indian governments have always accepted the realities of standard English and foreigners, informally West Indians spend a lot of energy objecting to the privileges given to foreign 'experts', foreigners and speakers of foreign English.

3 · *Creole English*

It is easier to use the term 'Creole English' than it is to use the term 'English Creole', for most of those who have studied Creoles will disagree about the reality of Creoles in the West Indies because of the great amount of variation between speakers, the spectrum of varieties, the competence of speakers and the differences between the territories. Laymen also will disagree because they seldom regard non-standard language as anything but language which is not standard; that is, as bad grammar, sporadic mistakes or slips. In other words, language which is not standard English in the West Indies is so wide and varied, sometimes apparently English, sometimes clearly not, that to try to present it as an entity would be contrary to the interpretation of both linguists and laymen. The term 'Creole English' allows for a number of notions: firstly that one is dealing with forms of English that are not 'normal'; secondly that these forms are the result of the experience or history of the West Indies; and thirdly that in addition to the English element there are common threads in what appears to be unending variation.

The term 'Creole English' also allows one to establish a connection between the same or similar threads occurring outside the West Indies either in the Caribbean or elsewhere, without having to set up a language type called 'Creole'. Therefore, the contention whether there are clearly separable Creole languages in the West Indies does not prevent one from identifying features individually. In addition, by identifying a feature as part of Creole English it counteracts the tendency to dismiss features as special or restricted or typical of only a certain small segment of the population or as slips or mistakes.

The common view that a feature is a mistake because it is contrary to a stated pattern is very often unhelpful in that it often prevents one from seeing the frequency and distribution of the feature and also from seeing that it might be something more than a 'mistake'. Objective analysis of non-standard language in the West Indies shows quite clearly that there are a number of features outside the English language which recur in a patterned way and even if these features are not regarded as or cannot be put together as a relatively homogeneous entity, they are there and form a normal part of the language and competence of West Indians. These features therefore can be described according to linguistic principles.

Features that will be identified as elements of Creole English do not necessarily occur, or occur with the same frequency, in all the West Indian territories. However, because certain features can be identified as Creole features based on their occurrence in the West Indies and elsewhere, it is more informative to give all the major Creole features which occur in the West Indies rather than only those common to all the territories. In general, differences in word and sentence structure make such fundamental distinctions between dialects and languages that where they exist in significant number the forms of speech are seldom regarded as the same language. Such conclusive distinctions are not easily reached in the case of the West Indies, however, because the features of pronunciation, vocabulary and meaning in Creole English are more perceptible and more ambiguous.

In this presentation of the features of Creole English there is no doubt that identification of features as Creole features is in many cases dependent on a judgement about acceptability as well as linguistic differences in form and structure. In other words, the presentation tries to conform both to linguistic principles and lay perceptions. This analysis is based on actual, current, everyday speech. It neither selects out the 'ideal Creole' type features so beloved by linguists nor does it try to promote the traditional layman's position that they do not exist, for as Craig (1971) says:

> 'At present it would seem that the spontaneous as well as careful speech of a majority of school-age children lies entirely within the interaction area. That is, it is neither Creole nor standard West Indian, nor yet again does it represent a discrete, stable speech norm of its own.'

If there is a leaning towards a specific section of the population, it is towards younger, urban people, because they represent the overwhelming majority in all the territories. However, the actual everyday speech of old, uneducated, rural people is not significantly different. This is quite clearly suggested by Beryl Bailey who, in an analysis of Jamaican speech in 1971, concludes:

> 'There are three social dialects represented here, the two most extreme represented by a single household, with the grandmother [a 60-year-old in an isolated village in the middle of the island] and not the grandson, manifesting the socially more accepted behavior.'

The quality of vowels very often provokes negative reactions among social groups. One however has to distinguish between different negatively perceived features and Creole features. For example, when a Dominican reverses the vowels of *sleep* and *slip*, this can be regarded as non-English, because it is not characteristic of any other English-speaking community. When a Barbadian produces *tremble* as *trimble* or *catch* as *cetch*, this is non-standard English, not only because it is indeed an older form of English (which is no longer standard) but also because in pronunciation it is not clearly removed from all other varieties of current English. The simple fact that such features are not standard English does not automatically mean that they are Creole features, for Creole features are general throughout the West Indies and elsewhere, whereas these are simply characteristics of specific territories, and every territory has its own characteristics.

The sounds of Creole English
Vowels

Vowels are identified by linguists on a horizontal–vertical chart which is meant to correspond roughly to the forward–backward, high–low movements made by the tongue in the articulation of vowels. For example, in the word *see* the tongue is pushed forward and upward to articulate the vowel; in *cool* the tongue is pulled backward and upward. The word *see* therefore has a high front vowel and *cool* a high back vowel.

Creole vowels generally are characterised not so much by special individual sounds but in terms of the system they present as a whole; i.e. the number of vowels, their relation to each other and what they occur next to. Figure 3.1 is a diagram of Creole English vowels, covering sounds that occur across the territories. As is the case in all languages the specific articulation of each vowel changes slightly depending on the nature of preceding and following sounds; the nature of gliding (gradual change of vowel sound within the same syllable) and the extent of nasalisation (amount of the airstream coming through the nose) also differ from other varieties of English.

	FRONT	CENTRAL	BACK
HIGH	i		u
	ɪ		ʊ
MID	e	ə	o
	ɛ	ʌ	
LOW		a, a:	ɔ

There are also the following vowel glides:

	FRONT	CENTRAL	BACK
	ie		uo
			ou
		aɪ	

Fig. 3.1 Creole English vowels.

Standard varieties of English usually have more low vowels, either low front or low back or both. For example, formal preaching and praying style, which is not a normal context for Creole English, has a low back vowel, e.g. *Our* F*ather, who* a*rt* ... As far as the mid-vowels [e] and [o] are concerned, there is a difference in their realisation in Creole English, colloquial English and non-West Indian varieties of English, which can be illustrated as follows:

British	Colloquial	Creole English	Word
eɪ	e	ie	w*ai*t, c*a*ke
ɛə	e	ie	h*ai*r, c*a*re
əu	o	uo, ua	c*o*ke, n*o*
uə	o	uo, ua	c*u*re, m*o*st

Nasalisation is much less easily illustrated principally because it is much more subjectively perceived and because it does not make significant meaning distinction between words. Speakers of one territory in the West Indies may recognise nasalisation, identify it either as 'speaking through one's nose' or by mimicking, and associate it more with another territory than with their own. Yet generally all the territories in the West Indies are said to have more nasalisation in their non-standard speech than is characteristic of other varieties of English. Nasalisation occurs in the vicinity of nasal consonants or where nasal consonants existed in the original English word (etymon). For example, the etymons *can't* and *man* have produced [kyãã] and [mã] respectively, the latter being specifically used as in a tag (i.e. tacked on before or after the clause), e.g.

Mã, a kyãã duu it, mã   'Man, I can't do it, man'

Nasality, or the impression that more air is escaping through the nose consistently in all utterances, is even more difficult to characterise. The impression is certainly not a response restricted to non-standard West Indies speech, but has been variously identified as a general characteristic of Creoles, and especially in story-telling, one of the major cultural domains of Creoles. There is little evidence, however, that it is an outstanding and clearly identifiable characteristic of Creole English as opposed to a vague or idiosyncratic trait.

Consonants

The articulation of consonants is a much clearer mark of Creole English than that of vowels. There are consonantal correspondences between Creole English and standard English, some of which are vibrant and consistent and others waning and inconsistent. The examples most cited by linguist and layman alike are the standard English sounds represented by the spelling *th* and their equivalents in Creole English. The correspondences can be symbolised as follows:

Standard English	Creole English	Word
θ	t	*th*ief, tee*th*
ð	d	*th*at, ba*th*e

Although out of all the features of a language these correspondences relate only to two consonants, their general salience over all other features is explained by the fact that the words in which they occur are the most frequently used and unavoidable ones in the language. It is virtually impossible to produce a coherent chain of sentences in English without using articles, pronouns, possessive adjectives and adverbs. The high frequency of the words *the, this, these, those, they, them, their, there, then* ensures that the correspondence between [d̪] and [d] together with that between [θ] and [t] remains very prominent.

Less consistent and declining are the correspondences between [l] and [r]; and [b] and [v]. The two liquid sounds [l] and [r] are historically related in a considerable number of the world's languages. The phonetic similarity which causes a Chinese to produce the English word *rice* as *lice*, much to the amusement of English speakers, is also responsible for the Saramaccan in Suriname producing *Rasta* as [lasta]. This correspondence is rare now in Creole English, but exists still in words like [fingəl] < *finger* = 'handle or touch' and [flɪtaz] < *fritters*. The correspondence between [b] and [v] is not as rare, but is declining. It occurs in a number of words, e.g. [nebəl] < *navel*; [bɪtl] < *victuals*.

Another correspondence, which is just as strong as the *th* one and for the same kind of reason, is that which can be called the *ng* correspondence. In phonetic terms, the sound [ŋ], spelled *ng*, corresponds to the sound [n] in Creole English. In contrast to the *th* correspondence which is general (i.e. Creole English replaces [d̪] and [θ] wherever they occur), the *ng* correspondence is restricted. It occurs only in what is or originates as the present participle ending in English (i.e. *-ing*). In other words, the *ng* correspondence is not simply a matter of pronunciation; it relates only to specific word endings. To illustrate further, Creole English and standard English both have the nasal sound [ŋ] in *thing, sing, sting, ring*, etc., but Creole English does not have it at the end of the words corresponding to the standard English words *singing, ringing, eating*, etc. However, it must be understood that whereas the citation form of the English word (i.e. the word in isolation) has the nasal sound [ŋ], represented in spelling *-ng*, in actual speech the precise sound of the consonant in standard English varies according to the context.

Examples of Creole English in some territories which seems to contradict the rule given are two combined forms of the word *thing* deriving from *something* and *nothing*. In Creole English these are realised as [sʌmn] and (nʌtn] with the nasal at the end of each forming a second syllable. The reason for these two words having [n] at the end is that the vowel [ɪ] in the original word weakens and disappears, and Creole English adopts the pattern of English generally in not having [ŋ] but [n] occurs on its own as a syllable. Where a form like [nutɪn] or [nufɪn] occurs, it represents a movement from the basic Creole English form back towards standard English.

The salience of [n] as a replacement for [ŋ] in Creole English is a direct result of the high frequency of occurrence of the participle form. Since the verb is the most important element in the sentence and since the -*in* participle form is used in Creole English to render aspects of future, present and past, and also as a noun form, it means that although one is dealing with a single consonant, its high frequency in its occurrence as a suffix makes it more noticeable than most other features of Creole English.

Structure of syllables

Another area of phonology which shows salient Creole English features is syllable structure. The lack of an absolute limit to the length of a syllable in English spelling is not necessarily preserved in English pronunciation, but English pronunciation still allows for syllables with a number of consonants. For example, *sixths* [sikθs] and *strengths* [strɛŋθs] are both monosyllabic words with four and six consonants respectively, even if all the consonants after the vowel are not often articulated. This kind of clustering of consonants is not characteristic of Creole English, especially when the cluster occurs after the vowel. Creole English reduces or restructures English consonant clusters within and across syllables by either rearranging the sounds, increasing the number of sounds or decreasing the number of sounds. However, in most cases today when the consonant cluster occurs before the vowel in standard English, it is more or less the same in Creole English.

The loss of [s] at the beginning of words like *strong*, *string*, *split* is not common in Creole English today as it was before. However, its loss at the end of many words is quite normal and related to factors which are not purely a matter of pronunciation but are more of word and sentence structure. For instance, the [s] which indicates third person singular in the verb, possessive and plural in the noun is weak, if not completely absent, in Creole English, whether the verb or noun ends in a consonant or not. Its weakness or absence is therefore better explained in terms of word structure than in terms of pronunciation alone. It is certainly not the case that Creole English speakers do not or cannot produce a consonant cluster with an [s] at the end, because they clearly do in common words like *box*, *mix*, *fix*, *axe* (the written symbol *x* is actually pronounced as [ks], and there is absolutely no case for even suggesting that writing is a crucial factor).

Clusters of two consonants after a vowel, except those with a liquid sound [l] or a nasal [n] not followed by [d], are usually reduced to one consonant in Creole English; that is, the last consonant disappears. The following are examples:

Standard English	Creole English
ask	[as]
last	[las]
blind, kind, find	[-ain]
bend, bond, band	[b-n]
mild, cold	[mail] [kuol]

The disappearance of [d] in the last examples is a result of its closeness in articulation to [n] and [l] – this means that they are identical sounds except for the fact that in their articulation the airstream comes through the mouth in the former and the nose in the latter. [l] and [d] are both orally produced, but in the production of [l] the airstream flows over the sides of the tongue whereas in [d] it comes over the tip.

In contrast, clusters after the vowel are usually maintained in cases where the consonants are more than minimally different, as for example in *milk, pelt, chink, bench, lamp, pint, lunch.* One common Creole English word which at first seems to contradict this rule is that derived from *want.* In reality in this case the nasal [n] caused the vowel to become nasalised and lengthened and then both consonants disappeared or only the [t] remains – *want* > [wãã] or [wããt].

There are many past-tense verb forms in English which have consonant clusters at the end in their spoken form, e.g. *spent, went, asked*, which are not preserved in Creole English. This is a result of word structure rather than merely pronunciation. In other words, the Creole English verb form comes from the basic form of the verb in English (usually the uninflected 'dictionary' form), e.g. *spend, go, ask*, and the past tense is rendered in accordance with the rules of syntax of Creole English.

Standard English also has a number of negative contracted forms with an [nt] cluster at the end, e.g. *wouldn't, won't, couldn't, can't*. These words do not occur in Creole English with final clusters for reasons of word structure rather than for reasons of pronunciation. Basically in Creole English negation in these auxiliary verbs is rendered by nasalisation of the vowel, e.g. *kyãã, wʌ̃, dĩ, kʌ̃, shʌ̃*, or with a nasal consonant *wudn, kudn, shudn, didn, musn*. The history of the structure of negation in auxiliaries is not straightforward or without contention, and is not a simple matter of consonant cluster reduction.

It should be quite clear therefore that Creole English does not indiscriminately reduce all the consonant clusters of standard English, but that certain clusters may not occur as a result of the word and sentence structure of Creole English and that where reduction occurs it is according to phonological principles and, contrary to popular belief, it is the 'harder' clusters, the ones in which the consonants are more different, that are preserved.

The case of [r] after a vowel and before a consonant, as in *hard*, is one of the most common features of English dialectology, dependent as it is on the varying pronunciations of [r]. It is better dealt with as a dialectal difference between the West Indian territories than as a consonant cluster feature of Creole English.

In addition to consonant cluster reduction, Creole English restructures English words by inserting a vowel, thus called *epenthetic*, between consonants. This can happen whether or not the consonants are in the same syllable, as in [pubəlɪk] < *public*, [ɪngəlɪš] < *English* or [wʌrəm] < *worm*, [heləm] < *helm*. The last two examples follow the same pronunciation rules as standard English [prɪzəm] *prism*. The English word *film* occurs in Creole English either as [fɪləm], thus in the pattern of the last examples, or is metathesised as [flɪm].

One other salient feature of Creole English which occurs under syllable structure is the relationship between consonants and vowels that results in the development of what is called a palatal sound between them. Development of a palatal sound, or palatalisation, is normal in several languages including English. In fact, it distinguishes some dialects of British speech from some of American speech, as for example in the production of words like *news* and *tune*: ➥

British	American
nyuz	nuz
tyun	tun

Palatalisation is normal in all dialects of English in a number of words where [k] and [p] occur before [u] as in *cube, cure, queue, cue, pure, puke, pubic, pupil*. And it is optional in *lure*.

Creole English has the palatal [y] after the velar consonants [k] and [g] before a central vowel [a], e.g.

kyar	'car'	gyardən	'garden'
kyāā	'can't'	gyas	'gas'
kyat	'cat'	gyaŋ	'gang'

The salience of this feature in Creole English is in part due to the fact that other varieties of English do not have any or at least no strong palatalisation between [k] or [g] and [a], and in part to the high frequency of commonly used words beginning with this combination, e.g. *can* (verb and noun), *can't, carry, cat, cart, card, candle, catch, canvas, cap, capture, captain, cash, gallon, gallop, gamble, gang, gap*. Palatalisation is noticeable in Creole English, not because it is un-English but because there is more of it [$p, k + y + u; t + y + u; k, g + y + a$] than in other dialects of English.

In relation to standard English, in its pronunciation Creole English shows decreases (consonant cluster reduction), increases (epenthetic vowel and palatalisation) and substitutions (ŋ>n, ɖ>d, θ>t and nasalisation instead of nasal consonant). In other words, Creole English shows a normal evolutionary relationship with English generally.

The structure of words, phrases and sentences

Word structure (morphology), sentence structure (syntax) and vocabulary are integrally related to each other and to meaning. In the languages of the world, morphology, syntax and vocabulary each have varying loads in the rendering of meaning. For example, Chinese depends more on vocabulary than on word structure. Chinese words are almost exclusively monosyllabic and in many cases words which would be spelled in the same way are differentiated from each other only by distinctions in pitch. Latin, on the other hand, depends heavily on morphology, which means that words are related to each other, having a base or root and a changeable affix (prefix or suffix). As a result, most Latin words are not monosyllabic.

In the evolution of Romance (Latin-derived) languages and Germanic languages (including English) there is an unmistakeable loss of morphology. In other words, when compared with their predecessors, French and English historically show a gradual decrease in grammatical inflections (morphology) and a corresponding increase in dependence on syntax. Such changes are often regarded by laymen as evidence of 'corruption', but viewed objectively there is no proof that such changes increase or decrease the expressive power of a language. Such changes in dependence on different areas of grammar are always facilitated by redundancy, which is a part of all languages. For example, in current English *whom* is declining in favour of *who* because the inflection -*m*, which previously was a strong indicator of non-subject function, is now much less so and is redundant since the non-subject function is indicated by word order or in some other way.

Redundancy as a feature of language can occur in any area of grammar and clearly contradicts lay beliefs about the totally logical nature of the standard language, when compared with non-standard. For instance, teachers of English grammar try to claim that standard English indicates the negative only once because it is 'illogical' to do otherwise, e.g.

I am going nowhere   is said to be 'logical'
I am not going nowhere   (meaning negative) is said to be 'illogical'

Explanations of language structure will founder if they are based on notions of logic which contradict redundancy. The Spanish language has double negatives to express negative and it would be foolish to claim that this is illogical. In fact, redundancy is one of the most crucial factors in facilitating understanding in speech and just as the load for rendering meaning is variously distributed over pronunciation, word structure and sentence structure, redundancy is also variously distributed over these three areas in the languages of the world.

The structure of words

In relation to standard English, Creole English shows much less dependence on morphology (word-endings) for expressing meaning. Many of the grammatical inflections which characterise standard English are either not a part of Creole English or are inconsistently used. The inconsistency is in most cases a result of redundancy or differences in social usage. Standard English morphology is concentrated in the verb, but occurs also in the pronoun, the noun and in the comparison of adjectives. Creole English generally makes no distinction in form between adjective and adverb as standard English does.

Creole English preserves both of the methods found in English for the comparison of adjectives, and in contrast to standard English combines them. For the comparative and superlative of adjectives, standard English either adds a suffix *-er* and *-est* respectively or has a separate word, *more, most*, respectively, preceding the adjective. In addition, two of the most common adjectives have forms for comparative and superlative which show little resemblance to the basic adjective form:

good	*better*	*best*
bad	*worse*	*worst*

Double marking, or redundancy, and single marking for comparative and superlative are both normal in Creole English, e.g.

big	*(more) bigger*	*(most) biggest*
tall	*(more) taller*	*(most) tallest*
beautiful	*(more) beautiful-er*	*(most) beautiful-est*

When comparative and superlative are single marked in Creole English, it is the suffix method which is preferred for all adjectives in contrast to standard English which makes a distinction between long adjectives and short ones, e.g.

bigger, biggest	*more/most beautiful*
taller, tallest	*more/most unusual*

The standard English comparative and superlative forms of *good* and *bad* occur in Creole English and are used alone – *bɛtə*, *bɛs* and *wʌs* – or with additional marking *muo bɛtə* and *wʌsə*, *wʌsɪs*. Double marking for 'best' is not common, whereas in the case of *wʌsə* and *wʌsɪs* what may seem at first like double marking is really a way of differentiating comparative from superlative as a result of the fact that the words *worse* and *worst* phonetically become identical in Creole English *wʌs*.

The noun in Creole English shows little of the morphology of standard English, which has basic inflections for number and possession and other suffixes for gender, e.g. *lions, lion's, lions'; lioness*. It is quite evident that in most cases English spelling indicates relationships which English pronunciation does not – *lions, lion's, lions'* are identical in pronunciation. It is only when the plural is marked other than with the normal suffix that the possessive forms are accordingly distinguished as in *men's, oxen's*. It is also quite evident that plural does not have to be marked in the noun itself for plural to be understood as, for example, in *sheep*. In fact, there is redundancy in the marking of plural in most cases in standard English; i.e. the noun is plural, sometimes preceded by a plural demonstrative, and the verb that goes with it is also plural, e.g. *those men are fat*.

Basically Creole English does not mark the plural in the noun phrase unless the context of the utterance is not clear, in which case it uses the third person pronoun before or after the noun, e.g.

di dog dem   dem dog

The third person plural pronoun when put before the noun may in most cases have an additional demonstrative force ('those'). The associative plural, in most cases restricted to persons, is also very common in Creole English and either has the structure of the normal plural or has *an* ('and') inserted between the noun and *dem*, e.g.

Mieri dem   Mieri an dem

Pressure from standard English and other social requirements of course are indicated by the use of English suffixes or forms for the plural. This is not to be confused however with English plural forms which have given the Creole English basic form, e.g.

teeth > [tit] (sing or pl)
mice > [maisi], [mais] (sing or pl)

or more typical in Jamaica

drinks   > [drɪŋks] (sing or pl) 'soda' or 'soft drink'
prayers > [prayaz] (sing or pl) 'prayer'
hops   > [aps] 'beer'

Possession is marked in standard English not only by using the suffix *-s* but also by putting one noun next to another as an alternative to the prepositional method, e.g.

trunk of the tree	*tree trunk*
cap of the knee	*kneecap*
end of the week	*weekend*

Creole English also uses this method of juxtaposition, but unlike standard English uses it generally. Creole English therefore does not depend on morphology for indicating possession, but solely on juxtaposition of nouns.

Juxtaposition is also used in Creole English to indicate gender when necessary, seeing that gender is often part of the basic meaning of the word, as in *gyal* 'girl'. Examples of gender and of possession therefore coincide in structure:

man book,   woman horse,   woman doctor,   bull cow,   girl child

The third example has the ambiguity of standard English in that *woman doctor* can also mean 'gynaecologist'.

As is the case with the noun, the pronoun in Creole English shows little morphology and where it does have any, the rules for changes are not immediately apparent, which often gives the impression that there are no rules. In addition, the pronoun is more subject to gradual approximation to standard English than most other Creole features because of its frequency of occurrence. Also, because it is in most cases monosyllabic and unstressed in the sentence, the many slight variations cannot be systematically represented and accounted for in easily understood or traditional terms.

The forms of the pronoun and possessive adjective are many and varied throughout the West Indies, but the following are the most widespread:

	Singular	**Plural**
1st person	*ə, mı, mi*	*wi, awi, abi*
2nd person	*yu, yə*	*unu, wənə, ayu*
3rd person	*(h)i, ım;*	*də, dem*
	shi, ar;	
	ıt, əm	

These pronouns are used for the pronoun as subject, as direct or indirect object, in isolation (e.g. as in a reply to a question), as possessive and for the possessive adjective. When used for the possessive pronoun they are usually followed or preceded by another word, e.g.

wi oon, *wi wən,* *fi wi* 'ours'

Whereas each territory differs in its choice, articulation and use of these forms, in general two of the forms are restricted in case: *ə* and *ər*. The form *ə* rarely occurs outside the subject position and *ər* rarely occurs as subject. All the other forms are used interchangeably for the six functions given.

In a broad perspective, choice of pronoun form in Creole English is determined by social and to a lesser extent by syntactic factors. However, choice is also dependent on factors of pronunciation. For example, *ə* is not used if the subject is being stressed. Nor is it used immediately preceding negative *nə/na/no*, e.g.

ə nuo 'I know' : *Mi no nuo* 'I don't know'

When the pronoun occurs in isolation, as in response to a question, certain forms do not occur, or if so, rarely – *ə, yə, i, də*. In the case of *ə, yə, də*, this is consistent with English phonology in that tense vowels (in which the muscles in the mouth are taut) tend not to occur in an exposed position. In the case of *i* (as opposed to *hi*) this form of the pronoun is not used because *h* resurfaces in a context of stress in all territories except Jamaica where in any case neither *hi* nor *i* is the preferred form in Creole English. Other variations in choice of form are not general, but territory-specific.

In contrast to standard English, Creole English shows little morphology in the verb, and where it does it may be regarded as an approximation to standard English. The only inflection of the verb in Creole English is *-in*, which is derived from the standard English *-ing* form. In Creole English the *-in* form of the verb varies interchangeably with another verb construction which is not morphological. Both constructions will be dealt with in the next section because generally function and meaning of verb constructions are best understood in the context of sentences and utterances.

The structure of phrases and sentences

It is in the area of syntax that Creole English has many outstanding features, some of which differ markedly from corresponding features in standard English. The first notable characteristic of Creole English sentences is that they are verb-centred in contrast to standard English, especially the written variety, which distributes the load over noun phrases, verb phrases, adverbial phrases and prepositional phrases. For example, the standard English sentence

The sleeping village was disturbed by the hunters' shooting in the dead of night

packs a lot of information into one sentence and contains three verb-related forms *sleeping, disturbed, shooting* with only one finite verb form *was*. In addition, it has a noun phrase preceding the verb, one following and a prepositional phrase at the end. Such sentences are not characteristic of the spoken language, as for example in a conversation, even in English, and would never be found in Creole English. The information in the sentence given would be conveyed in shorter sentences involving more finite verbs. It is not surprising, therefore, that the outstanding features of Creole English syntax are directly related to the verb.

Predicative adjectives

Since there are almost no inflections in the verb, meaning depends on the interrelationship of verb forms, and the relationship between the verb and other parts of the utterance, including context. One of the best-known features of Creole English is a structure which the normal observer identifies as having no verb. It occurs in a sentence of the type

Di cat fat	*Di boy sick*
Di cat no fat	*Di boy in sick*

There are two major considerations in the analysis of sentences of this type – firstly to decide whether the sentences are meaningful and secondly whether they are full sentences. It is quite obvious that the sentences are meaningful. For if only by comparison with standard English it will be seen that the *is* < *be* in the equivalent standard English sentence is meaningless. To decide whether the Creole English sentences are full one has to look at the structure of similar sentences in other languages. Such a search reveals that sentences of the same structure occur in Arabic, Russian and Yoruba, among other languages. It can hardly be claimed that sentences with this structure are not full sentences in such 'major' languages. Finally, theoretical analysis of the specific structure of these sentences and equivalent sentences in languages, including English, indicates that the adjective has verbal qualities and in many cases derives from the verb.

Consider the function of the word *disturbed* in the following sentences and its movement from one sentence to the next:

The noise disturbed the man
The man was disturbed
The disturbed man was angry

In the Creole English sentences, as in the Arabic, Russian and Yoruba equivalents, the adjective is said to be functioning as the verb and predicate of the sentence and is thus called a *predicative adjective*. Sentences with predicative adjectives are universal in Creole English and most other Creoles.

Serial verbs

The next notable feature in the syntax of Creole English is what is best known as serial verb constructions. This feature occurs in most of the West Indian territories, although its frequency of occurrence varies from territory to territory. It is a feature that occurs in other parts of the world but only minimally in spoken English. A serial verb construction is the occurrence of two or more verbs in a clause without intervening conjunctions. In spoken or conversational English, *go* and *come* are sometimes followed directly by another verb, e.g.

Go get it   Go fetch   Come see it

In Creole English, serial verb constructions can be much more elaborate in structure and not restricted to clauses with the verbs *go* and *come*.

In Creole English, serial verb constructions can be subdivided into three types:

– clauses involving verbs of motion;
– clauses with instrumental constructions;
– clauses with *gi(v)* < *give* as the last verb in the construction.

Serial verb constructions may have as many as four verbs going together without intervening conjunctions, although other words which are nouns, pronouns, adjectives and adverbs may intervene. Examples of serial verb constructions are as follows:

Example	Type	No. of verbs
carry it *come*	1	2
run come see it	1	3
carry go bring come	1	4
I would *use* it *buy* dress	2	2
di man *tek* whip *beat* di children dem	2	2
i *tek* it *giv* ar	3	2
run fast *go tek* it up *gi* me	3	4

In sentences in which *go* or *come* occur, the word gives the direction of motion. For example, *carry come* means direction towards the speaker, whilst *carry go* means direction away from the speaker. Detailed analysis of serial verb constructions in Creole English shows that the verbs used and their relationship to each other are not random or haphazard, but clearly rule-governed. Serial verb constructions also show that the verb has the major focus in the Creole English sentences, especially when one compares the instrumental construction in Creole English, rendered with two verbs, e.g. *tek* . . . *beat*, with the instrumental construction in standard English, rendered with one verb plus a prepositional phrase, e.g. *beat . . . with . . .*

Sentence focus

In many of the world's languages there are two main ways of highlighting an element in the sentence, either in pronunciation by using heavier vocal stress or syntactically by putting the specific element in a prominent place in the sentence, usually at the beginning or the end. The syntactic method may involve the simple movement of the specific element to the beginning of the sentence without affecting the rest of the sentence, e.g.

I will go tomorrow   Tomorrow I will go

or it may involve a change in the structure of the sentence, e.g.

It is tomorrow that I will go

Creole English favours the syntactic method and uses it more extensively than does standard English. In addition, Creole English uses a syntactic structure which is different from either of those just given for standard English and thus is one able to focus on any element in the sentence. In Creole English the element to be highlighted is moved from its normal position to the beginning of the sentence, if it is not already at the beginning, and may or may not have *a/iz* in front of it. Examples:

John eat di mango yesterday
Iz John eat di mango yesterday
Iz di mango John eat yesterday
Iz yesterday John eat di mango

Where the element to be highlighted is the verb, it is put to the beginning, but also remains in its original position. This rule also applies when there is a predicative adjective. Examples:

Iz eat John eat di mango
Iz sick John sick   (< John sick)

Front focusing, which occurs in either positive or negative sentences, can be contrasted with back focusing in negative sentences specifically, which occurs in some territories. Back focusing is in most cases restricted to the verb, including the predicative adjective. Examples:

I in eat no eat
She in sick no sick
Yu kyāā bat no bat

Back focusing may have the strong negative meaning 'not at all', but it usually gives the meaning 'not really/very well'. The construction *It is . . . that . . .* which is used to highlight elements in standard

English sentences is related to impersonal constructions introduced by *it*, e.g.

It is possible that that is so
It is possible to go
It is raining

Creole English does not favour such constructions and either uses another construction or another pronoun, e.g.

Dat musi true
You can go
Rain falling

Creole English prefers to use the third person pronoun (the singular in some territories, plural in others) where standard English favours the *there is/are* impersonal construction. In all cases the Creole English pronoun is normally followed by a verb with the meaning 'have'. Examples:

It have a lot of ting in dere
Dǝ got a lot of ting in dere
Dem have a lot of ting in dere

The use of a verb with the meaning 'have' in this construction is characteristic of most Creoles and also of French and Spanish (*il y a*; *hay*, *ha*). It should be quite evident that constructions used for highlighting elements and for impersonals are not reflections of standard English, but contain structures that are outside English syntax.

Verb meaning

Tense, aspect, modality and voice are universal grammatical categories in that they are represented in some ways in the languages of the world. Their universality springs from the fact that their meanings are virtually indispensable for human communication. These four grammatical categories are presented in no two languages in exactly the same way, no matter how close historically the languages are, and languages have one or the other of these categories more prominent than the others. Languages depend on pronunciation, word and sentence structure to varying degrees to render the meanings of the four grammatical categories, and there is no linguistic evidence to suggest that any one of these meanings is better rendered by a specific form or structure.

Of the four categories tense is the simplest to define. Tense in a strict linguistic sense, as opposed to its loose use in most grammar books, refers specifically to the time of speech. There are three tenses: past tense refers to time before the time of speech, future to time after the time of speech (in other words, not yet arrived when the speaker is speaking), and present to the time of speech. Present tense itself is more of an illusion than a fact because it cannot last over a whole sentence or utterance – when the speaker is in mid-sentence, the beginning of the sentence is already past and the end is still future. Present, in people's minds, is a continuity from immediate past into immediate future. It is probably because of the transience and brevity of present that it is neutrally represented in a number of languages. For example, in English, French and Spanish the present tense form normally coincides with the stem of the infinitive form with endings added for person-number, in contrast to the future or past for which there is a specific word or inflexion, e.g. *will*.

Aspect, as a specific linguistic term, refers to the nature of the action of the verb. There are many possible aspects, but only a few of them commonly occur positively represented as part of the verb in the world's languages. The aspect of continuity, variously called 'continuous', 'durative', 'progressive', is one of the commonest, as is the aspect of completion, variously called 'perfect', 'perfective', 'completive'. Another common aspect is that of repeated or habitual action. Other aspects referring to concepts like beginning, growing, decreasing and dying occur in some languages but are not represented as part of the verb in most languages.

The word 'modality' is related to the normal English word *mood* and although the two words are not synonymous, they still share a common thread of meaning. Modality in most cases refers to feelings, desires, beliefs, conditions and attitudes of the speaker reflected in the verb and is usually contrasted with what is factual in the eyes of the speaker. In many languages, however, modality has been formalised and is no longer directly relatable to specific meanings. In standard English it is represented principally by auxiliary verbs (*may, should, must*, etc.) and residually in a morphological way in sentences with the verb 'to be', e.g.

If I were you . . .
Were it not for that, . . .

The notion of voice is both semantic and grammatical in nature. It involves the grammatical concepts 'subject' and 'object' and the semantic concepts 'agent' (or doer) and 'patient'. The voice of the verb tells whether the subject of the sentence is the doer of the action (agent), or the patient, or neither. Where the subject of the sentence is the agent, e.g.

Bill struck Bob

the sentence is said to have active voice; where the subject is the patient

Bob was struck by Bill

the sentence is said to have passive voice. In some languages there is also a middle or benefactive voice, in which cases the subject cannot really be said to be agent or patient, but 'in the middle' or benefiting from the action. English grammar does not have middle voice, but the English sentence

Bob is sleeping

best illustrates this relationship. The notion of 'transitive' (verb having a direct object) and 'intransitive' (not having a direct object) is integrally related to the notion of voice. Creole English positively (i.e. by a form or construction) represents tense, aspect, modality and voice, but in all cases without the many forms and structures that are characteristic of English. Since Creole English is mostly spoken language, it depends more heavily on context of utterance as a supplement or as a redundant feature. In other words, any of the four categories may not be positively marked or may be said to be zero marked. When they are positively marked, Creole English depends almost exclusively on syntax in contrast to standard English which employs both morphology and syntax.

Verb particles

For all four categories Creole English uses the same basic structure:

verb particle/auxiliary + unchanging form of the verb

In all cases the verb particle/auxiliary may be zero, or alternatively two or possibly three particles may occur together as long as their meanings are compatible. Since zero particle can be used for tense, aspect or modality, it should be quite evident that it is not restricted to any one meaning. In fact, both in standard English and in Creole English, tense and aspect are indicated normally outside the verb, whether or not they are indicated inside the verb. For example, future tense is given outside the verb by the adverb or conjunction of time in the following standard English sentences:

Tomorrow we conquer the enemy
When I go there I am coming back at once

and habitual aspect in the following:

I always go there
Whenever I go there I faint

There is therefore nothing unusual or deficient about non-specification of tense or aspect in the verb itself. In fact, flexibility in structure allows the speaker a choice of style in order to be more precise, less precise, or deliberately ambiguous, to distribute the focus in the sentence in different ways and to make use of the immediate context to varying degrees. In analysing tense and aspect, therefore, the function of linguistic forms and structures must be considered in conjunction with adverbial phrases while bearing in mind the potential of the immediate context.

Figure 3.2 gives a schema of the major forms and structures for expressing tense and aspect available to the Creole English speaker, and Fig. 3.3 gives a list of the most commonly occurring adverbs and conjunctions that complement them. Of course, there is variation in choice from territory to territory and from individual to individual as well as variation in the pronunciation of the forms.

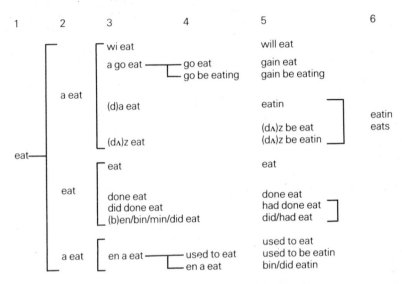

Fig. 3.2   Creole English: the major forms and structures for expressing tense and aspect.

sometime	in time	tomorrow	after
everytime	first time	soon	just now
anytime	same time	yet	as
in the day time	next time	till	long time
nuf time	one time	ever	later on
all the time	now	again	never
always	already	when	since then

Fig. 3.3   Creole English: common adverbs and conjunctions.

Figure 3.2 shows that the verb form alone (column 1) together with the right adverbial in the right context can give any tense or aspect, or that more specifically (column 2) it can be any completive past. The structure *a + verb* with the same conditions (column 2) can give any future, continuous or habitual, or more specifically (column 3) may simply be continuous. Figure 3.3 also shows that the Creole English speaker has a choice of a number of precise forms which are basically the same as or not very different from the standard English forms. It also shows on the contrary that in situations which require formality the Creole speaker may use *verb + s* (column 6) for any person-number for habitual, as in

He works at Harrisons
I gets up to a time
They teaches there

or that the Creole speaker may use *verb + in* (column 6) for continuous or habitual as in

We workin at Bata
He playin guitar now
We teachin there

It also shows that *had + verb* (column 5) may be used for a past that is not present or perfective, as in

She had come home last year
She had gone when I come

Figure 3.3 also shows that although the English words *go, does, done, been, did, had* are presumably the original form of some of the Creole English verb particles, there are structural and semantic differences between the way the words are used in Creole English and the way they are used in standard English. For example, *does* in standard English is vocally stressed, is third person singular, is emphatic, and used in response to a contrary meaning or used with a negative (*not*), whereas in Creole (*dʌ*)z is unstressed, is used for any person-number, and has a meaning (habitual) as opposed to merely a function.

In addition to verb particles/auxiliaries, adverbial phrases and conjunctions and context, interpretation of tense and aspect is also dependent on the meaning of the verb itself. There are a number of verbs, called 'psychological' verbs, which have as part of their meaning the idea of continuity. When the particles are used with these verbs there is usually a difference in interpretation. For example, zero particle with a non-psychological verb, without a specifying adverb, normally refers to past, whereas zero particle with verbs like *feel, know, believe*, refers to present continuous. Contrast *I eat it* (past) with *I know it* (present). Creole English can of course highlight the continuous when necessary, as in

She still a believe that? / She still believe that?
Yes. She en a believe / did believing that long time now

Although there is no absolute restriction about using *be + -ing* with psychological verbs in standard English, it is less frequent than *a + / -in*

+ *psychological verb* in Creole English, especially with reference to the past. This of course depends on the specific verb itself.

No simple analysis of the interrelationship between verb forms, structures and adverb expressions can account fully for the intricate relationship between tense and aspect which is a part of all human communication. It is even more complex in Creole English in which stylistic and social choice is constantly being influenced, negatively and positively, by standard English.

Modal auxiliaries

The notion of doubt and uncertainty which attends modal usage must be looked at not only in terms of the speaker's view of reality but also in terms of his view of social success or achievement. Politicians are forced to speak about the world in a clear-cut style without making too many commitments. Diplomats are forced to equivocate in order not to make unshakeable commitments. Poor people, very often because of the attendant circumstances of ignorance and uncertainty which they seek to mask, react in an unequivocal manner. In addition, one of the accepted paths to success is to be confident at all times. One of the greatest social achievements, therefore, is to be able to manipulate language in such a way that truth must be deduced rather than be obvious and this must be done in a style that is quite clear.

Modal auxiliaries in English bear a heavy load in this respect and such auxiliaries as *may, might, would* are characteristic of polite and socially successful language. The Creole English speaker does not use the same degree of social cushioning in his speech, as a result of which equivalents of those three modals are not as frequent in Creole English. For example, sentences such as

May I go?
He might be able to do that
Would you please ensure . . .

would have *can, musi* and *zero* respectively in place of the standard English modals. Before examining modal auxiliary usage in Creole English, therefore, one must appreciate the fact that such usage is socially controlled.

Creole English modal auxiliaries can be classified in the following way:

Conditional	Imperative	Probable	Able	Moral
would	mus	musi	can	should
	ha/got fi/to	might	could	ought fi/to
	(i.e. hafi, ha to)	should		fi
	(got fi, fə to)			

Creole English modals differ from standard English modals first of all in that they are not bound by the sequence of tense agreements which characterise formal, especially written, standard English. Secondly, standard English modals have many more overlapping meanings conditioned by politeness than Creole English modals. Thirdly, the Creole English modal and its standard English phonetic equivalent are not always immediately related in function and meaning.

It is only in the case of *can* and *could* that Creole English has a tense relationship between modals, unlike standard English, which also has *will:would, shall:should, may:might*. In addition, in Creole English the use of *can:could* is determined by the meaning in the same clause rather than on a past-tense form in a governing clause. For example, compare Creole English

She tell me she can come

with formal standard English

She told me that she could come

Notice that the Creole English sentence is not ambiguous, whereas in the standard English sentence it is not clear whether the person 'is still able to come' at the time of speech.

In addition to the ambiguity caused by the sequence of tense relationships in standard English, complexity is increased by a politeness relationship between tense forms and also by the perceived degree of moral obligation appropriate to the context. Politeness and degree of obligation are not universally agreed on or rendered in the same way by all speakers of standard English and this in itself further complicates modal usage. On the whole, Creole English uses fewer modals and this avoids a lot of complication.

The auxiliary *would* is always a modal in Creole English, unlike standard English where it is also used for habitual aspect, as in

He would go there every Sunday   ('He went')

The Creole English *musi* has no phonetic equivalent in standard English functioning as an auxiliary. Its variant form *must be* cannot fit into standard English structure as an auxiliary verb. The form *mus* in Creole English is imperative not only in meaning but also in function. This is clearly seen in sentences which are reported commands, e.g.

She tell me mus wash out me mouth
Di man tell you mus duon touch it

The imperative force (mood) of the direct command is thus maintained in Creole English by *mus* in reported commands and by *mus* or *ha/got fi/to* in other cases.

As in the case of tense and aspect there may be no auxiliary used for modality. In these cases the 'tone of voice' or intonation of the speaker establishes modality. This is of course possible in all languages and the extent to which this is used by one speech community compared with another is not easily determined.

Passives

Zero marking is also used for the passive voice in Creole English, but this may best be understood, when compared with the specific passive structure of standard English, as zero structure. However, before examining the nature of passives in Creole English, it must be borne in mind that there are no definitive boundaries in most languages between the lexical content of a specific verb, the syntactic structures into which it fits and the way people choose to use it. Consider the following standard English sentences:

Eggs are selling well nowadays
The army suffered great losses
The glass broke

The verbs *sell* and *break* themselves are active or passive in meaning depending on whether there is a noun following them in the same clause in a direct relationship. In other words, if they are used intransitively, they are passive and vice versa. In contrast, the verb *suffer* has the notion of passive as a feature of its very meaning, no matter whether it is directly followed by a noun or not. As far as usage is concerned, *break* is normally considered to be both transitive and intransitive, whereas *sell* is considered transitive, with its use as in the sentence above regarded as restricted. On the whole, standard English allows only a few other transitive verbs (e.g. *smoke, burn*) this kind of flexibility of occurrence, but speakers increasingly expand this flexibility to other verbs.

In Creole English, in contrast, flexibility of the verb in syntactic occurrence is the norm and the relative frequency of the verb in transitive as opposed to intransitive sentences may be more a matter of what the speaker wants to focus on (semantics) than on syntactic constraints.

The meaning of certain verbs in both standard and Creole English of course limits them to being principally intransitive verbs, e.g. *come, go, sleep, rain*. Sentences in which such verbs occur therefore have the basic structure *noun + verb*. The same structure also appears when verbs are used transitively with the object not expressed, but understood, e.g.

The men ate
I see

The same structure occurs with verbs which can be used either transitively or intransitively, e.g.

The man was smoking
The house was smoking

It is not the structure itself that determines the function of the verb, it is the meaning of the subject. Unless the subject is animate and, under normal circumstances, human, then the verb must be intransitive. In other words, it is the semantic relationship between subject and verb that determines the basic structure of the sentence, either *noun + verb* or *noun + verb (+ noun)*. Consequently, when the semantic relationship between the subject and the verb is ambiguous, then the structure of the sentence is not clear.

Creole English specifically, because it allows more flexibility in the verb, has more intransitive sentences of the type

The car hit
The sugar use already
The water hold in the bucket

Since there is nothing different in the structure of these sentences, they cannot be said to have a passive structure. Whether they are passive in meaning is a matter of semantic interpretation depending on the meaning of the subject and the verb.

Ambiguity may result when the meaning of a noun allows it to be either agent or patient, e.g.

Man going destroy   ('to be destroyed' or 'destroy something')
The child bite bad   ('bites' or 'has been bitten')
Shark can eat   ('eat a lot' or 'be eaten')

In real life contexts, however, such sentences are hardly ever ambiguous. To prevent ambiguity Creole English has a specific construction involving the use of the word *get*, which is distinct from the simple intransitive structure. The semantic voice of sentences with the intransitive structure in Creole English is debatable, but the construction with *get* is clearly passive in meaning. However, the construction with *get* does not refer to a state of being, as the intransitive structure may do, but involves more action. For example, the sentence

*The water get hold in the bucket

is virtually impossible (hence the asterisk) because *get* and *hold* are semantically incompatible in this sentence. The semantic distinction between the two structures is further seen in sentences such as

The boy frighten	vs	*The boy get frighten*
The child bite up	vs	*The child get bite up*

It is clear in such contrasts that the sentences with *get* refer to a specific point whereas the intransitive structure gives the idea of a continuous state. In other words, an adverb referring to a specific point in time is normal in sentences with *get*, but is not always so in the other structure.

A normal alternative to intransitive, *get* and passive constructions of other types is the use of an indefinite pronoun in a transitive sentence. This is characteristic of a number of languages, including French (*on*), and standard English (*someone, somebody*). Creole English, as is the case also in standard English, also uses the third person plural pronoun *dem/də* as an indefinite to perform this function, e.g.

Dem kill she
Də tek way he licence again
Də tear out me book leaf

Negatives

Negation is one of the areas in which non-standard varieties of English generally differ from standard English. The difference is that non-standard varieties usually allow double and triple negation, i.e.

not . . . none/nobody/nowhere/nothing

This is also a characteristic of Creole English. Negation of the verb itself in Creole English involves a number of forms which vary from territory to territory and reflect different semantic, social and stylistic choices. The most general negative forms used with the verb are *nə/na*, *in*, *ɛ*, *not*, *duon*, *neva*, and with the auxiliary verb + *n* or nasalisation of the final vowel.

Although there is a great degree of uniformity in the structure of Creole English, there is no question that levels of Creole English can be distinguished according to the placement of the negator. Creoles which differ in the extreme from European languages have the negator coming before the verbal particles and auxiliaries. Extreme forms of Creole English make a distinction between the tense and aspect particles on the one hand and the modals on the other, putting the negator before the former and attaching it to the end of the latter, e.g.

him na a come
him no ben do it
him wudn do it
him kyāā do it

This distinction disappears when past tense forms like *din* or *wazn* are used. In addition, *ɛ/in*, which is the general negator in some territories, is not totally unlike *ain't*, the common negator in non-standard English.

In spite of what appears to be a gradual approximation towards standard English, Creole English negation is at times significantly different. This however will be dealt with when the specific characteristics of individual territories are being dealt with.

Words and meanings

The vocabulary of a language, like all other parts, is a stage in an ongoing process. However, looking at it from a static point of view, the structure of the vocabulary can be said to consist of a core of basic words and a capability for increase which is always at work and which produces non-basic words. Basic words in a lexicon are those words which refer to features common to all human communities. Such words are names for parts of the body, the elements, food, clothing, family relationships, animals and plants.

Basic words, and consequently non-basic ones, are not absolute and independent entities, but are arranged in hierarchical and contrastive relationships arising out of the notions of abstraction and specialisation. This can be illustrated as in Fig. 3.4. Further abstraction and specialisation are possible above, below or at any point within this diagram or any other such diagram. It is evident then that a word does not occur simply to identify and name what are already isolatable entities in Nature, but in order to fit into a system of hierarchies and contrasts, i.e. to say something different, or the opposite, or to point out a detail, etc.

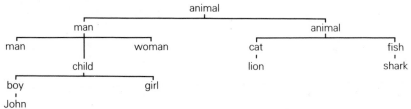

Fig. 3.4   An example of hierarchical and contrastive relationships.

Abstraction itself is a property of all words. No word is made up to name a single specific entity – even proper names are divided into parts to relate to other persons or things. The word *apple* does not refer to a single fruit that grew on a tree once in history, but to a kind of fruit. In other words, *apple* is an abstraction consisting of a number of features and this abstraction may be manifested concretely, with each manifestation being different but at the same time similar to other manifestations of *apple*. The notion of being 'abstract' must be differentiated from the notion of being 'tangible', specifically when 'tangible' is extended to include all five senses (touch, see, feel, hear, taste). Words in all languages refer to things tangible and intangible, but languages differ in the number of these words in the vocabulary and the way they are formed.

Non-basic words and meanings in a language are created by internal methods, by external ones and by a combination of both. In the first place, a word is not restricted to having only one meaning, and the more frequently it occurs, as basic words do, the more meanings it tends to acquire. Secondly, the word may be modified phonologically by stress or pitch without changing its consonants and vowels, e.g. standard English *'contrast* (noun), *con'trast* (verb). In other cases, words can be formed by syntactic and morphological processes which are a basic part of the language or in other words by internal processes.

One of the most common syntactic processes in the expansion of the lexicon is the usage of a word for more than one part of speech, e.g. *man* (n) *man* (v); *sharp* (adj) *sharp* (n); *fast* (adj) *fast* (adv) *fast* (n). Another common syntactic process, which in itself does not result in single words but is commonly used for meaning modification and precision, is adjectival and adverbial modification, e.g.

a personal computer, conditioned reflex, skills training programme, fast-breaking news item

There is often little difference between this process and what is called morphological compounding except that in writing the words may be written as one (*armchair, taperecorder*) or hyphenated (*mother-in-law, tape-recorder*) or separately (*news item, tape recorder*).

Although syntactic processes for lexical expansion are very common and formal, in European languages the morphological process of affixation is the most basic process and this is because of the inevitability of grammatical inflections in sentence formation. Derivation, as a morphological process, may not be in the most fundamental sense as inevitable in word formation in English as inflection, but such a distinction is more philosophical than real, for the acquisition of English knowledge of derivational affixes like *in-*, *un-*, *-al*, *-ness*, is just as useful as knowledge of *-s*, *-ed*, *-ing*.

The process which comes closest to the spirit of 'making up a new word' is the one that is least common, but even so it is significant in the area of commerce where new products daily come onto the market. Coining of words is seldom totally unmotivated. In other words, the name of a new product may retain a trace of its composition and also conform to English phonology, e.g. *nylon, rayon, cotton*, or it may be an acronym, e.g. *radar, laser*. Even a word like *xerox* is not unmotivated (it derives from *xerography* < Greek *xeros* + *graphe* 'a dry printing process' – the Greek word *xeros* means 'dry').

Contrasting with these internal processes for lexical increase is the practice, common to all languages, of borrowing words from other languages. The process very often reflects the history of associations of the users of a language. The English language is the best example of a language that has increased its vocabulary from a myriad sources, thus showing the worldwide historical associations of speakers of the language. In fact, it is ironic that the development of the English dictionary arose directly out of the need to explain the meaning of foreign words that were being used normally as part of the English language by educated speakers. The argument that a language borrows because of a deficiency is not always logical. Words are very often borrowed because they are more colourful. For example, the pronoun in some form is basic in Creole English, but a speaker today may find it much more appealing and fashionable to say

Don't mess with the I ('... with me')

Compare this with a standard English sentence which starts,

The ego is ...

in which one can claim that English borrowed the Latin word *ego* ('I') and used it in a way in which it is not used in Latin, but in a way that originally stood out.

Words borrowed into a language may or may not retain their original meaning, but their pronunciation is usually changed to suit the language they are borrowed into. In addition to this change in pronunciation, the words are usually given the morphological endings of the borrowing language and over a period of time the fact that the words were originally borrowed is known only by historical linguists. In contrast to this kind of historical levelling there is an ongoing practice, favoured by scientists generally, of getting the roots for new words from Latin or Greek and attaching the endings of their own languages to them, e.g.

phlebitis, telepathy, symbiotic, sinusitis

The vocabulary of a language gives a clear picture of the preoccupations and aspirations of its users. This is especially relevant in considering the size of a vocabulary. The more varied and the more sophisticated, technologically and otherwise, a society is, the more non-basic words it will have and consequently the bigger the vocabulary will be. However, the absolute size of a vocabulary is to a certain extent an illusion in that words are always coming into and going out of existence. In addition, all the words, as for example in the English language, are not characteristic of any one individual, group, class or society. In fact, it is more important to assess the normal methods, their potential and efficiency, which are available to every speaker for discovering or creating non-basic words than to compare the absolute sizes of vocabularies.

Creole English has a much smaller vocabulary than standard English because it is characteristic of fewer societies and also within those societies it is restricted in its domain of use and channels of use. In other words, because it is not widely written, not normally used for formal functions, and not the language of general education, it does not have words that are characteristic of these areas. Its preferred methods of creating non-basic words are fewer in number than those of standard English. The number in itself is less significant than the nature of the methods employed.

Creole English has a number of basic words each of which covers a greater semantic area than the same word does in standard English. For example, *foot* and *hand* refer to a much greater part of the anatomy than they do in standard English and the word *tea* refers to a much greater variety of beverages and times of the day than it does in standard English. Width of reference of this type is also characteristic of commonly used verbs like *hold* and *take*.

Of the methods generally used for creating non-basic words, Creole English has a strong preference for the syntactic ones as opposed to the morphological. Changing syllabic stress from first to last syllable according to part of speech is also possible in Creole English (e.g. *'compliment* vs *compli'ment*), but again is limited in scope.

Creole English allows a great amount of flexibility of occurrence of words across grammatical parts of speech. Bearing in mind the heavy interdependence of syntactic function and semantics in all languages, Creole English may be regarded as a case where the word is under less pressure (than for example standard English) to add suffixes and prefixes to suit its syntactic function. For example, *sweet* can be used as an adjective, a noun and a verb; *give* can be used as a normal verb and in the same way that the preposition would be in standard English (p. 64); *make* can be used as a normal verb or to join sentences like a causal conjunction, as in

Im drop di ball make di man no out

or it may be interpreted, according to Bailey (1966), as a causal verb with a clause as object. Prepositions also may be used as verbs as in

and she into grade 5 and she pass ar exam and go to Papine School and she out Papine School and go to a different school and she out it again . . .

The word *out* is also generally used in Creole English as a verb to mean 'extinguish (a fire or light)' and *out out* to mean 'erase'. Note that although *out* is usually a verb complement or preposition in standard English, it occurs as a verb in

The truth will out

and the word *down* is also used as a verb in

The workers downed their tools

and the word *up* as a verb in

They have upped the price of gas

Creole English is therefore not breaking down syntactic barriers, but simply making greater use of words in different syntactic positions. Flexibility has also been commented on in the analysis of passive and intransitive sentences.

Flexibility of occurrence of words is matched only by syntactic modification as a process of increasing vocabulary in Creole English. This method depends heavily on the combination of basic words to achieve specialisation and abstraction. Combinations such as *man dog* 'male dog', *cry water* 'tears', *bush tea* 'traditional liquid herbal medicine' are examples of specialisation, whilst *hard ears* 'persistently disobedient', *sweet mouth* 'given to flattery', *big eye* 'avaricious', *hand to mouth* 'never having enough to put aside some for another day' are examples of abstraction, resulting from metaphorical extension. Lists of such combinations have always been the favourite items in short glossaries of West Indian speech. Combinations may in fact be simply repetitions (*little-little, holey-holey*) which give different shades of meaning, or there may be repetition of words of the same class – *bull-cow, boar-pig, ram-goat, rock-stone, glass-bottle* ('broken glass') – which give more precise information. They may of course be of the type which also occurs in standard English, e.g.

a mash mouth woman (adj + noun)   ,   *a brek up thing* (verb + adv)

Qualifiers, modifiers and compounding are used in most languages as a normal method of being more precise and to distinguish similar things. However, abstraction and intangibility are most often rendered in European languages by word endings (e.g. *-ness, -ity*). In other words, to use a periphrastic method depending on the combination of basic words to give the meaning, for example, of 'intangibility' is not normal in standard English. It is not that morphology is used by all languages to give the meanings '-ness', '-ity', etc., but that Creole English seems to have only the syntactic method available for this purpose, a method which appears inefficient. This is one of the oft-stated weaknesses of Creole English.

Creole English has its own peculiar words which are inherited, evolved or mutated, e.g. *unu/wənə, um, toto, nʌkə, preke, jook*. Some of these words, e.g. *jook* and *unu/wənə* have survived very strongly in spite of the fact that they are non-English and frowned upon in higher social usage. The claim that their strong survival is a result of the fact that standard English does not have immediate equivalents is appealing but again not easily proved. It is true that standard English has no distinct form for second person plural, but non-standard varieties of English overcome this by using some combination of *all* and *you*. In the case of *jook* one has to consider why the meaning embraced in this word is necessary to West Indians and not to speakers of all other varieties of English. It is clearly not a basic meaning; it must be that *jook* is syntactically and semantically more versatile than any English equivalent. In short, it is typical of Creole English in that it carries a heavy load, as many common words do.

Words peculiar to Creole English deal with the specific and the tangible. An 'intangible' word like *stupidness* which survives in Creole English from archaic English is rare, but even in this case the word refers to stupid things and acts rather than to a 'quality'; in other words it does not mean 'stupidity'. Borrowing as a process of increasing vocabulary does not make the vocabulary more diverse, because borrowed words generally also refer to the specific and tangible. In any case, the concept of borrowing is difficult to substantiate in Creole English because of the fact that the formation and constant development of the language involve so many varied contributory sources from across the Caribbean. Furthermore, to claim that Creole English borrows words from English would be to set up an impossible lexical distinction between the two.

Reference to the intangible – that is, to philosophical projection and reflection – in Creole English is achieved mainly by the use of proverbs. In proverbs concrete words are used to put over timeless truths, experience and wisdom. This is done principally by using the noun with a generic meaning; that is, syntactically without an article, e.g.

Time longer than rope
Rockstone a river bottom never feel sunhot

The use of set expressions is of course characteristic of general discussion rather than of specific analysis of theoretical or hypothetical subjects in formal disciplines such as mathematics, sociology, economics, formal logic, etc. In fact, such analysis is mostly outside the domain of Creole English.

The present worth of a variety of a language and its future development are realistically measured not by the actual and potential linguistic capability of the language itself but by the social and economic standing of its speakers. This standing can be calculated and summed up after examining both internal and external factors, involving the perceptions of the speakers themselves as well as those of others. An assessment of Creole English will show strongly contending negative and positive forces among speakers with the negative probably being greater. Among non-speakers the negative prevails because of the internationally low status of speakers of Creole English in the face of the extensive and considerable power of the speakers of standard English.

There is no doubt, however, that social and economic forces have a significant effect on the range of uses of a language and so on the actual range of linguistic structures actively employed. This is very true in the case of Creole English. The fact that Creole English exists in West Indian societies alongside standard English in a diglossic relationship – that is, with standard English performing the 'high' functions and Creole English the 'low' ones – means that the full potential of Creole English is not being realised. For example, Creole English does not have a fully exploited written style, with the result that the explicitness and formalism of the written medium, as opposed to dependence on context and shared experience which is typical of the spoken, is not a part of Creole English. And it is precisely because there is a general belief in most communities that the written is a superior form of the spoken that Creole English will continue to be regarded as inferior.

Rasta English, profane English and foreign English are dominant influences in the West Indies, but they are not real choices for many West Indians as part of their normal, everyday speech. On the other hand, almost all West Indians are faced with having to choose between colloquial English and Creole English in different contexts. Such a choice is in the mind of the speaker and not necessarily revealed conclusively by what is actually said. Some of the oldest and most common stories in all the West Indian territories are told about natives returning home after studying or working overseas who continue to speak as if they were still overseas, but then are suddenly confronted by some great danger and uncontrollably express their fear in the 'deepest' Creole. Such situations highlight major differences between spontaneous language and monitored language, but normal everyday interaction between West Indians for the most part does the opposite – it masks the extremes and causes differences to appear small by making minimal shifts in form and structure. In other words, in spite of the acute perception of social class and types of language, the level of mutual intelligibility is high. In fact, a high level of mutual intelligibility is required if social marking in language is to be meaningful – it would not make sense for an upper-class speaker of French to speak typically if the social significance of the 'high' level of French is totally lost on a hearer who barely understands French.

The acute perception of social distinction and type of language together with the high level of mutual intelligibility makes for maintenance and slow change. There is therefore little possibility that Creole English will disappear in West Indian individuals or communities. Whether passively or actively used it is a factor of social and psychological stability. In addition, it is the most widely used type in all West Indian communities and the extent to which it is used by those who assume they are speaking an 'international' form of standard English is grossly underestimated. As is the case universally, beliefs and prejudices about different types of language are very often determined by a few extreme linguistic and many non-linguistic factors, rather than by an objective and precise knowledge of linguistic differences between types.

The relationship between Creole English and colloquial English presents itself in the following way: West Indians perceive a sharp distinction between the two as a result of a few, prominent features. In actual fact, West Indian usage unites the two into a complex, multi-dimensional and inseparable relationship with the few prominent features having major social but minor linguistic significance. The actual lack of clear distinction between the two, together with the prominence of stigmatised features, causes West Indians to view Creole English solely as 'bad' English or as mistakes or as lack of success in speaking English rather than as a separate, viable system with its own rules. In other words, the unconscious competence in the multi-dimensional reality contradicts the conscious perception of difference.

The multi-dimensional and inseparable relationship between Creole English and standard English can be illustrated in a number of ways. Looking first of all at the relationship between form, structure and meaning, an examination of formal English used by West Indians will reveal a higher incidence of the auxiliary *had* in past-tense contexts than in comparable contexts in non-West Indian English. In addition, most West Indians would regard the isolated sentence

He had come yesterday

as more formal than or just as formal as

He came yesterday

Few West Indians will immediately reject the first sentence as ungrammatical and not having the same meaning as the second in the same way that they would if *He does teach* is used for *He teaches.* The fact is that the difference between the two sentences, which theoretically in standard English is clear (past before past vs simple past), which in English worldwide is generally but not always maintained, in West Indian English is very indistinct as a result of the confluence of Creole English and colloquial English (see Fig. 3.2). The Creole structure *ben come* is gradually changed to look like standard English (*ben > did > had*) *had come* without a corresponding restriction in context. Such lack of distinction is replicated in other auxiliaries, *does, done, could, must,* thus making Creole English and colloquial English inseparable over a wide area.

Looking secondly at the relationship between social usage and stylistic usage, one sees that even the most lowly, uneducated and socially immobile speaker has a repertoire which cannot be one-dimensional. Speakers in all languages change the form of their language to suit the subject matter or the speaker's mood on the one hand and the external context and the perceived social rank of the hearer on the other. Although this distinction cannot always be consistently maintained, the former may be regarded as stylistic and the latter as social variation. In the West Indies by and large the changes in form which are made for social variation are the same changes that are made for stylistic variation and this is overwhelmingly a matter of shifting from Creole to colloquial. The important point is that there is no way that normal speakers in normal communities can interact without both social and stylistic variation. Therefore the variants are in an integral relationship with each other and not an evolutionary one.

Because such variation has to achieve all degrees of subtlety, it means that the change in form and structure from Creole to colloquial will show all degrees of subtlety, that is, from most subtle to most crude. Thus developmental-evolutionary changes and social-stylistic variation have together made the relationship between Creole and colloquial an inseparable, multi-dimensional and integral one. These two types are therefore not pulling in different directions in spite of the belief of many people that they can be separated into 'good' and 'bad'. In addition, although a lot of emotion is vented in the press and elsewhere about the low level of proficiency in standard English, the belief that this is caused by the presence of Creole English, and that Creole English should be eradicated, is less prevalent now than it was thirty years ago.

Language is a stumbling block in the way of progress for many West Indians both because the individual is conscious of linguistic difficulties and because official standards have to be achieved. West Indians have accepted and exaggerated – principally as a result of feelings of inferiority – the Englishman's sensitivity to language and class, rather than evolved with the American's freedom towards language which resulted from heterogeneity in development and feelings of security and confidence. It is only since the middle of the 1960s that West Indians have grown in confidence enough to accept increasingly their own language patterns with greater appreciation. At the same time they have also become increasingly aware of the practical applications and benefits of literacy and (standard) English.

4 · *Linguistic differences between the West Indian territories*

Rivalry between the West Indian territories is historical and traditional, ranging from acrimonious to friendly in all fields, especially politics, economics and sport. Sometimes this rivalry is so intense that the similarities and shared experience between the territories have been overshadowed by the differences. No two islands have an identical history. The two islands of the state of Trinidad and Tobago have substantial differences and a history of friction. The formerly three-island unit of St Kitts, Nevis and Anguilla had to be separated into two because of differences of opinion. In the West Indies political associations have engendered ceaseless hostilities both among rival politicians within and across different territories and among the people they lead, thus indicating that the colonial policy of 'divide and rule' seems to have had little resistance.

To West Indians and some non-West Indians the linguistic differences between Jamaicans on the one hand and Trinidadians on the other are noticeable and easily explained; the differences between Kittitians and Anguillans are not, but the perception of difference by the people of these two last islands is no less intense than in the case of Jamaica. The fact that similarity is in most cases unconsciously processed whereas difference is strikingly perceived means that difference, however small, assumes greater importance.

Perception of linguistic difference in the West Indies is, as anywhere else, negative and positive in nature. The individual, under normal circumstances, distinguishes native from foreign speech and in many cases identifies the foreign speech with varying degrees of accuracy. Accurate identification of foreign speech, when this speech is not immediately neighbouring, depends partly on the experience of the individual but more on the prominence of the dialect generally, which itself results from the prominence of the people who speak it and a few outstanding linguistic features. For example, speakers of English would easily succeed in identifying British speech, but would find greater difficulty with Canadian or New Zealand speech (unless of course they were Canadians or New Zealanders respectively). In the West Indies, then, speakers have notions about the speech of most territories, but some territories, for historical reasons, have identifying characteristics known to all West Indians.

In the West Indies territorial prominence is closely linked to economic development, population size and feelings of superiority.

This is clearly revealed in the way the territories are designated and grouped together. The names, official and unofficial, used for territories and groupings not only reveal assessments and attitudes but have served to smother the individuality of some territories. Barbados, partly for historical reasons and partly because of the perceived presumptions of its people, has long been referred to as 'Little England', a designation which is ambivalent in nature because although it is used negatively to suggest a colony or satellite of a major power, it also suggests achievement of characteristics which are to some extent beneficial in nature. In addition, Barbadians are the only West Indians to have a well-known nickname – Bajans (derived from the word *Barbadians* without the first syllable). Ambivalence towards Barbadians is also revealed in the use of this word. Many West Indians consistently use the term with a negative connotation or preceded by a derogatory adjective and also believe that in less prejudiced and objective contexts the term *Barbadian* should be used. Barbadians themselves do not show any decided preference for one term over the other.

Jamaicans refer to all the other territories as 'small islands', even though Guyana is not an island and in land area is much bigger than Jamaica. Barbadians refer to the Windward Islands as 'low islands', not for geographical reasons, but to try to establish superiority over their close neighbours. The term *Islands*, without a preceding adjective, is often used to refer to any or all of the Windward and Leeward Islands, as a result principally of cricket in which the Windwards and Leewards for a time functioned as a single unit and also as a result of political/economic grouping of the same islands as the Lesser Developed Countries.

The linguistic significance of the term *Islands* is that the users are not making any distinctions between the territories, may not see any significant differences, or regard them as unimportant. For example, the characteristics of Antiguan speech are not well-known, not because there are none, but because Antigua for many is indistinguishable generally from a number of other islands. In spite of the fact that most West Indians would find difficulty differentiating between non-standard speakers of Jamaica and those of Antigua, Antigua – linguistically – is not thought of in the same way as Jamaica. Within the West Indies only two territories are notorious linguistically: Jamaica and Barbados. It is Jamaican Creole, perceived as different in all areas of grammar, which makes Jamaica stand out and it is the characteristic pronunciation, standard and non-standard, which marks Barbadian speech. Trinidadian and Guyanese speech are recognisable because of the numbers and importance of these people in the West Indies, but their speech is not identified with the same enthusiasm as is the case with Jamaica and Barbados.

Subjectively identified characteristics are important, but should not be allowed to overshadow objectively identifiable ones, which clearly demonstrate similarities between territories which are not well-known. Figure 4.1 seeks to illustrate perceived markedness and historical and linguistic relationships between the characteristic speech (principally non-standard English) of West Indians.

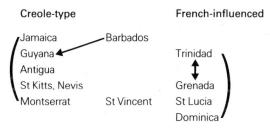

Fig. 4.1   Historical and linguistic relationships between the characteristic speech of West Indians.

There has always been migration between territories, but the arrows in Fig. 4.1 are added to indicate that during the formative years of the characteristic speech of the people, migration was on such a scale that it contributed a number of features or affected speech generally. In fact, Alister Hughes (1966) goes so far as to say:

> 'Grenada has her closest links with Trinidad. The populations of the two islands are kept in such close touch through newspapers, radio, trade and travel, that they share a large common non-standard English vocabulary and may be regarded as a single linguistic entity.'

In the case of Guyana and Barbados, of the 40,000 immigrants who went from the islands to Guyana between 1835 and 1893, Barbados contributed the greatest percentage.

On the vertical scale Jamaican and Barbadian speech are the most easily recognised (by West Indians themselves), then Trinidadian and Guyanese; the others are less easily recognised. The brackets in Fig. 4.1 indicate in both cases that there are close linguistic similarities between the territories with a decreasing strength in Creole features going from Jamaica to Montserrat and an increasing strength of French Creole features from Trinidad to Dominica. Barbados has the fewest Creole features and St Vincent more than Barbados.

Guyanese and Trinidadians generally are more familiar with names for East Indian dress, food, festivals and other cultural items than most other West Indians. The word *curry* is a general English word and is familiar to all West Indians, whereas *roti* is less well known throughout the English-speaking world but still familiar to most West Indians, with the possible exception of Jamaicans. Words such as *daalpuri* and *masala*, however, are not well known outside Trinidad and Guyana except in Indian-influenced communities. In the same way, with reference to dress, *sari* is a well-known word, whereas *dhoti* is not well known in the West Indies outside Trinidad and Guyana. In both Guyana and Trinidad, Indian religious festivals are officially recognised, with the effect that the non-Indian part of the population has become aware of their significance.

Ethnic vocabulary in the West Indies is quite evident but is not problematical mainly because of the cosmopolitan history of the region and the tolerance of the people in this regard. In fact, paradoxically it is the non-ethnic vocabulary that is current or idiomatic which presents greater problems, both for interpretation and acceptability. For example, if a Guyanese says

The children keeping nuff noise

the verb *keep* in this context tends to jar those who say *make*. Or, if a Jamaican uses *all* to mean 'even', as in

All the ceiling she paint   'Even the ceiling she painted'

it tends to be disconcerting to those other West Indians unfamiliar with it. In short, therefore, ethnic vocabulary is not provocative, because the reason for its existence and usage is quite clear; on the other hand unfamiliar usage of basic words is often regarded as illogical and ungrammatical.

Linguistic similarities, linguistic distinctiveness and linguistic complication between the territories can be illustrated more precisely by using the selected features of vocabulary, pronunciation and syntax presented in Table 4.1. These features are significant and except for *wi* have been broadly commented on in chapter 3. The first conclusion to be drawn from the table, one that would be further strengthened if more features were added, is that there are no exclusive subgroupings covering all the features. The feature *wi* (< French *oui* 'yes') used after sentences as a tag, as in

I going home, wi

can be attributed to French influence, but tense vowels rather than lax ones, represented by the feature i/ɪ, especially in final position, e.g.

tɪ, plɛ, nɔ instead of *ti, ple, no* 'tea, play, know'

and replacement of lax by tense, e.g.

slɪp, shɪt instead of *slip, shit* 'sleep, sheet'

cannot be easily attributed to French influence, especially as the former occurs in Montserrat and the latter is not characteristic of French. The negator *no*, the word *say* used to introduce a clause after certain verbs, and the continuous particle *a* clearly divide the territories into two.

Table 4.1 *Selected features of vocabulary, pronunciation and syntax in the West Indies.**

Feature	Ja	Ant	Guyn	St K	Mon	Bar	St V	Trin	Gren	St L	Dom
1	+	+	+	+	+	−	−	−	−	−	−
2	+	+	+	+	+	−	−	−	−	−	−
3	+	+	+	+	+	−	−	−	−	−	−
4	−	−	−	−	−	−	−	+	+	+	+
5	−	−	−	(+)	+	−	−	(+)	(+)	+	+
6	+	+	+	+	+	−	+	+	+	+	+
7	−	+	+	+	+	+	+	+	+	+	(+)

* Features: 1 *a* (continuous); 2 *say* (+ clause); 3 *no* (negator); 4 *wi* (tag); 5 *i/ı* (tense vowel); 6 *a/iz* (topicaliser); 7 *does* (habitual)

    Symbols: + indicates that the feature is normal and widespread
            (+) indicates that it occurs in some people's speech
            − indicates that it is not normal or widespread

(*Da*, a variant of *a*, occurs in Barbadian speech but it is not widespread.) On the other hand, *does* used for the habitual shows no pattern of distribution in keeping with other features across all the territories and the fact that it has never been a feature of Jamaican speech distinguishes Jamaica from the others. The one feature in Table 4.1 which can be termed an indispensable West Indian Creole feature is *a/iz* used as topicaliser. Its absence from Barbadian speech (and there is no trace that it ever was in Barbados) raises the problem whether speech in Barbados was ever fully Creolised.

The occurrence of significant features across the territories shows complex interrelationships and vague subgroupings. However, each territory has its own peculiarities, which are predominantly but not exclusively in pronunciation and vocabulary. These peculiarities are the ones that are usually overdone when people attempt to portray the non-standard speech of their own territory or try to imitate the characteristic speech of another territory.

Jamaica

Jamaican speech has a number of peculiarities, some pervasive and strong, others not. The strong and pervasive ones are in pronunciation. The omission and addition of [h] at the beginning of a word or syllable have occurred in the history of many languages (e.g. English *herb*: [hərb]/[ərb]; French *hotel*: [otɛl]; Spanish *hay*: [ay]), but in the West Indies specifically this usage is characteristic only of Jamaicans. It is prominent because it occurs at the beginning of words, because it is complementary in nature – [h] occurring where it does not in standard English, and not occurring where it does in standard English – and because it often occurs in formal contexts apparently uncontrollably when the speaker is under emotional strain. The indignant schoolmaster reprimanding his pupil with 'Hemphasise your haitches (h's), you hignorant hass' is a traditional joke in Jamaica illustrating the difficulty which some Jamaicans have controlling *h's* in a context where words beginning with a vowel are being stressed. In addition, there is the general problem that speakers may not know which words actually begin with *h* in standard English.

Another feature of Jamaican speech, which although it is not categorically different in some other territories is clearly stronger, is the use of [a] where standard English has [ɔ], e.g.

[aas]   comes from *horse* not *ass*
[aan]   comes from *horn* not *hand*
[batəm], [waatə], [(s)tapə] come from *bottom, water, stopper* respectively

As a result of hypercorrection, when the speaker is trying to correct what he sees as a problem, the reverse occurs, e.g.

bad, man, Dagwood become [bɔd], [mɔ], [Dɔgwəd]

A strong feature of Jamaican non-standard speech is the insertion of [w] after [p] or [b] before [ay] in the words [bway] *boy*, [bwayl] *boil*, [pwayl] *spoil*. This feature is prominent in spite of the small number of words it occurs in because of the frequency of the words themselves in normal everyday speech.

The consonants [t] and [d] preceding [l] change to [k] and [g] respectively. This is also fairly prominent in Antigua, and less so in St Lucia, e.g.

little, bottle become [likl], [bakl]
needle, middle, model become [nigl], [mɪgl], [magl]

In the area of morphology the outstanding feature of Jamaican non-standard speech is the use of *(h)im* in the subject position, in contrast to *(h)e* used in the other territories.

In the area of syntax the outstanding features are in the use of some prepositions/adverbs and in the function and meaning of *mek* (< *make*) in some contexts. In the following the word *from* is used more as a conjunction than a preposition; that is, it is followed not by a noun but by a clause:

From I see him, I know that . . . 'From the time I saw . . .'

This usage is not restricted to non-standard speakers in Jamaica but also occurs in educated formal speech.

Adverbs or verb complements also differ in some cases in Jamaican speech, as in the following:

The children laugh after her '. . . laughed at her'

laugh + after is also common in Antigua. The word *mek* is used in non-standard Jamaican speech where standard English has *let*, as in

Mek me tell you something 'Let me tell you something'
Im wudn mek me do it 'He wouldn't let me do it'

Peculiarities of a geographical area are most typical, other than 'accent', in vocabulary, especially that referring to flora and fauna. This is no less so in Jamaica when contrasted with the other territories, but such words are not of major significance as outstanding features of Jamaican speech. Words that really do characterise Jamaican speech are *pikni, raatid, maasta* (master), *face(t)y* and to a lesser extent *jinal*. *Pikni* is in widespread use and is not always restricted to the informal and non-standard; in more formal usage *child/children* is normally used. The word *raatid* is not strong enough to be regarded as obscene or even impolite. However, it has the same freedom of occurrence syntactically as obscene words do, as for example in

Cho raatid! Im move it
Im move it to raatid
The boy gone and move the raatid thing

The word *maasta* is a form of address employed when the speaker does not know or prefers not to use the addressee's name. It is equivalent to *you, mister, sir* used in other English-speaking communities and also as alternatives in Jamaica. It is not normally used in Jamaica today to concede superior status to the addressee, and of the four alternatives it is the most neutral, not being intentionally offensive or aggressive and not being friendly.

For Jamaicans *facety* or *facey* is more related to *face* in *bold face* and *barefaced* than it is to an older English word *feisty*. The word means 'brazen and insubordinate', but it can be used as a serious reprimand, a mock reprimand with a touch of admiration, or in jest.

The word *jinal* ('trickster'), equivalent to *smartman* used elsewhere in the West Indies, is significant both in its form which is peculiar to Jamaica and in its meaning which identifies a character or person well known in the folklore and history of the West Indies.

The foregoing features of Jamaican speech are the most prominent because of their frequency and distinctiveness. The overall sound of Jamaican speech – that is, what is referred to as the 'Jamaican accent' –

and the degree and frequency of use of Creole structures cannot be explained and illustrated briefly and in a simple fashion, but the features given here are to be understood as situated within the general context for the total picture to be better appreciated.

Barbados

The prominent features of Barbadian speech are mainly in pronunciation. Other West Indians notice above all in Barbadian speech a high and consistent level of nasalisation ('talking through one's nose') and glottalisation ('swallowing the ends of the words' or, more precisely, under-articulating consonants) which together produce a unique and strong 'accent'. For example, the sentence

I am not going to tell you what I am going to do

is heard as

a ē gā te? yu wa? a gā? du

which seems to involve minimal movement of the lower jaw. (The symbol ? indicates that the vocal cords merely come together momentarily to separate two sounds rather than there being a full articulation of the consonant.) In addition to the nasalised vowels marked in the sentence, it appears as if throughout their utterances Barbadians have more of the airstream coming through the nose than other West Indians. This however is only an impression and is not easily verifiable.

Another feature of Barbadian speech, not readily perceived by Barbadians themselves, is the production of the vowel glide/diphthong [oy] where other varieties of English have [əy] as in *I, my, rice, might, bite*. The reverse [əy] for [oy] is familiar to Barbadians but they regard it as geographical variation in Barbados, as in *pəynt* (< point), homophonous with *pint*, and *nəynt* (< anoint). However, the articulation of *poison* as *pəyzən* and *boil* as *bəyl*, the latter homophonous with *bile*, is not geographically restricted but general in Barbados.

A feature which is prominent in Barbadian speech because it contrasts with all other West Indian speech, with the possible exception of Guyanese, is strong retroflexion, or in other words maintenance of [r] in front of consonants, as in *card, cart, horse, George*.

A feature of Barbadian speech, also occurring in St Lucian English, is the use of [f] and [v] at the end of a syllable and word where other West Indian territories have [t] and [d] respectively and where standard English has the two pronunciations [θ], [ð] for the writing symbol *th*. Examples of the feature in Barbados are *birfday, paf* (*path*), *brof* (*broth*); *bave* (*bathe*), *teeving* (*teething*).

In the area of vocabulary Barbadians use three unique exclamations: *bo*, *kəder* and *wələs*. *Bo* is used at the beginning or at the end of utterances, and in meaning is like *alas* expressing disappointment or sorrow or mild fearfulness about the future. *Bo* has a diminutive endearing form *bosie*. These two are comparable to *bʌ* and *bʌdi* used in St Kitts. *Kəder* expresses sympathy for someone (second or third person) who is being reported as having suffered in some way. *Wələ:(s)* is an exclamatory reaction to a disaster, slight or serious.

Barbadians use a profane oath which, without being identical to it, sounds much like the British English expression *cor blimey*. It is interpreted and said by Barbadians as *God blind me*, but the characteristic glottalisation brings it close to the British expression. Barbadians do not use the word *pikni*, but their most common pronunciation of the word *children* [trildrən] distinguishes them from other West Indians.

In Barbados, as in other territories, polite language among the folk shows the avoidance of sometimes quite normal words referring to natural functions as if they were taboo and their replacement by bland expressions. For example, in Barbados the word *use* often replaces *eat* in the context where a visitor is offered a meal. The meal itself is seldom referred to as *food* or given the specific name of the food but as *this* or *the thing* or *something*. In other words a question such as

You used the thing I gave you?

is regarded as the right and polite form of speech among the folk. The words *thing* and *something* are also extensively used to refer to alcoholic drinks. There is a great deal of sensitivity attached to language in these contexts.

Polite language is of course quite normal in most societies in the context of sexual relations, but in Barbados deliberate vagueness is fostered in a word such as *talk* (this is not a case of a bland word with a known meaning). For instance, the expression

They does talk

can refer to anything from a platonic relationship to a long-standing sexual relationship. Such vagueness of course allows the user on the one hand an escape route and on the other the freedom to make insinuations.

Barbados and Guyana

The freedom of stress and pitch in West Indian English (pointed out earlier under colloquial English in chapter 2) allows for a contrastive pattern of words which is characteristic of Guyanese and Barbadian speech especially. The contrast is between words in which stress and pitch go together and the same words with stress and pitch separated, producing a difference in meaning which is consistent throughout the following pattern:

Heaviest stress and highest pitch on first syllable		Heaviest stress on first syllable and highest pitch on last syllable	
fáther mother sister brother	} 'blood relative'	fathér mother sister brother	} 'member of religious body' } 'member of religious body and nursing rank'
fármer butcher mason baker	} 'occupation'	Farmér Butcher Mason Baker	} 'proper name'
úgly beautiful wicked foolish	} 'description'	uglý beautiful wicked foolish	} 'jocular name'

There are two notable features of variation in form and function of the words in the second column. The words in the first column all have a generic descriptive meaning and a constant pronunciation pattern. The words in the second column do not have the same type of meaning now and the pitch pattern varies depending on whether the word is in isolation in its phrase. The pattern and meaning of the first three words in the second column derive from the form of address for priests and nuns (*brother* fits in by analogy), which means that all the words in the second column have the common function of title, name or form of address. The first four words in the second column are produced with the pattern of the corresponding words in the first column if they are followed by a name, e.g.

'sistér   becomes   'Síster Smith or 'Síster Mary

The next four words in the second column (and other words of this group) are produced with the pattern of the corresponding words in the first column, if they are preceded by a name, e.g.

'Farmér   becomes   Tony 'Fármer

The last four words do not change their pattern according to context, e.g.

'beautifúl   Miss 'Beautifúl   beautifúl Mary

The last three words in the second column represent a productive type in that virtually any relevant descriptive adjective can be changed to a jocular form of address by changing the pitch pattern.

There are other words, not of the types above, which have the same contrastive pitch-stress pattern and in some cases are examples of geographical and social variation without change in meaning. The only other word used with a contrastive stress-pitch pattern and a corresponding change in meaning is *as*. However, since the word is monosyllabic, it is difficult to determine whether the crucial distinction is one of pitch or one of stress. The word *as* when produced with weak stress and low pitch means 'because' or 'since'; with heavy stress and high pitch it means 'as soon as', e.g.

As you came, I went   'Because you came . . .'
'Aś you came, I went   'As soon as you came . . .'

Guyana

Guyanese speech is not characterised by many outstanding phonological features when contrasted with other territories except firstly for the use of [ɔ] instead of [ʌ] in words such as *another, brother*, which Guyanese pronounce as [ənɔdər] and [brɔdər] respectively, and secondly that the first vowel in words such as *dirty, thirty, further, Thursday* is produced further back in the mouth to sound like the vowel in *door*, i.e. [o]. In both cases therefore there is a move away from the [ʌ] sound. Claims have been made that this has been substantially caused by the widespread presence historically in Guyana of speakers of Hindi, which does not have the [ʌ] sound.

Like Jamaica, Antigua and St Kitts, Guyana has [a] in many cases where British English has [ɔ] as in *jab* 'job', *smaal* 'small', *dag* 'dog', *gat* 'got', *baks* 'box'.

In syntax, as in Jamaica where *from* can normally be used as a conjunction (i.e. in addition to its use as a preposition), e.g.

From I was a boy . . .

in Guyana *by* can be used in the same way, e.g.

By them meet the steling, the gas use out   *[1]
'By the time they reached the jetty, the gas was all used up'

Guyanese, like Jamaicans, use *mek* to link clauses establishing cause and result, to give sentences of the type

He cuff she up proper mek she lef he   *[1]

However, Guyanese also have a variant *mek so*   *[2] as in

Them take way the thing mek so me no got none no more   *[1]
'They took away the things, so I don't have any any longer'

*[1]   These examples are taken from Bickerton (1972).
*[2]   In Tobago *mek so* is used as a question to mean 'Why?'

It is of interest to note that Guyana had the conjunctions *whichin* 'as a result of which' and *becausin* 'because', which are also regarded as quaint forms in Barbados.

Guyana is more outstanding in its vocabulary in that besides the many words of ethnic origin it has words that relate to its terrain, land use and construction. In addition to the word *sea-wall*, there is *steling* 'jetty, wharf', and *dam* 'a strip of land between waterways', which are household words to Guyanese. One of the most familiar examples of Guyanese usage, however, is in the case where other West Indians more frequently use the semantically empty *man* before and after clauses. In this case Guyanese use *boy*, pronounced [bay] (which rhymes with the English word *aye*) as in

Boy, I going home   or   *I going home, boy*

For the first and second person plural pronouns, Guyanese non-standard speech has respectively *awi* (< all we) and [ayʌ] (< all you). These forms are also normal in Antigua, St Kitts and Montserrat.

There are a number of English words used in Guyana, the meanings of which are totally unfamiliar to people outside Guyana. Take, for example, *uplift* and *transport* in the following examples:

Mary gone a post office fu uplift one parcel   *
'Mary has gone to the post office to collect a parcel'

I bin at me lawyer to uplift the transport   *
'I went to my lawyer to get the title-deed'

The word *pikni* is used in Guyana, but *cɪrən* is more common.

Trinidad

Two strong features of Trinidadian speech are the exclamation *eh eh* and the use of *go* before the verb to indicate future. The *ɛʔɛ* and *mʔm* exclamations, described earlier, are variously distributed across the West Indies, but there is no question that *ɛʔɛ*, high-pitched and sudden, is pervasive and strong in Trinidad and used by both men and women. In other territories *ɛʔɛ* is used more by women than by men.

Where other West Indians, in order to indicate future, use *a go*, *gain*, or *gwain*, Trinidadians use *go* as in

I go eat now

Trinidadians also use a specific associative plural with the words *man* and *boy(s)*, as in

I eh know what the man and them go do
I went down by the boys and them

* These examples are taken from Bickerton (1972).

In other territories, although the associative plural *and them* is not absolutely restricted to following proper names, e.g. *Mary and them*, it is more normal in this context. In Jamaica specifically the associative plural does not necessarily contain the conjunction and so is not distinct in structure from the normal Creole plural, e.g.

di man dem: *Mary dem*

In its vocabulary Trinidad speech is outstanding in cultural items relating to Carnival, supernatural beliefs and folklore, and also in words for fruits, plants and animals. These areas of Trinidadian vocabulary overwhelmingly show words of French Creole and French origin. Words like *jouvert* (< *jour overt* Fr.), *ligarou* (< *loup garou*) and *pomme citerre* are only single examples from these areas.

In the more general vocabulary of Trinidadians are the words *mamaguy* (< *mamar gallo* Sp.), 'to tease, especially by flattery' – Laurence (1971). There is also the word *picong* (< *picon* Sp.) which is explained in Laurence (1971) as 'the exchange of teasing and even insulting repartee, generally in a lighthearted, bantering manner'. Both of these words have been so widely and prominently used that they have spread to other territories, and as Laurence says, 'no Standard English words can adequately replace them with their undertones of lighthearted and good natured teasing.' Another typical Trinidadian word is *maco* (noun/verb/adj) which refers to a special kind of or undue inquisitiveness.

In Trinidadian speech also the word *children* is significant because of its pronunciation [cɪrən].

St Lucia and Dominica

In Dominica and St Lucia, English varies from being a second language to most people to being a native language for some, with others in between. It therefore shows great influence in its pronunciation, syntax and vocabulary from French Creole. Best known generally are features, also common in Grenada and Trinidad, such as the following:

i   *It have* (standard English 'there is'), e.g. *it have a man in town who . . .*
ii *It making* (standard English 'it is') describing the weather, e.g. *it making hot.*
iii *Wi* (< *oui* Fr.) – as a tag, e.g. *it making hot, wi.*
iv Strong stress on the penultimate or final syllable in a phrase.

In St Lucia specifically the correspondence between standard [θ], written *th*, and [f] goes even further than in Barbados – it also occurs at the beginning of words, e.g.

[fri] 'three'; [fɔt] 'thought', [fiŋ] 'thing'

In general in Dominica and St Lucia the intonation pattern of utterances has more rises and falls than other varieties of West Indian English.

In St Lucia the tag *wi*, given in Table 4.1, occurs normally as [i] as in

We do it, i	'We did it, you know'
It turning, i	'It's turning, you know'
She dat give it to me, i	'It is she who gave it to me, you know'

Other tags in use in St Lucia are [ō] and [ɛ̄]. [ō] is normally used after negative statements and requests, as in

I don know, ō	'I don't know, you know'
She din give me cake, ō	'She didn't give me any cake, you know'
Let's go, ō	'Let's go'
Put it on for me, ō	'Put it on for me'

[ɛ̄] is normally used after positive statements and statements requiring reassurance, as in

I going, ɛ̄	'I am leaving'
I put it on the table for you, ɛ̄	
We'll go this afternoon, ɛ̄	

In St Lucia the word *children* is pronounced [cɪlrən].

Another prominent feature in both St Lucia and Dominica is the use of prepositions in a way that differs from other West Indian usage and from standard English. Firstly where other West Indian usage would have an additional *from*, St Lucia and Dominica have zero, e.g.

Move your foot there	(W.I. Move your foot from there)
Move in the middle of the road	(W.I. Move from in the middle)
Take your hand in my pocket	(W.I. . . . from in my pocket)

There are also changes in the actual preposition used, e.g.

She threw it behind me	'. . . at me'
The limes are on the fridge	'. . . in the fridge'
If they speaking patois for me,	
I speaking patois for them	'. . . to me/them'

In both islands prepositions used for direction and location vary from usage elsewhere, e.g.

I going at home	'I am going home'
Let's go on the beach	'Let's go to the beach'

In St Lucia *does* is normally used to express habitual meaning but in Dominica it is restricted. St Lucians also use the *-ing* form to express habitual, as in

The cookin the breadfruit with the skin
'They cook breadfruit in the skin'

French-Creole influenced structure occurs in

How many years you have? 'How old are you?'

In St Lucia specifically the French Creole *kōsa* (< French *comme ça*) translated *like that* occurs before noun clause complements, as in

My mother tell you like that to send the ice for her

I tell you like that to not to go and bring it for her *

The fact that English is a formally learnt language for many in these two territories shows up in more formal contexts when standard English and specifically the English auxiliary verbs *be*, *do*, *have* are being used. Spoken formal English is characterised by constructions such as *I'm, he's, don't, hasn't*, but in Dominica and St Lucia the full forms *I am*, etc. are more frequently used.

Much of the profanity and many of the exclamations of Dominicans and St Lucians when speaking English are from French Creole. One exclamation typical of St Lucia and Dominica is *egas*, which is used to accompany blows (as in a fight at the cinema).

Antigua

The general structure of non-standard speech in Antigua is very much like that in Jamaica, but Antigua has its own specific characteristics. Antiguans produce the consonant cluster [tr] as [c]; that is, the sound normally represented in English spelling by *ch*. The words *three* and *truck* therefore sound like *chuck* and *chee*. The related cluster [dr] changes in the same way to [j]; that is, English spelling symbol *j*. The words *drink* and *drunk* sound like *jink* and *junk*.

In order to indicate past tense, where Jamaicans use *ben/en* Antiguans use *min*, e.g.

You min eat   'You ate'
You min a eat   'You were eating'

(Note that *min* is also attested for Jamaica, but it is not now as common as *ben* and *en*.)

In prepositional usage Antigua demonstrates features in common with other islands:

- with Jamaica it has *laugh after* meaning 'laugh at' and *look pon* 'look at';
- with Jamaica it has *for* to indicate possession, e.g. *anybody for me* 'any of my relatives';
- with Barbados, St Lucia and other territories, *by* is used to mean 'at the home of', e.g. *I went by you yesterday.*

* The St Lucian examples are taken from Alexander (1981).

In its vocabulary Antiguan speech of course has a number of peculiarities, but words which stand out are as follows:

- *dikti* 'fancy', a word not generally known outside Antigua;
- *grandy* in the expression
  You think you have grandy legs
  'You think you are better than everybody else';
- *walk with* meaning 'bring'
  when you coming, walk with two limes;
- *wonderful* meaning that a person tends to over-react and is therefore lightly dismissed, as in
  She too wonderful;
- *empty* meaning 'only, nothing but', as in
  She doesn't have any mangoes, she has empty figs
  'She doesn't have any mangoes, she has only bananas' *[1]

St Kitts

Kittitian speech is basically in the same camp as Jamaican and Antiguan. The one significant feature of St Kitts pronunciation which stands out is the tendency for [v] to become [w], e.g.

weks	'vexed'
wery	'very'
Newis	'Nevis'
grawy	'gravy'

In its sentence structure to signal past tense where Antigua has *min*, St Kitts most often has *di* (< standard English *did*), but it also has *iin* and *bin* used in different parts of the island.

To signal future, St Kitts speech has both *gon* and *an* (both derivable from standard English *going*), e.g.

He an go town fi you	'He will go to town for you'
A gon do om soon	'I will do it soon'

In all the territories the relative pronouns usually derive from *that*, *what*, *who* and *where* and are pronounced in different ways, but St Kitts also has [sʌ] as in

Dat a di woman sʌ tief di mace	'. . . woman who stole . . .'
Bring di buk sʌ you just read	'. . . book which you just . . .'

In its vocabulary it is the specific sentence tags used in St Kitts which stand out: *bʌ, bʌdi, daadi-bʌ* as in

He lef he wife, bʌdi/bʌ	'He left his wife'
Let me show om, daadi-bʌ	'Let me show him'. *[2]

---

*[1] This example is taken from Evelyn (1982).
*[2] These examples are taken from Martin (1982).

Another word which other West Indians would not easily understand, especially if taken out of its context, is *gutless* which in St Kitts means 'greedy' (together with its noun form *gutlessness*). Where Barbadians use *above* and *below* to mean 'east of' and 'west of', Kittitians use *upperside* and *lowerside*. Note that Barbadians also say the *lowside part* to mean the western part, which may account for the development of the term 'Low Islands', a term used by Barbadians to refer to the Windwards which are west of Barbados. In Berbice in Guyana *lowside* is also used to mean the western or southwestern part.

Montserrat

Montserrat is another of the Leeward Islands group which has a number of features in common with Jamaica. Specifically Montserratian in pronunciation, however, is the tendency to pronounce [ʌ/ə] as [u], e.g. *should* > *shu*, *could* > *ku* and *for, a, of* normally occur as *fu, u, u* within sentences.

As in Jamaica, *boil, boy, spoil* are pronounced *bwayl, bway, spwayl*, and *oil* as *ɔyl* as in Barbados. The word *from* becomes either *fan* or *farm* and *children* is pronounced *trɪldrm*.

Does is used to render habitual meaning but the negative of it differs from both Trinidad and Barbados, e.g.

Montserrat:	*Me no does do that*
Trinidad:	*I doesn do that*
Barbados:	*I does dont do that*

For the past tense where Antiguans use *min*, Montserratians usually have a shorter *mi*. The verb *be* is also more commonly used, as in

A what e be	'What's wrong?'
A what um be	'What is it?'
A who them be	'Who are they' *

The associative plural of the noun shows a slight distinction in Montserrat which is not typical of all other islands. For example, *Mary dem* can be restricted to mean 'Mary and her family' or 'Mary's family' whereas *Mary and dem* means 'Mary and her friends'.

The two exclamations which stand out are *oh-gaam* which expresses sorrow or regret and *sudden out* which expresses disappointment.

In the general vocabulary of Montserrat, words that would not be intelligible to most other West Indians are *cherry* 'cashew', *crabbit* 'intelligent', *doo doo* 'idiot'. *Chups* meaning 'a kiss' is related to Jamaican *troops* with the same meaning and also to the general West Indian word

---

*   The Monserratian examples are taken from Irish (1985).

Table 4.2   *A comparison of words in the different territories of the West Indies*

Source	Antigua	Barbados	Dominica	Grenada	Guyana
gossip	melee	—	[bɛf]	gossip	talkname
tamarind	tambran	tambrin	tambrin	tambran	tambran
firefly	firefly light-a-light	firefly	label firefly	firefly	candlefly
cutlass	cotlis	cutlʌs	cutlʌs	cutlish	cutlish
(various)	box	meeting turn	sub	sou sou	box
quenepo (Amer. Sp.)	ginip	ackee	kenip	skenep	ginip
—	dums	dunks	—	—	dunks
fast 'inquisitive'	fas interference (adj)	gipsy (adj) malicious	fas	fas	fas
ɔdɔkono Kaŋgi (Afr.)	dukuna	conkee sweet dumpling	conkee-dumpling	—	conkee
beverage	brebich bebich	sweet water swank	sugar water beverage	sweet water	sugar water swank
funži Kuskus (Afr.)	funji	cou-cou	—	cou-cou	cou-cou
strike (someone)	bang	hit	hit	hit	knock
craving lickerish	[rebm]	likrish	greedy	badways	scraven likrish
homosexual	antiman	buller	bogerer	bullerman	antiman
lesbian	zami (adj)	wicker	zami (v)	zami mattie	sadamite
prickle	cassie	plimpler	prickle	picker	plimpler
barata (Sp.) la nyapa (Amer. Sp.)	braata	—	rangement (Fr. Creole)	—	overs

Jamaica	St Kitts	St Lucia	Montserrat	Trinidad	St Vincent
cass-cass	tori	roro	melee	commes	commes
—	tamon	tamarin	taman tomoon	tambran	tambram
peenie-walli	lampfly	firefly	firefly	candlefly	larbel
machete	machete	cutlas	cutlʌs	cutlash	cutlis
pardner	pardner-hand	sou-sou	box throw hand	sou-sou	sou-sou
ginep	skenip	ackee	ginip	chenet	—
coolie-plum	dounce	—	—	dongs	—
fas	fas jeps	indiskwet (Fr. Creole)	fas	fas	commes
ducka-noo tie-a-leaf	conkee	[pɛmi]	dukna	pay-me	dukunu
sugar water	swank	sweet water	baybridge	—	sugar water
turn-cornmeal	corn	—	turn-corn	cou-cou	cou-cou
lick	bang	hit	bang lash	beat	lash
craven	gutlis	vowas (Fr. Creole)	craven likrish	likrish	likrish
battyman	auntieman	buller antiman	antiman bullman	bullerman	bullerman
—	flap (v)	—	flapper bapsa	—	zami
macca	casha	pichet prickle	prickle cusha	picker	cashie
braata	commission	—	mek up braata	lanyap brata (Tobago)	—

translated as 'suck teeth' (the lip formation is the same for the kiss as for the 'suck-teeth').

The word *above* is also used in Montserrat to mean 'the eastern side of'.

A comparison of words across territories

The great variety in pronunciation and word choice in the West Indies is illustrated in Table 4.2, in which seventeen different items are compared in eleven territories. The word(s) given for each territory are in a number of cases only a sample of the variants within the territory. In Jamaica for the words *firefly* and *cutlass* there are a great number of variants, all of which could not be represented in the table. Table 4.2 therefore merely gives an indication of the total variety.

It may be surprising to those of some islands that other islands know nothing or very little about the fruit variously called *dums*, *dunks*, *dongs*, *coolie plums*. It may be surprising to some Barbadians that *cou-cou* is not restricted to Barbados and that in some territories it has little prominence. In the case of *dukuna/conkee/pay-me* this item also varies in prominence and in almost every case is made in a different way.

It may appear to the outsider that with so many differences, West Indians find difficulty communicating with each other. However, this is more apparent than real, since West Indians are good examples of sociolinguistic variation in that they change their speech, often significantly, to correspond to local level, national level and international level. Such changes have always been a part of the linguistic repertoire of West Indians.

5 · *Linguistic sources of West Indian English*

Popular notions about language development in the West Indies

Before dealing with objective evidence and well-based theories about the linguistic sources of West Indian English, it is necessary to account for, if not dispel, popular notions about the way in which West Indian speech came to be what it is. The idea that the reason for something is 'obvious' or a matter of 'common sense' is usually the function of the prejudices and level of ignorance that obtain in a society. In the same way that it seems 'obvious' to the individual that the world is flat (and it was once heretical to believe otherwise), many notions about language structure in the West Indies are a legacy from slavery, colonialism and racism. Notions that racial differences (actual or assumed) in lips, nose, tongue, mouth, throat, lungs and brain, or the external factors of nature such as the heat of the sun, the noise of the wind, trees, rivers and the sea, or that the sounds of animals have significant influence on linguistic structures, are groundless. Such notions are strong and persistent, however, because prejudice and myth-making are an inescapable part of man.

Evolution and change in the sounds, word structures, sentence structures and meanings of a language are neither 'obvious' nor a matter of 'common sense'. They require accurate documentation and research, close analysis, and analogical reasoning based on a sound theory. The task becomes more difficult when languages come into contact and leave little or no record of what happens. In short, it requires even closer analysis of the available material and sounder reasoning to determine development in such a case.

Two of the oldest notions about the development of English in the West Indies are a straightforward reflection of the political, social and economic relationship between the West Indies and Britain, a relationship born in the master-slave era and maintained through colonialism. These notions emerged in two ways: in the mouths of laymen and native speakers, and from the pens of early linguists, based on what seemed 'obvious' to both sets. In the case of the former the 'obvious' was contradicted by a lack of knowledge about the way in which languages evolve and in the case of the latter by a lack of knowledge of the very languages that were being talked about. Another difference between the two was that the native speakers of these languages, who obviously have never considered themselves sub-human and foolish, believed and still do that West Indian non-standard English is simply a consistent case of falling short of the target as a result of laziness, not being provided with a good example, and lack of motivation towards uplift. Early linguists, on the other hand, brought up in a tradition which regarded European languages and cultures as superior to all others, viewed West Indian language as resulting from initial simplification of European languages by Europeans who thought that the simplified forms would be easier for the Africans to understand. In both cases an element which seemed 'obvious' was inflated into a total theory to account for linguistic systems, in spite of the more obvious fact that these linguistic systems which were supposed to be simplified or reduced versions of the European language were not understood by Europeans themselves. The response to this fact of inability to understand, whether it was (and still is) European talking about West Indian language or West Indian about West Indian language, was to regard whatever could not be understood as gibberish. In other words, the full assessment of West Indian language was that it was either simple language or wrong (reduced) or gibberish. In addition to the fallacies just indicated in these notions of simplicity and reduction, conclusions made were erroneous because the language learning situation – and specifically one or two elements in it (motivation of learners, attitudes of Europeans) – were being taken as identical to the totality of language that was being spoken and the full linguistic ability of speakers. So a few prominent factors in the learning situation were being used to represent and characterise the full range of a highly varied linguistic situation.

The notions of simplification and ungrammaticality held respectively by early linguists and West Indians are based on a direct comparison of the European language with only those elements which were comparable with it in the Creole language. It is as if one were to take the language of 'Spanglish' speakers in New York City, select the English elements, regard them as a non-standard variety of the English language, and compare this variety with standard English. In the West Indian situation conclusions were based on a comparison of the following:

- the length and form of words in the two varieties;
- the length of comparable syntactic structures in each variety;
- the total number of words in each variety;
- a spoken language (Creole English) with written English.

In addition, conclusions were based on a theory of simplification which implied that whatever is shorter and smaller is simpler.

Consider the following few examples of comparison:

West Indian Creole English	Standard English
(a) written symbols *t, d; -in*	written symbols *th; ing*
des	*desk, desks*
love	*loves, loved*
(b) *he bad*	*he is bad*
go eat	*go and eat, going to eat*
the food eat	*the food has been eaten*
(c) short sentences joined by *and, but*	long sentences with dependent clauses
(d) smaller vocabulary	larger varied vocabulary

In (a) and (b), conclusions about simplicity are erroneous either because forms are being compared without reference to their full function, meaning and relationship to other forms being used by speakers, or because of ignorance of linguistic facts. In (c) and (d) the conclusions relate to difference in societies, social classes and domains of language use rather than to the expressive potential of varieties, and so go far beyond the scope of language.

Even if the comparisons had greater validity, one would still have to deal with the notion of simplicity from a theoretical point of view. To explain the notion of simplicity the idea has been put forward that human beings make certain adjustments in their language in order to make it easier, for example, for a foreigner to understand. Two such adjustments are identified as the reduction in inflexions and the omission of the verb *to be* (or its equivalent), both of which imply that reduction, or being shorter and smaller, brings about simplicity. These two adjustments and the idea behind them seem reasonable if your language is inflexional and has a verb like the verb *to be*, but if your language does not, adjustments for simplicity must be different. In short, then, the absence of inflections and the verb *to be* is not a universal feature of simplicity or an indication of simplicity.

In any case, to claim that reduction achieves simplicity is to state a half-truth, for reduction also brings ambiguity and complication, as for example when one changes

old men and old women   to   *old men and women*

Also, in research work on the development of language in children, no clear and unequivocal relationship is demonstrated between on the one hand the adults' perception of simplicity (i.e. the kind of language parents use when talking to babies) or the grammarian's analysis of simplicity and on the other hand language produced at different stages as the child grows older. In other words, the 'simplicity' of child language is not the same as 'simplified' language produced by adults. These facts alone show that what the speaker intends as simplification may be either simplification, or complication, or irrelevant.

The notion of ungrammaticality used by some West Indians to explain the language situation is based on the assumption firstly that standard English should be used or is actually the intended target, and secondly that with effort the target is achieved. This assumption disregards the realities of language learning for the child and the adult. It assumes, for example, that a West Indian individual to whom standard English is presented explicitly (as in school) or casually (by radio, television, etc.) with a little effort should be able to produce standard English when required, in spite of the fact that in the course of any one day over 90 percent of the contexts in which this individual finds himself do not require the production of standard English exclusively. In short, the amount of actual practice required for the production of standard English is grossly underestimated and the actual usefulness of standard English to some individuals is grossly overestimated.

Linguistic theories and development of language in the West Indies

In contrast to the commonsense types of notion put forward to explain the development of West Indian language, there was a major theory which held sway for some time, which was quite scholarly and arose out of research work done in different parts of the world. To those who developed it, it came like a brainwave or a revelation. Nowadays it is generally dismissed as relying on limited and inadequate evidence and poor knowledge of language learning. This theory, familiarly called the 'Portuguese Pidgin Theory', is based on the idea of maritime transmission of a single embryonic language to all parts of the world initially by Portuguese traders who made the language so useful as a tool of trade that it was eventually used by all other trading nations. To explain language in the West Indies, the theory claims that the embryonic language was introduced all along the slaving coasts of West Africa, came across with the slaves, and while retaining its basic structure in every territory, used the words of the European language that was the official or major language in the territory at the time. This theory was inspired by the presence of Portuguese-derived words in Creoles in diverse parts of the world (principally some form of the words *sabe/savvy* and *pikin/pikni*). The main goal of the theory was to account neatly for features that are common to Creoles all over the world by giving them a single source. The proponents of the theory, in their zeal for homogeneity and carried away by what at the time seemed like a powerful theory, never really addressed the problem of language learning in adverse conditions and in greatly varying situations. When this was eventually done, the theory was gradually deflated.

Theories about the development of West Indian language which today enjoy a measure of respectability refer to one or a combination of three areas: the linguistic structures of languages known to have been involved in the contact between European and African, research data and conclusions from monitored first- and second-language learning, and hypotheses about the human brain and the nature of linguistic ability. No one theory is stated in such a way as to account for the totality of the linguistic situation in the West Indies today; theories concentrate on what the author considers most crucial or interesting, and, because of academic tradition, each one is stated in such a way as to contrast with or exclude all others. The three areas mentioned, even though they overlap, can be respectively situated in three major traditions of formal linguistics: historical and sociolinguistics, language learning or psycholinguistics, and general or theoretical linguistics. Since these traditions evolved from relatively stable and homogeneous language situations, West Indian language has presented and continues to present great challenges to linguistic theory as well as to West Indian speakers themselves and West Indian educators.

Whereas theories based on the notions of simplification and lack of grammaticality have as their immediate starting point a comparison of West Indian language with English, the more 'respectable' theories do the opposite – they concentrate on features that are non-English. The reason for this is that it is believed that West Indian language is better understood if it is situated in a historical perspective and this historical perspective indicates that even if West Indian language does not seem distinct from English today, it was once quite distinctive in its basic structure and also that it is closely related to other Creoles which are today quite distinct from European languages. In other words, West Indian language is seen as deriving not principally or solely from English, but – for some – principally from West African languages and – for others – from a language contact situation in which many differing factors operated.

Some theories have concentrated for the most part on West Indian language and have tried to explain all the non-English features. Other theories have situated West Indian language in the general context of Creole languages and have tried to account principally for those non-European features in West Indian language which are common to all Creole languages. Of course the very assumption or suggestion that a feature is non-English bristles with difficulty because of ignorance of many regional features of European languages and English specifically that have been used from the earliest years up to now in the development of West Indian language. One of the implications of using one starting point rather than the other is that when West Indian non-standard English is immediately related to English, it suggests that the differences between the two are superficial, whereas when it is not, it suggests that those differences are substantial.

Those theories which, in the tradition of historical linguistics, use specific details of languages and also make use of general historical and sociological facts, have a fertile field, because they are not constrained by well-known and documented features in the development of West Indian language. In other words, reconstruction is based on careful selection, or selectivity, and argumentation to support a theory. Those theories which refer to the data and conclusions of psycholinguistics rely on an inductive leap from an observed case to a historical one which can never be identical. In addition, experimentation, data and conclusions in language learning research are not always so scientific or objective as to be beyond argument. Those theories which refer to the brain and human linguistic ability are overwhelmingly speculative in nature and either do not claim to directly represent reality or are as difficult to prove conclusively as they are to disprove. In summary, there is no way that linguistic theory can recover West Indian linguistic history totally or precisely. The theories must be judged according to the extent of evidence and logic they are based on.

The most controversial element in the theories of development of West Indian languages put forward by linguists is the role of the child *vis-à-vis* (the role of) the adult. The traditional and most tenacious interpretations of the word *Creole* itself accord a crucial role to the child. So too does the most recent theory. However, most theories explicitly or implicitly regard the initial formative period of West Indian language as second-language learning by West African speakers with then a second stage which involved first-language learning by children born into a slave society. The traditional interpretation of the term *Creole* contains the assumption that the children learned the language they heard in the situation, but it specifically claims that the children expanded what they learned in order to deal with all the domains of human experience. On the other hand, the most recent theory claims that the role of adults in the early formation of West Indian language was minimal and that it was the child who performed the crucial formative role with a minimal or no model to follow.

Appeal to non-linguistic historical facts, because it has some measure of conjecture, will not resolve the problem, but it does not provide strong evidence in support of the role of the child. History of social structure under slavery presents a picture of the individual as chattel whose worth was assessed according to immediate, current output in a situation rigorously controlled by economic factors. In this situation the adult male had the greater value and adult females did secondary and minor jobs. The old and the young were economic liabilities, but never became a major problem because of economic policy and harsh reality. Severe working conditions during the most fruitful years of the slave's life militated against longevity. The high mortality rate of slaves is well documented. Pregnancy and child-rearing were not encouraged because they reduced the economic output of women during their strongest years and also because it was cheaper and quicker to get adult imported slaves than it was to depend on a protracted system of child-rearing. In addition, the infant mortality rate must have been very high in the early years.

This picture suggests that in the formative years of West Indian language the role of the child was minor because there would not have been many children. This picture can be further developed by comparing the situation of Jamaica with that of Barbados during the formative years. Statistics for Jamaica show a consistent and heavy dependence on importation of slaves from Africa up to the 19th century as a method of maintaining an adequate labour force. Statistics for Barbados show a gradual decrease in dependence on importation and a corresponding increase in dependence on child-birth from the 18th century. The Jamaican language situation shows a high level of Creole features and the Barbadian situation a low level. A possible implication of this is that it was adults who were primarily responsible for Creolisation in West Indian language. Such an argument, however, has to be tempered by the myriad other factors in the situation of slavery in the West Indies and the differences between the territories.

Social factors in the development of West Indian English

Theories of development and specifically those dealing with the role of the child *vis-à-vis* the adult highlight what is in full a complex interrelationship between language contact, language learning and language evolution in the history of the West Indies. Figure 5.1 outlines this interrelationship by identifying major contributory factors.

Whether or not there were any intermediary languages involved in

Language contact	Language learning	Language evolution
Variety of languages	Conditions of learning	Socially determined:
Social and geographical dialects	Attitudes and motivation	function and domains
		education
	Strategies of learning	modernisation
Lack of source standardisation	Limitations on achievement	Linguistically determined:
Contemporary linguistic structure		principles of structural change

Fig. 5.1   Factors in the origin and development of West Indian English.

the development of West Indian language, there is no question that English and West African languages came into contact. However, whereas English, the target, was a single language, and can be recovered to a great extent from British literature, the West African languages present a much greater difficulty for recovery. A difficulty for recovery in both cases is the exact provenance of the people, but in the case of the British there is no doubt that colonists and servants came from all parts of England, Scotland and Ireland. The bond servants who would generally have been in closer contact with the slaves than the masters were often poor or debt-ridden people and were thus generally speakers of lower-class dialects of various geographical regions. There were also many 'black sheep' of upper-class families who were sent to the colonies as a form of punishment or to be kept out of further trouble. Such people, although their dialect would have been basically upper-class, might not have projected themselves as models of linguistic sophistication.

On a more general level it must be remembered that the unit, Great Britain, did not come into existence until 1707 and that the period 1760–1830 was one of major industrial transformation which brought about a higher level of urbanisation and national homogeneity in Britain. In other words, although London and the Court may have claimed to have a standard version of English developing during the 18th century, the effect of this standardisation was limited and the regional dialects were vibrant and respectable. In addition, the very notion of a national standard for all is much more recent, catering as it does to general education and wide communication, which were not normal earlier. The British colonists who came to the West Indies therefore not only spoke many different social and regional dialects but also were under no external pressure to do otherwise. The low level of literacy which has been a factor in the black population up to today in most territories is paralleled by a level which was not substantially higher among the white plantation administrators (owners, bookkeepers, overseers) throughout slavery and colonialism. Thus the variety of English which the slaves came into contact with most often, especially in the early years, was regional and colloquial. The general regional dialects of the British Isles given in Fig. 5.2 represent distinctions which were significant during the 17th and 18th centuries.

The slaves themselves came predominantly from West Africa, but one can deal only in generalities when trying to pinpoint the exact sources in West Africa. In the 17th century the majority of slaves are said to have been taken from the coastal area from modern Senegal to Sierra Leone (area A in Fig. 5.3). In the 18th century, the most important period for the West Indies, the majority are said to have come from the coastal area from modern Liberia to Nigeria (area B in Fig. 5.3). In the last period of slavery, when slaves were more difficult

Fig. 5.2   British dialects of the 18th century.

to obtain, the slave ships were forced to go as far down the west coast as Angola (area C in Fig. 5.3). Areas A and B specifically contain many forms of speech, which today are variously classified by experts on African languages as dialects, subgroups, groups, languages and language families. There is general agreement, however, that area A is dominated by the Mande language group and area B by the Kwa language group. The languages and some major dialects of the Kwa and Mande groups are given in Fig. 5.3.

The linguistic competence of the West African slaves coming to the West Indies and the nature of their languages have been presented by experts in a paradoxical way: great variety with basic homogeneity. In addition, it is claimed that as a result of the system of keeping slaves in 'factories' at the shipping ports on the West African coast for varying periods of time, it was possible for interlanguage communication between Africans to have been significant. On the other hand, it is claimed that slaveowners in the West Indies tried to get slaves speaking different languages in order to minimise general communication which could lead to mass insurrection. However, not

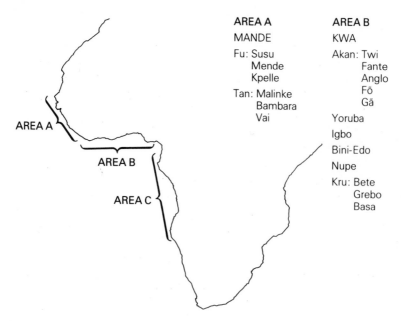

AREA A	AREA B
MANDE	KWA
Fu: Susu	Akan: Twi
Mende	Fante
Kpelle	Anglo
Tan: Malinke	Fō
Bambara	Gā
Vai	Yoruba
	Igbo
	Bini-Edo
	Nupe
	Kru: Bete
	Grebo
	Basa

Fig 5.3   West coast of Africa: language groups and languages.

only did price and limited availability of slaves nullify the slaveowners' intentions, but maroonage and rebellion were so frequent that communication did not seem to have been a major problem among the slaves. In spite of the contradictions and the variety of languages in West Africa, the fact that the two major areas from which slaves were imported (areas A and B) are classified by experts on African languages (who have no direct interest in language in the West Indies) into two basic groups according to structure shows that historically West African linguistic homogeneity could have played a significant role in the development of language in the West Indies. Linguistic homogeneity and specific structures of 17th- and 18th-century West African languages now have to be posited or reconstructed from modern descriptions of West African languages, in contrast to those for regional English for the same period for which there is sufficient literature and documentation.

In considering language learning historically in the development of West Indian language, one must take into consideration not only general factors in first- and second-language learning but also the special circumstances of slavery and colonialism. The plantation society of the West Indies was essentially an economic unit, giving low priority to European cultural practices while trying to deny West African ones. Those owners and administrators who were interested in education and social niceties sent their children to England for such instruction; the others allowed their children to grow up and follow in their footsteps, safeguarding their future by maintaining a family-run business and a colour bar. Nepotism and racism therefore virtually removed the need to strive for excellence in all areas of life among West Indian whites. Formal language and literature were not a major preoccupation of plantation slave society in the West Indies, and national and international standards of English were aspired to by few and discussed only by visitors or those coming from abroad. In any case, negative comments on local peculiarities only served to provoke hostility and resentment.

Formal instruction of slaves was systematically opposed by slaveowners, which meant that for the most part the slaves learnt English according to the exposure to it afforded them by their job, function or closeness to speakers of it. In the case of the adult African, since there was no longer a community speaking his native language, the language became limited in usefulness, and he was forced to learn some English in order to perform his duties successfully with minimum punishment. The field slaves, who were greatest in number and least in contact with speakers of English, learnt the least amount of English; the house slaves, who were in constant contact with English, learnt the most; and those who were trained to perform skilled jobs fell somewhere in between. In addition, the fact that all slaves were quartered in lodgings separate and distinct from whites and had a limited life of their own meant that the slaves developed a dialect of their own.

Therefore, the situation in each territory allowed for the development of a local dialect of English with varying degrees of Creolisation without strong pressures toward literate standards but at the same time evolving into a cohesive and identifiable national variety. However, though literate and 'sophisticated' standards were not of paramount importance in the early years, these still filtered through with a time-lapse, and were preserved or admired locally when they were no longer current or admired in London. This was a direct result not only of the distance from and the slow speed of communication with the mother country but also of the fact that the educational system tended to teach the values and language standards of the preceding era rather than current ones. Time-lapse differences also resulted in misinterpretations by later teachers who, through ignorance of features which were current and even admired in Britain and London itself, regarded the same features which were still contemporary in West Indian language as aberrations of intelligence and race.

As far as attitudes and motivation towards language-learning on the part of the slaves are concerned, one is dealing with a situation in which initial language contact was sudden, development was fast and the target was unstable. Instability in target was caused by changes in masters, rebellions, maroonage and social function. Pressures to learn the new language or to abandon the native language varied from psychological (often exerted by peers) to physical (usually in cases where the person was failing at his given task), or, in contrast, many 'learners' were completely disregarded. In spite of the fact that most of the data on language acquisition refer to 'normal' situations (i.e. formal instruction in or out of school or learning a second language by association with speakers of the language), differences in learning situations and differences in motivation (pressures to learn) are acknowledged and dealt with not only as a part of language learning but also as a part of education generally. The differences therefore between early West Indian situations and 'normal' situations are differences of degree, and there is no likelihood that strategies for learning a language change from one set of human beings to another. The findings of language-learning research then are directly applicable to the development of language in the West Indies.

Psycholinguistic factors in the development of West Indian English

Second-language acquisition research data outline the following basic learning strategies:

1	Transfer	This is interlanguage in nature and principally seen as the retention by the learner of many of the devices and distinctions of the native language in producing the target language.
2	Overgeneralisation	The use of analogy in regularising all the patterns of the target language leading to hypercorrection and similar 'errors'.
3	Avoidance	This is psychological and idiosyncratic. It may be restricted to simple avoidance of 'difficult' structures of the target language or it may extend to avoidance of as much of the language as possible while relying on non-linguistic methods of communicating.
4	Creativity	The human brain on its own works out patterns which are not a direct reflection of patterns heard or seen. Creativity therefore has a certain universality in character.

It is said that in very early second-language learning, the learner depends more heavily on transfer, whereas in later learning the learner changes more to overgeneralisation. The one strategy, however, does not necessarily totally exclude the other. In addition, where conditions of learning are adverse and where the learner is forced to use the target language very quickly, the learner depends heavily on transfer. The last two strategies – avoidance and creativity – are employed at the same time as the first two, and are not ranked in order of prominence. Creativity is always present in the learning process and is presented by some on the one hand as idiosyncratic, thus accounting, for example, for differences between fast learners and slow learners, and by others on the other hand as universal, thus determining order of acquisition of structures and possibly kinds of structures.

Interlanguage transfer or heavy dependence on native language implies that in the case of the Africans, whether on the west coast of Africa, or in the early days of slavery in the Caribbean, or those late African arrivals in the Caribbean, their language, as they attempted to learn English, was dominated by features of West African languages. This was so not only in the early stages of second-language acquisition but also because of extremely adverse conditions and the necessity to function quickly in English. In the case of the English who came in contact with the slaves, their identification of the language of the slaves, as attested in the literature, was in terms of 'broken' or 'corrupt' English, because what they were identifying was really their own conception of the developing language. This conception was in keeping with one of the strongest social practices in the West Indies and a mark of British colonialism – the assertion of superiority of class (and previously race) specifically by the use of language. This is still done at all levels of society, and social distance between perceived inferiors and the speaker is achieved by formal, full language. In the days of slavery this was certainly just as strong, because there was no need in a rigidly authoritarian structure to use 'softer' methods to coax or encourage 'inferiors' to perform duties. The British and their descendants in the West Indies therefore lorded it over their 'charges' using English, and were quick to pass judgement on the speech of the black population, whose interlanguage was pounced upon as a clear sign of inferiority. They themselves did not realise that their own language was diverging from that of Britain and converging with that of the African population as a normal consequence of geographical separation.

Early stages of second-language acquisition prominently featuring the transfer strategy were not restricted to a specific stage in the period of slavery, because for example in Jamaica many adult Africans were still arriving up to the middle of the 19th century. The idea of crystallisation of a Creole, meaning that a great number of features were characteristic of the majority of individuals not only in a (given stratum of) society but also in all similar (strata in such) societies, cannot be interpreted in terms of, for example, a fifty-year period, but must be seen in terms of relative stability in a society and in terms of the relative number of arrivals in and departures from the society.

Early stages in second-language acquisition therefore relate more to individuals than to a historical stage of West Indian society.

As to what features are transferred in second-language learning, there is no consensus. General claims are made that the phonology (consonants, vowels and intonation) and morphology (affixes) of a second language are not easily learnt, and that the learner compensates for these by using equivalent-meaning devices in his native language. However, the equivalent-meaning devices may themselves be phonological, morphological, syntactic or lexical. Claims are also made that the syntax of the native language is so strong that it is constantly transferred; that is, maintained by the learner as he attempts to produce the target. Analyses of different contact situations and specifically the West Indies show that in transfer there is an element of selectivity – that syntax is maintained and lost and that in all areas of grammar certain features seem 'fitter' for survival than others. Interlanguage transfer, then, cannot be characterised by identification of universally valid general or specific features of grammar.

The second phase of language learning, that dominated by overgeneralisation, can be seen to produce convergence in Creoles as opposed to the first phase which is more divergent in nature. Overgeneralisation is evidenced in two ways. The first is of the linguistic evolutionary type that is a feature in the development of all languages. It involves regularising based on analogy – the learner notes that a feature occurs in more than one context and generalises it to most or all contexts, e.g. *sheeps, hitted* produced by learners of English. What started out as an error in analogy or hypercorrection has become standard usage in many languages. The second type of overgeneralisation is linguistically less powerful, but nevertheless very prominent. It can account for many of the stylised examples in the early literature as cases of overuse or exaggeration. An example of this is the case of a non-native speaker of a Creole called upon to illustrate it, or a native speaker of a Creole, who, in order to achieve an objective, uses the 'appropriate' form of speech, or the speech expected of him. In these cases the individual packs as many 'exotic' features into as small a space as possible, thereby distorting the normal patterns of the Creole. This tendency is common especially in 'dialect' columns in newspapers and in 'dialect poetry'. Note, for example, the following from Louise Bennett's *Jamaica Labrish*, in which a considerable number of Creole features are packed into four short lines:

> 'Me did a-dead fe bus out laugh,
> But me tun me y'eye look roun',
> An as a me one ben deh-deh,
> Me dis 'queeze me foot a groun'.'

Because of the pervasiveness of this kind of overuse, most people, including the Creole speakers themselves, come to believe that this distorted speech is the 'real' or 'pure' Creole. Linguistically therefore it may have some feedback effect on the Creole and the perception of it. There is no doubt that this partly underlies attempts to describe 'pure' Creole, an entity distinct from English.

The effect of generalisation is, as was said, convergence. It can be used to explain some similarities occurring across West Indian territories. The reason for overgeneralisation of certain specific features and not others in different territories is just as difficult to account for as the retention or transfer of certain specific features from the native language in early second-language learning. For example, one cannot easily explain why *dont* is generalised as a tag question in Jamaica, but nowhere else in the West Indies. (*Dont* is used in Jamaica where standard English has to use a variety of forms to ask a question at the end of a sentence, e.g. *don't you, isn't it, weren't we*, etc.)

The strategy of avoidance characterises all stages of language learning. It may be looked at in a general way in the asymmetric contrast between comprehension and production, and it may be looked at more particularly in terms of deliberate choice. Even if it is assumed that a speaker cannot habitually use all the devices and distinctions of a language (native or target), his choice of some (his idiolect) may be considered a positive reaction to those chosen and a negative reaction to the ones not chosen; in other words, avoidance of the latter. Non-use, both in a general sense and the particular sense of deliberate choice, is motivated by social and psychological factors. An individual's speech patterns are not necessarily a direct reflection of what he hears most often, but choice to suit self-image, group identity and solidarity or peer pressure, and other such affective forces.

In the days of slavery, to avoid being branded a 'salt-water negro', the newly arrived slaves had to conform quickly to the practices, especially linguistic, of the other slaves. Throughout the history of the West Indies and up to today, migrants from some of the poorer territories who have gone to those which seem better off disguise their native speech in order not to be branded as foreigners. Also, many West Indians going to Britain and North America mimic the speech of people of those places for the very same reasons. This kind of avoidance is really avoidance of features of the native language, but the motivation is the same, although reversed, when a West Indian youth of today uses Rasta speech or refuses to speak 'proper English'.

The avoidance strategy is also used in the later development of Creole speakers mostly in a formal setting as a method of escaping punishment or ridicule. For example, a child in school, in order not to make mistakes and seem a fool in the eyes of peers or in order not to be reprimanded by the teacher, relies exclusively on those devices of English which he is sure of, or uses non-verbal communication, or resorts to silence, implying in this latter case that it is better to be thought stupid or ignorant than to speak and risk showing oneself to be so. Although avoidance varies among individuals, in situations where speakers are generally considered inferior simply because of their social position, there is obviously an increase in the tendency on the part of these speakers when dealing with social superiors to avoid certain structures and features of the standard language in order not to be confirmed as inferior or worsen the reaction. In addition, avoidance is employed not because of incompetence, but in order to avoid charges of insubordination, 'getting besides yourself', 'getting too big for your boots', or other such charges made by social superiors or elders.

Certain devices of standard English have been identified as not occurring in non-standard West Indian speech. Some of these are the verb *to be* in sentences where the predicate is adjectival or adverbial (e.g. *He fat, He down the road*), the passive construction, nominalisations or clauses as subject of sentences (e.g. *The fact that he went bothers me, His going bothers me*); abstract words, and certain types of dependent clauses introduced by *although, whereas, since*. Similar 'absences' are also noted generally for English speakers as characteristic of lower-class speech *vis-à-vis* middle- and upper-class. Although these 'absences' have most often been explained in terms of the questionable notion of simple versus complex structures, there is no question that affective forces (generally identified as the learner's motives, attitude, needs, emotional state) are much more evidently the cause than cognitive ones (the level of development of the thinking processes and the brain).

Affective forces can also be used to explain the low incidence of psychological verbs in non-standard West Indian speech. Sentences of the type

I believe (feel, think, etc.) that so-and-so is the case

are much less frequent than the same sentences without the introductory

I believe (feel, think, etc.) that . . .

when the speaker is really not certain about his assertion. There are two explanations for this. Firstly, in some cases uncertainty is rendered phonologically rather than syntactically; that is, by inflections of the voice. Secondly, in other situations revelation of uncertainty is incongruous with a social context which requires bold rather than guarded assertion. This latter explanation parallels teenage and 'macho' behaviour, both of which are very strongly marked in the lower social class situation. Avoidance, then, as a strategy in language learning and use, is clearly related to social and psychological forces.

The strategy called 'creativity' is hard to characterise in detail both in second-language learning generally and in West Indian language specifically. Most of those who deal with it refer to possible or assumed innate and universal properties of the human mind or brain. Whereas some regard these properties as abstract methods of processing language, providing constraints on language by limiting the possible ways that structures can represent meaning, such properties therefore being essentially regulatory and non-specific in nature, others believe that under certain circumstances the human brain will reveal itself concretely by producing those specific structures which are basic, innate and natural. Arguments about 'creativity' have much in common with religious belief. They are prominent and powerful, although speculative, because total human experience cannot be explained by clinical, tangible or objective analysis and conclusions. Scholars throughout history have been divided about speculation into the human mind, some regarding it as outside 'serious' academic research, others as the peak of scholarship. The role of 'creativity', then, in language is recognised, but the extent of the role has not yet been well understood.

One of the major limitations on achievement in second language learning is that learners seldom achieve native speaker competence in the target language, especially in its phonology. In the learner's language the native language surfaces sporadically and unpredictably, sometimes in situations of stress, sometimes in situations where there is little pressure. It is widely believed that there is a critical stage of maturation (puberty) after which language learning, and specifically second-language learning, differs markedly in nature as a result of reduction of creativity and heightening of dependence on already acquired linguistic knowledge and experience. For example, in the same way that illiterate people can get by in a developed society by depending on extra linguistic clues (without having to read signs, roads, names, notices, etc.), the late learner is said to operate with the basic and functional. There is no conclusive proof from research, however, whether the late learner in most cases does not go far beyond the basic and functional because he does not need to, or whether it is because he cannot. In the case of early Africans in the West Indies, the possible role of maturational factors is unimportant in a social situation in which 'un-slave-like' fluency in English would have been a doubtful asset.

Language evolution in the West Indies has been a process of growth in stability and homogeneity, or conversely a lessening of the instability and variety which characterised the language contact and language-learning situations. Language from different sources had to evolve to perform normal communicative functions and reflect the interrelationships of the society, thus becoming an integrated system. This evolution involved development to accommodate an increase in social functions, in change and growth of society, the levelling of input languages, and other kinds of internal historical change characteristic of all language development.

All the children born into the early West Indian situations had to acquire a language – a linguistic system that was flexible and suitable enough to represent their total experiences in the society. It would be misleading and frustrating to think of this language as a pure, exclusive entity with a specific name, or as another variety of a known language. Names given to languages and the homogeneous concepts they conjure up in the minds of adults are not in the mind of the child learning his native language. The child, in whatever situation, learns a system of meanings and functions out of a multitude of sounds (linguistic and other) to become a unit in a society. The fact that adults have difficulty naming some systems and not naming others is not a reflection of the viability of existence of one as opposed to the other.

The West African brought to the West Indies could lie down at night and reflect on life in his own language. Children born into slavery also had to have a language to do the same. Children later on acquired, from formal instruction, language to suit the educational and modernisation process, building on the language which evolved from contact and language learning. The model for first-language learning of children born in the West Indies therefore arose out of transfer, overgeneralisation, avoidance and creativity. It is not necessary to isolate the inputs and strategies which went into the development model of West Indian language and assign primacy to one of them, because at all stages the individual would have had a system of interdependent or mutually influencing elements, no matter how heterogeneous or inconsistent they may seem to us today, which allowed for varying types of communication.

Linguistic development in West Indian English

One kind of development which unquestionably took place is expansion in vocabulary. On the other hand, the idea of expansion or net increase in other areas of grammar is difficult to demonstrate by data and theory. In other words, to claim that first-generation slaves in the West Indies had only a half (or less) of a language and that succeeding generations have expanded it gradually into a full (or almost full) language is to claim that successive generations have been gradually becoming full human beings. Development is better looked at as an increasing number of blacks principally, but whites and others also, acquiring more and more English over succeeding generations – language change concomitant with social change. The speed and extent of this change have varied from territory to territory.

Another kind of development is that which results from social-maturational change. It is believed by some that the child growing up in the West Indies learns a single variety first – for the lower-class child this is said to be the basilectal or Creole variety – and with age learns more varieties. However, closer examination shows that variation occurs from a very early age and that there is not a significant increase in the total number of forms used, unless the person becomes socially mobile. Rather than there being early basilectal acquisition followed by gradual mesolectal (near to English) acquisition, there is early acquisition of most variants, which are used from an early age for stylistic reasons (emphasis, refutation, anger, etc.), with growth in social awareness gradually bringing consistency in usage of the same variants to correspond to degree of formality of context. Social-maturational development is therefore an increase in consistency rather than an increase in number of forms. General comments about major structural developments in West Indian language from start to finish, suggesting a pidgin stage, then a Creole stage, and projecting a non-Creole dialectal stage are conjectural or based on scanty evidence.

Levelling of input languages is normal in all situations of language contact and is captured in the linguistic notion of 'koine'. This notion is based on the observation that in a situation characterised by variation, a single variety evolves or is chosen for general communication. A koine can be a language, e.g. English in India; a marked dialect, e.g. standard English in Britain; or an unmarked dialect, e.g. network standard in the USA. A koine can also evolve out of many varieties of the same language among immigrant groups, e.g. Yiddish among the Jews in America. Although there is no set formula for the way in which a koine evolves, it is generally believed that those features which are common to all varieties have a greater chance of survival than peculiar and limited ones. However, the striking or special nature of a feature may make it stand out and become popular, as happens with slang expressions in all languages. The use of Jamaican-type speech in Britain by children of West Indians from all territories illustrates this latter tendency.

In the early development of language in the West Indies, levelling of the dialects of both whites and blacks took place. The various British dialects gradually lost their identity with specific geographical regions of Britain. Except where there were heavy concentrations of speakers of a specific African language (and this was more so in big non-West Indian countries in the New World like Brazil), levelling of specific African languages was not a major factor even where it took place. It was rather that West Africans had to depend on general, common and special rules (structures) in acquiring English, rules that were present in West African languages and those that were present in the varieties of English they heard.

Levelling also involved the modification and mutation of forms and structures, and in cases of similarity across languages, syncretism took place. Levelling as a process is in no way separable from historical change in isolated communities. In the same way that dialectal peculiarities are suppressed and lost in communication between immigrant groups coming together in a new location, irregular features (e.g. nouns without an overt plural, verbs with unusual tense forms) have disappeared (that is, they have been replaced by regular ones) in the evolution of many languages. In contrast, in the same way that special or striking features have become a part of a koine, irregular features (plurals like *sheep* and past tenses like *hit*) have remained in many languages. Levelling therefore does not result in or denote total internal linguistic symmetry, but rather homogeneous use as an instrument of communication.

'Normal' language change is of course a part of the evolution of West Indian language. However, the timespan for the evolution of West Indian language (200–300 years at most) as distinct from and following early language contact, is not long enough in terms of historical linguistics for substantial changes to have taken place. In any case, there is difficulty in determining changes in consonants, vowels, syllable structure and intonation patterns because poetry and other types of literature from which one could get an idea of rhymes and word pronunciation are not abundant. The whole of the colonisation period is within the era of Modern (*vis-à-vis* Middle and Old) English, and the major structural changes in English and other European languages took the greater part of a millennium. A brief look at general developments in these languages is informative for the understanding of development of West Indian language.

Where once functional and semantic relationships between words (subject, object, agent, possessor, instrument, etc.) were rendered totally or partially by inflexions in Old English and early Romance languages (French, Spanish, Italian, Portuguese), as the languages evolved many of these inflexions disappeared and the relationships were expressed increasingly by prepositions, other function words, and a strict word order. From a phonological point of view many of the inflexions and also many prefixes and other syllables disappeared because they were in a position of weak stress – that is, immediately preceding or following strongly stressed syllables or at the extremities (end or beginning) of words. From a morphological point of view the reduction in number of inflexions is attributable to the regularising or levelling of many inconsistent inflexions. On the other hand, derivational morphology and especially word compounding increased in English to accommodate expansion in the vocabulary of English as it became a language of colonisation and – eventually – a world language.

Promotion of proficiency in language as basic in general education and international communication has in modern times caused many languages to be relatively fixed, even frozen, in their written form (spelling, punctuation, grammatical agreements) in comparison with spoken forms, which vary extensively. The picture of standard English presented by traditional school grammar as a matter of preserving or safeguarding inflexions and details is counterbalanced by evolution which has witnessed attrition of these very features.

Parallels between West Indian English, British English, and West African languages

This section is a presentation of significant selected features of West Indian language with parallels in British regional English of the colonial period, and in West African languages. The purpose of presenting these parallels is threefold – to show that:

- certain features occur normally outside West Indian English and are not aberrant or necessarily caused by a special situation;

- the West African and British parallels could have been the source of the West Indian features;

- there could have been more than one source for certain features.

These parallels should serve to counteract generally misguided and misinformed opinions about West Indian language and also provide specific information to show that West Indian English has a history and structure relatable to different traditions. It has to be borne in mind however that it is virtually impossible to demonstrate a direct line of descent of any feature.

Phonology

1   i:ɪ   Dominica, St Lucia, etc.:   e.g. *bit: beat, tick: teak.*
British: Brook, 1963:89 refers to a proverb from 1636 in which the word *sheep* because of its dialectal pronunciation is later misunderstood and reinterpreted as *ship*.
West Africa: Cassidy and LePage, 1967:xlv suggest that [i] and [ɪ] seem to be variants of the same vowel in Twi and Ewe, and this is partially supported in Turner, 1949:15.

2   ɪ:ɛ   (a) Barbados, and others: e.g. *ɛf* 'if'.
British: Wyld, 1920:229 gives as examples of 17th- and 18th-century London and Court English the following : *tell* 'till', *sence* 'since', *ef* 'if'.

(b) Barbados, and others: e.g. *trimble* 'tremble', *kittle* (drum) 'kettle'.
British: Wyld, 1920:222 gives *Gintlemen* 'gentlemen', *atinding* 'attending', *opprision* 'oppression'.

3 e:i General *: e.g. Frid*i*, Mond*i*.
British: 17th-century English has *Frydy* 'Friday', *Mundy* 'Monday'.

4 a:ɔ Jamaica, and others: e.g. *waant* 'want', *kaal* 'call'.
British: Brook, 1963:112 says that Irish English has [a] in some cases where other British varieties have [ɔ].

5 ʌ:ɔ Barbados: e.g. *bondle* [bɔndl] 'bundle', *yong* 'young'.
West Africa: Turner, 1949:18 for West African and Gullah.

6 oy:əy Barbados: e.g. *bəyl* 'boil', *pəynt* 'point'.
British: This pronunciation is identified by a number of authors. Examples are *byled* 'boiled', *implyment* 'employment'. Homophones: *I'll–oil*; *line–loin* (Wyld, 1920:223, 224).

Consonants

7 θ:t, f   t – General, f – Barbados and St Lucia: *ting* 'thing', *teef, teet* 'teeth'.
British: Wyld, 1920:291 gives the following examples: *erf* 'earth', *helfe* 'health', *kiff and kin* 'kith and kin', *frust* 'thrust' (f initial occurs in St Lucia, e.g. *fing* 'thing'). Brook, 1963:112 gives *trote* 'throat' as typical of Irish speech.
West Africa: [θ] does not exist in these languages.

8 ḍ:d, v   d – General, v – Barbados: e.g. *bade, bave* 'bathe'.
British: Brook, 1963:112 gives *dere* 'there' as typical of Irish speech. Wyld, 1920:291 points out *bequived* 'bequeathed' in a letter written by Queen Elizabeth I. Zachrisson, 1927:107, 111 gives [d] for [ḍ] as characteristic of East Sussex and Kent, e.g. *dis* 'this', *dat* 'that', *dose* 'those', *farder* 'farther'.
West Africa: [ḍ] does not exist in these languages.

9 ŋ:n General: e.g. *eatin* 'eating'.
British: This is still a normal feature in English today. Wyld, 1920:289 points out for 17th-century English *seein, comin, shillins* 'shillings'.

10 k:ky,   g:gy   General: e.g. *cyar* 'car', *gyarden* 'garden'.
British: Wyld, 1920:310 gives the following examples: *cyan, cyard, gyearl* 'girl', *gyet*. Walker, 1801, quoted in Wyld, 1920, says that [y] gives a smooth

---

* (General) means used generally in the West Indies.

and elegant sound which distinguishes the polite conversation
of London from that of every part of the country.
West Africa: Cassidy and LePage, 1967:lvii point to this as a
feature of Twi.

11   h:ø   ø:h   Jamaica: e.g. *im* 'him', *hask* 'ask'.
British: Elphinston, 1787, quoted in Wyld, 1920, gives the
following example of contemporary London English: 'So
hamiabel however iz dhis yong lady, dhat, widh her fine air,
sweet hies, quic hears, dellicate harms, above all her tender art.
She would giuv anny man a ankering to halter iz condiscion.'
'So amiable however is this young lady that with her fine hair,
sweet eyes, quick ears, delicate arms above all her tender heart,
she would give any man a hankering to alter his condition.'

12   hw:w   General: e.g. *wat* 'what', *wich* 'which'.
British: Normal in many dialects of English today. Wyld,
1920:311 gives the examples *any ware* 'anywhere', *wite* 'white',
wen 'when'.

13   w:ø   General: e.g. *uman* 'woman'; compare Barbados *wənə*
and Jamaican *unu*.
British: Brook, 1963:97 gives the example *ooman* 'woman' and
says that [w] disappeared in some dialects.

Syllable structure

Consonant clusters

14   cc:c   General: e.g. *bes* 'best', *lan* 'land', *mas* 'mask'.
British: [d] and [t] not pronounced in many words, e.g. *chilren*
'children', *bline* 'blind', *cole* 'cold', *granmother, husban, friten*
'frightened', *own* 'owned', *gretis* 'greatest', *respeck* 'respect', *nex*
'next', *Papeses* 'Papists' (Wyld, 1920:303).
West Africa: The syllable structure in West African language is
predominantly CVCV or CVN (there are no consonant clusters).

15   r+c:c   General: [c] (i.e. r disappears); Barbados [r + c] *haat*,
hart 'heart'.
British: Brook, 1963:113, 118 says that Irish English and
Scottish English have [r] in all positions, whereas in other
dialects of British it is generally silent before consonants.

16   r/l + m:r/l + v + m   General: e.g. *worəm* 'worm'.
British: Brook, 1963:113 says that in Anglo-Irish a vowel
develops between [r] or [l] and a following [m], e.g. *arəm* 'arm',
filəm 'film'.

17   *vcv:v?v*   (glottalisation)   Barbados.

> British: Strong glottalisation, i.e. replacement of [t] and [k] by a glottal stop is characteristic of cockney up to today, as well as the dialect of Leeds and other parts of Britain.

Intonation, stress and pitch

18   Lexical pitch   Barbados, Guyana: e.g. brother, sister.
West Africa: Pitch to distinguish between words is characteristic of most of these languages.

19   Stress and vowel quality – [e], [o], [a] > [ə].
Jamaica and others have purer vowels in unstressed syllables; Barbados, Trinidad have [ə].
West Africa: These languages have purer vowels which may be relatable to syllable timing.
British: Stress timing causes weakening of vowels to [ə] in unstressed syllables. But Brook, 1963:98 says that Northerners give secondary stress to syllables which in other dialects are unstressed causing the vowels to be 'pronounced as they are spelled', e.g. *con*demn, *con*fuse, state*ment*, in*du*stry.

Word and sentence structure

20   -s:ø   (3rd person singular)   General usage has ø.
West Africa: Most of these languages do not depend on verb inflexions to mark person-number.
British: Wyld, 1920:337 says: 'At the present time such forms may occasionally be heard from vulgar and uneducated speakers. I noticed, some years ago in Essex, that such phrases as "he come everyday to see me", "he always take sugar in his tea", and so on, were very common.'

21   -s:ø   (possessive)   General usage has [ø], e.g. *the man cow*.
West Africa: Most of these languages do not depend on word inflexions to signal case relationships in the noun phrase.
British: Wyld, 1920:316–318 dealing with usage from 1600 onward says that the suffix is often omitted in the following cases:
 – in words ending in -s (e.g. horse, ass) where [iz] is now used;
 – before a word beginning with s- (*the quen sister*);
 – in old feminine nouns (*the Scotish Quene letter*);
 – in groups (e.g. *the King of England hat*);
 – in old -r words (e.g. *father*, *brother*);
 – in other words where no special reason can be assigned.

22   Subject–verb agreement – one form for singular and plural. General usage.
West Africa: See 20.

British: This is common in non-standard English up to today. Wyld, 1920:356 notes that 'a tendency to extend the use of *is* to sentences in which there was a plural subject is traceable in the sixteenth century and continues among educated people well into the eighteenth century' and that '*you was* was apparently much more common, and there are indications of a more general tendency to extend the use of *was* to 3rd person plural also.' Wyld also notes the use of *we was* and the suffix -s with a plural subject among educated and upper-class speakers.

23 Pronominal inflexion for case: no inflexion.
General usage is sporadic, e.g. *tell she, im book*.
West Africa: See 21.
British: Brook, 1963:105 gives the following as dialectal usage for the possessive only: *me pen is as good as me paper; we held we breaths*; and Shakespeare's Hamlet I, 2, 216 *It lifted up it head*.

24 Double : single comparison – *more* + -*er*, *most* + -*est*.
General usage has a tendency toward double marking, e.g. *more better*.
British: Brook, 1963:103–4 notes that *more* and *most* are often used to intensify regular comparison and produces double comparatives and superlatives as in Shakespeare's *Julius Caesar's* famous *most unkindest cut of all*. He also gives as dialectal usage *betterer, worser, baddest*.

25 Plural of noun – noun + *dem* (3rd person plural pronoun).
Jamaica, Antigua, and others: e.g. *di man dem* 'the men'.
West Africa: Normal in some West African languages, e.g. Ewe *ame wo* (man + they) 'men', Twi *agya nom* 'fathers', Yoruba *awon omonde* (they + child) 'children'.

26 Demonstrative plural – (3rd person plural pronoun) *dem* + noun.
General: *dem dog* 'those dogs'.
West Africa: Yoruba *kini awon ni* (thing + they + that) 'those things'.
British: Some dialects have *them book (there)* 'those books'.

27 Predicative adjective – subject + adjective.
General: e.g. *the man tall*.
West Africa: Normal in many West African languages, e.g. Ewe *ati la ko* (tree + the + high) 'the tree is tall', Yoruba *olorun tobi* (God great) 'God is great'.

28 Serial verb structure – verb + verb (+ verb).
(a) General, except Barbados: e.g. *carry come*.
West Africa: Normal in many West African languages, e.g.

Ewe *wotsone yia keta* (one + carry + him + go + Keta) 'someone took him to Keta'.

(b) General, except Barbados: e.g. *im gone go eat it.*
West Africa: Twi *yɛreko akɔsra yɛŋ na* 'we are going *go* visit our mother' (*go* = 'to').
British: Possible comparison in Modern English *go get it*, which however is regarded as a shortened form of *go and get it.*

29 Topicalisation of the verb – *a/iz* + verb . . . + verb . . .
General, except Barbados: e.g. *iz drop it drop* 'it dropped'.
West Africa: Normal in many of these languages, even though the word order may differ. Alleyne, 1980:172 gives for Yoruba *gbigbe ni won gbe e lo* (take + is + they + took + it + go) 'they actually took it away', and Twi *hwe na Kwasi hwe ase* (fall is Kwasi fell down) 'Kwasi actually fell'.

30 Tense and aspect marked outside the verb form – no suffixes for tense and aspect.
General: *You eat?* 'Have you eaten?', *I does eat* (habitual), *mi a eat* (continuous).
West Africa: Normal in several of these languages, e.g. Fante *o ben* 'He approaches/He approached', *nna o ben* (then + he + approach) 'He approached'. Alleyne, 1980:163 referring to a work of 1883 by Lucien Adam says that the perfective is unmarked in Twi and Yoruba – Twi *mi ko* (I + come) 'I have come', Yoruba *emi ri* (I + see) 'I have seen'.
British: The future tense in English need not be marked as in *Today I bake, tomorrow I brew.* With reference to form only, in most cases the future and the modal auxiliaries are followed by the unmarked form of the verb, e.g. *I will eat, I can eat, I must eat.* With specific reference to *a*, marker of the continuous in Jamaica, etc. (*im a eat* 'he is eating'), and a similar form in some British dialects (*a hunting we will go; what are you a doing?*), the history given for the British dialectal form (Brook, 1963:107) is that *a* is a lightly stressed form of the preposition *on* preceding a verbal noun (i.e. a noun derived from a verb by adding -ing). In other words, the British dialect structure was originally *subject + verb + preposition + noun.*

Selected features of vocabulary

31 me/mi 1st person singular (subject) pronoun.
General: *mi no know* 'I don't know'.
West Africa: Ewe *me*, Fante *me*, Ga *mi*, Yoruba *emi*.
British: *me.*

32 eye-water 'tears'.
General.

West Africa: Compounding as a primary method of word-formation is normal. With direct reference to calquing, in Mandinka *nye ji* (eye + water) 'tears'.
British: Compounding as a method of word-formation is normal.

33 *big eye* 'covetous'.
General.
West Africa: Igbo *anya uku* (eye + big) 'covetous'.

34 sweet mouth 'flatterer'.
General.
West Africa: Twi *no ano yɛdɛ* (his mouth sweet) 'he is a flatterer'. Yoruba *ɛnū didū* (mouth sweet) 'persuasiveness'.

A perusal of British literature shows quite clearly that there has been from the beginning of the Modern period of English – and before – a history of strong prejudices against varying regional dialects, and that many authors acted on the belief that their mission was to preserve English as a pure, untainted language, especially in its formal spoken form. Many comments on regional usage deemed speakers to be ignorant, crude and rustic. As the British Empire grew, the comments were extended to cover the dominions and colonies, but at the same time created the belief not only that England was the standard for English but also that there was a single standard which was accepted and adhered to by the whole of Britain. Animosities, prejudices and linguistic differences between English, Scottish, Irish and Welsh were little known, especially in the colonies. Many of the comments made about English in the colonies, and in the West Indies specifically, have a long history – they were in large measure a transplantation of comments from Britain made about regional and lower-class varieties of English there. The notion of English as a pure, sophisticated entity has been so strong that linguistic works in the USA from Noah Webster's dictionary in 1804 to the *Webster's 3rd New International Dictionary* in 1962 which promoted American linguistic independence and documented the language of all the people have been strongly condemned as attempts to confer respectability on vulgarity and corruption.

Language purity and sophistication, or conversely the notion that English is corrupted in the mouths of rural, regional and unsophisticated people, should not be identified with the promotion of proficiency in English for general communicative purposes in the modern world. The former is essentially a class-oriented belief, whereas the latter sees as its goal increased, general (of all classes) efficiency. In the West Indies, however, because of sharp differences in class, and because of a history of language and culture contact, the two now seem to some inseparable. In addition, as a result of the fact that the power of language as a medium of communication is evidenced in artistry (techniques of persuasion) rather than in information, and that artistry and aesthetics generally are often dictated by class, it is clear that language learning involves acceptance of certain social values.

When the history of West Indian languages is haunted by the notion of English as a pure, sophisticated language, it diminishes into 'corruption'. On the other hand, when it is seen as resulting from contact between human beings from differing social levels, differing cultures, with differing elements of motivation and in a situation where human linguistic activity was severely and constantly tested in adverse conditions, West Indian language will be seen as a creation of positive diversity to match varying levels of achievement in emergent societies. In other words, language is maintained as a flexible human instrument, as it is in all societies.

6 · *Language and culture*

Culture in one of its interpretations includes all human behaviour, but in a more restricted sense it is used specifically to refer to the oral and written literature as well as other traditional social practices characteristic of a society. Culture in this restricted sense, while it tends to highlight folklore and practices which are seen as indigenous, historical, part of rural life, and not ostensibly transmitted by formal schooling, also includes the more traditional school areas of literature (prose, poetry, drama) and music (singing). For our present purposes, other areas normally included – e.g. painting, dancing, sculpture, playing musical instruments – are not immediately relevant here because they do not essentially involve the spoken or written language.

In the analysis of culture there is a history of distinguishing between aspects of culture in a hierarchical way, based on the belief that some are refined, requiring formal training and creativity, whereas others are normal, spontaneous or acquired incidentally. The fact that the dividing line between the two is subjective and impressionistic is paradoxically the very reason that it is preserved. In addition, the history of art criticism is tied to upper- and middle-class preoccupations, as opposed to folklore, which etymologically is the knowledge and beliefs of 'common' people. One factor, however, which tangibly has caused a division between 'refined' literature and folklore in language-based culture is writing. When elements of culture are written down, they have an existence separate from their author, are more accessible for criticism, and have a greater potential for more widespread influence. On the other hand, oral literature is not easily captured and preserved, is subject to greater changes from generation to generation, and has limited influence outside its immediate arena.

Culture in the West Indies has been especially vulnerable in this way in that in the early years the masters and the slaves were from completely different historical traditions: the culture of the upper class (masters and administrators) was fragmentary rather than coherent and vibrant, and was an extension of British and other European cultures; the culture of the lower class (the slaves) was under pressure because of adverse circumstances, because of schism from its historical source, and was almost exclusively oral in transmission. 'Refined' literature in the West Indies, that which revolves around the educated and the middle and upper classes, was seen as a rich and viable area only after the Second World War, and was produced and fostered in large measure outside the West Indies by West Indians who had migrated to Britain as a result of opportunities offered in the post-war reconstruction of Britain. It gradually received recognition in the West Indies and now enjoys such stability and prestige that it has taken its place as a part of formal education, as is the case with native literature in most developed countries.

Form of language and orthography

As a consequence of recent attainment of position and prestige in the educational system, critical appreciation of the literary aspects of West Indian literature is open-ended, shows all levels of perceptiveness in relation to themes, styles and other elements of art, and is generally available. More linguistically oriented elements have not been extensively treated and are not clearly understood, however. The major linguistic problem of literature in the West Indies is choice of form of language. The form of language of Chaucer, Shakespeare or Dickens poses no problem to the average reader today both because the English language has resolved most of its orthographical problems and because editors have a measure of freedom in changing classic texts to suit the modern reader. A perusal of the original texts, however, will show clearly that these authors were confronted with decisions about spellings and dialect usage. The same problems confront the West Indian author to a much greater degree today because of the high level of language variation in West Indian societies. However, unlike the classic authors just mentioned, West Indian authors face a situation in which the standard form of English is stable, full of conventions, powerful and dominant in all literature written in English. In addition, when colloquial varieties and regional dialects are represented in English literature, there are orthographic conventions used which are well-known. The problem that the West Indian writer faces is that West Indian literature is not fully satisfied or well served by a dominant standard form or heavy reliance on known orthographic conventions, because these tend to rob the literature of its essence as well as distort it.

West Indian writings show many methods of representing West Indian language. Some authors have stuck to standard English with minor injections or indications of West Indian language varieties. Some have tried to reflect the great variety of West Indian speech by known or idiosyncratic conventions. Some have depended more on indirect speech in standard language rather than try to render the speech of non-standard speakers. Others have tried to resolve the problem by identifying the social and educational level of their characters, using standard English, and leaving it to the reader's imagination or interpretation to give the appropriate form to each character. Still other writers have been more moral in intent, deciding for example that non-standard English has no educational value, and have eliminated it, while conversely believing that standard English should be promoted and reinforced at all times.

A consistently recurring comment made by authors presenting West Indian language and especially folklore is that the words or the text are those of the speakers, exactly as they were said, or that the author has given the characters their normal speech. This seemingly innocent comment, very often made with sincerity, is extremely misleading and shows a great ignorance of the relationship between sound and orthography. It suggests that orthographic symbols standing alone have a clear, objective and unequivocal meaning. It disregards the many obvious factors which are involved in communication – the intent and ability of an author of a literary work or the presenter of recorded folklore, the flexibility of the medium (in writing), the ability and imagination of the reader, and the total context of communication. In short, the interpretation of every word that is written varies according to these factors. In addition, one has to bear in mind that the artist specifically sees himself not as a recorder of the precise, objective details of society, but as provocative and catering to the emotional response in his audience by using suggestion and creativity.

Standard English orthography

The rigidity of English orthography should not be misinterpreted as paralleling a single, rigid, uniform variety of speech (actual or desirable) for all speakers of English. In fact, one of the functions of a writing system is to maintain general communication in a situation of diversity – the best example of this is the Chinese writing system which is generally used and understood, although the major dialects of the Chinese language are not mutually intelligible. Standard English spelling serves the same purpose of communication among the various dialects of English. More generally, the conventions of English orthography give first of all only partial information about the pronunciation of words; secondly they reflect the history of the English language to some degree; thirdly they show some underlying relationships between words; and fourthly they maintain general relevance by being conservative and stylised. In the representation of non-standard speech, because the conventions are being extended out of their rigidity to give principally more precise social and phonological information, there is a corresponding increase in idiosyncratic usage and a lessening of the ease of general communication.

The following are a few examples of conventions of English orthography, their meaning and the problems they pose:

1   The use of the symbol *e* at the end of a word to indicate that the preceding vowel is long or different, e.g. *sin* ~ *sine*; *man* ~ *mane*.

Although most readers of English by their production unconsciously understand what the vowel at the end (both its absence and its presence) does, they are led to believe that the use of *e* at the end means that the word is in some sense actually pronounced with a vowel at the end. In other words, not only is correct pronunciation not paralleled by a conscious awareness of the function of the symbol, but also the symbol maintains the illusion in the mind of the reader that it always represents a sound in itself.

2   The retention of a 'silent' symbol which serves to preserve a structural relationship with derivatives, e.g. *hymn ~ hymnal; damn ~ damnation; condemn ~ condemnation; solemn ~ solemnise; heir ~ inherit ~ heredity.*

In a number of base or root words in English ending in *mn* the symbol *n* is not sounded, but with the addition of a suffix this basic part of the word resurfaces in sound (*-nal, -nation*). In a word like *act* the *t* retains its normal sound when suffixes are added (*-or, -ed*), unless the suffix is *-ion*, in which case *t* combined with *i* stand for a different sound (roughly the same as that represented by *s* in *sugar*). The *t* symbol is retained in *action* however to indicate the basic root of the word. In most cases, readers, even though their pronunciation is normal, show little conscious awareness of the structural function of symbols.

3   The maintenance of a 'silent' symbol which shows the history of a word or its roots in a source language, e.g. *knight, psalm, pneumonia.*

The spelling of the word *knight* fossilises previous pronunciations of the word and exemplifies what most people normally think of as the 'inconsistencies' of English spelling, rather than being interpreted as giving information about the history of English. The word *pneumonia* can be used to represent a word-forming process, one which is very active especially in medicine and law – technical words are coined from Greek and Latin roots, with symbols and spellings specifically showing the classical connection, thus giving an air of scholarship, sophistication and precision. In other words, the symbols are used not for phonetic purposes but for historical and aesthetic ones.

4   The use of digraphs such as *th* in *that*, *ng* in *sing*, *ph* in *philosophy*, *sh* in *shoe*, to represent what are phonetically single segments of speech sound.

The digraph in itself is not a source of pronunciation difficulty even in elementary readers. However, as in (1) above, most people find difficulty in consciously analysing (not pronouncing) a digraph as a single sound, and persist in believing that *ng* stands for two consonant sounds and also that *th* stands for two consonant sounds in the same way that *sl* in *slide* and *pl* in *play* do. The problem here is that an author may deliberately omit one of the symbols in a digraph (*n* instead of *ng*) and so create the impression in his own mind and that of his readers that the 'speaker' has not fully pronounced the word, or, in other words, has simplified it by shortening it. It is not that the reader's phonetic interpretation of what the 'speaker' said is necessarily incorrect, but that the attendant connotations (simplification, 'swallowing' word endings) are incorrect and misleading.

English orthography also has conventions to represent colloquial standard English; that is, to indicate how the standard language is produced in normal conversation. Except for the use of question and exclamation marks, which will automatically cause the reader to alter the intonation of the sentence, orthography for colloquial English is characterised almost exclusively by the apostrophe. This punctuation mark shows that the only feature of standard speech which is suitable for recording orthographically is the shortening of words that is generally accepted throughout the English-speaking world. Spellings like *I'll, don't, they're, it's* are simply examples of a restricted number of combinations that are currently accepted; they certainly do not indicate that authors can use the apostrophe freely whenever words are shortened in spoken standard English. Regional and idiosyncratic pronunciation is therefore not represented in standard English orthography.

Eye dialect

To represent any variety of regional or idiosyncratic pronunciation, traditionally what has been used is 'eye dialect'. Although it has been employed most often for non-standard dialects, eye dialect is the only method of representing actual spoken language (standard or non-standard), without resorting to a specialised phonetic script. Unfortunately for clarity of phonetic representation, eye dialect brings with it emotional values which more often than not cloud any phonetic precision that the orthographic symbols themselves sometimes are intended to give. Whereas the standard orthography identifies words or lexical units, eye dialect attempts to give the precise sound of these units by giving the symbols greater phonetic significance than they normally have and by altering the standard spelling, in spite of the fact that the standard spelling itself is not totally or exclusively phonetic. Eye dialect, then, is an idiosyncratic orthography or an alteration of a partially phonetic orthography to make it more phonetic by people who generally have little knowledge of linguistic phonetics.

Below are some of the characteristics of eye dialect, what they are intended to do, and the problems they create in relation to West Indian English.

1   The apostrophe used to indicate absence of a sound, e.g. *fo'* (*for*), *o'* (*of*), *'em* (*them*).

The significance of this usage varies with context. In many cases it does no more than give an indication of the character or attitude of the 'speaker'. Take for example the two expressions *good-for-nothing* and *run-of-the-mill*. An author who writes *fo'* and *o'* instead of *for* and *of* is not giving the reader phonetic information, because *for* and *of* in these expressions would have their final consonant articulated only in unusual circumstances. When an author replaces the final consonant in these cases with an apostrophe, the effect is to create an illusion that goes beyond the sound of the single word, and indicates, for example, that he is using an informal style to evoke an informal context. In other cases, however, the apostrophe is phonetically significant, as in *'e* for *he* and *'em* for *them*.

Consider the following representation of Jamaican speech:

Mi jus' say, 'Cho', and mi just turn mi back . . .

The author writes the first 'just' as *jus'* and the second as *just*. The second 'just' occurs in a phonetic context (the next word begins with *t*) in which even in standard English the *t* at the end would not normally be articulated. The author writes the word *and* with the *d* at the end, when in such a context in Jamaican speech it is hardly likely that it would be articulated. Inconsistent and idiosyncratic representation by the author is therefore evident, and this leaves the reader with a more difficult task of deciphering the actual pronunciation. It also unconsciously gets the reader so preoccupied with sound that meaning is glossed over or not given full significance.

Although in many cases the apostrophe is used in eye dialect to represent the omission of a single consonant standing alone, it is also used to show the reduction of a consonant cluster (as in *jus'* above). Many authors however make no distinction between two neighbouring consonant symbols representing a single sound (*th*, *ng*) on the one hand and two sounds (*st*, *nd*) on the other, and use an apostrophe to represent omission in both cases. The problem here is that readers seldom stop to think that the apostrophe in each case is not indicating the same kind of change. For example, in *jus'*, *an'* and *don'* < (*don't*) the apostrophe indicates that the 'speaker' has not articulated the *t* at the end; in *clot'* (*cloth*) and *eatin'* there is nothing omitted phonetically after *t* and *n* respectively, so the apostrophe merely indicates that the pronunciation of the final consonant has changed to something else.

2   The apostrophe used to represent an orthographic change from standard orthography, but little or no phonetic change, e.g. *tho'* (*though*), *'nee* (*knee*), *g'os* (*ghost*).

The effect of this use of the apostrophe is clearly stylistic and social. The author in this case is indicating a context of informality and speech that is characteristic of such a context. The problem with this technique, however, is that it leaves in the mind of the reader the impression that non-standard English is being used with consequential conclusions about the speaker's level of education, intelligence and sophistication.

A variation of this usage, which although it seems more sensible from a phonetic-orthograpic point of view has traditionally been more insidious, is the omission of the apostrophe. Realising that no sound is really missing, the author does not use an apostrophe, as in *tho* (though), *thru* (through), *tru* (true), *gos* (ghost), *ded* (dead), *wach* (watch). In most cases of this kind of spelling the author uses the technique to match what he sees as simplification, corruption or distortion in the speaker, whether it is in his speech or in his general behaviour. Thus the author uses the technique to create a general picture of a character, catering to the social and other prejudices of the reader, more so than to give precise pronunciation.

3   The use of bracketed symbols to indicate absence of a sound which is not 'normal', at the same time attempting to make reading less difficult, e.g. *(h)arm* 'arm' or 'harm', *(h)im* 'he/him'.

The author in this case, realising that whenever normal standard orthography is altered it causes difficulty for the reader, tries to bridge the gap between traditional spelling and actual sound by putting the peculiarity of sound in brackets. The author, however, is at the same time making an etymological statement, which in a simple bracketed form can be misleading. For example, when an author writes for Jamaican speech

a don(t) do it   'I haven't done it'

it gives the impression that *don(t)* is simply a phonetic reduction of standard English *don't* (< *do not*). The gloss itself shows that such a suggested reduction is not the full and true picture of the Jamaican negative. In effect, brackets suggest to the reader historical derivations which in isolated words may be justifiable, but which placed in sentences can be deceptive.

4   Replacement of the symbols of standard spelling to reflect directly a specific regional or social pronunciation, e.g. *dem* (them), *wiv* (with), *swibel* (swivel), *faif* (faith).

This is undoubtedly the least objectionable aspect of eye dialect, in that the matching of symbol to sound comes over as more important than social and emotional elements. In this kind of replacement the author often has to respect the conventions and consequences of standard spelling. For example, in giving a non-standard West Indian version of *take*, the change of *a* to *e* necessitates the removal of *e* at the end (the function of *e* at the end is discussed above, pp. 135–136), resulting in *tek*. The opposite, the addition of *e*, also occurs, as for example in *chile* and *wile*, which result from the removal of *d* in *child* and *wild* respectively, and the addition of *e* to indicate that the preceding vowel remains a diphthong. Also, words like *fact, subject, respect* are respelt as *fack, subjeck, respeck* because in normal English spelling -*ck* as an ending is more frequent and normal than -*c*. (Note that some authors in this case use an apostrophe rather than a *k*, because in actual non-standard pronunciation there is simply a loss of a consonant *t* at the end when compared with standard pronunciation.) The same is also true when the non-standard Jamaican pronunciation of *little* is spelt as *lickle*.

The obvious shortcoming of this technique is that not only will it have the same inconsistencies of standard spelling but also that it is paradoxical in nature – its very conformity with the conventions of standard spelling may prevent the reader from immediately recognising the word as dialectal. If, for example, *sound* is respelt as *song* to conform to some non-standard West Indian pronunciations of the word, it will no longer be 'eye' dialect; and if *ask* is respelt as *axe*, the striking element caused by high visibility will be less. For this reason this technique is restricted by some authors to cases where difference from standard English remains immediately and strikingly clear. Other authors, however, clearly prefer to use the conventions of standard spelling, but in such a way not only to let the reader accurately interpret the sound but also to create a comic or at least interesting effect. If, for example, an author writes *Bahbaydus* for Barbados or *Fillup* for Philip, *bay*, *fill* and *up* are known pronunciations which will give a good idea of how the two names are actually produced by some speakers. There is no doubt however that the representation produces a comic effect and also that some authors regard this kind of writing as artistry or a kind of game, not unrelated to the kind of comic writing puzzle intended for children, as for example:

He 🐝 🍃🍃 u   r   pretty.

(sounded as)   He bee leaves you are pretty.
(meaning)   He believes you are pretty.

In actual fact this kind of representation is related to the Rebus method, which was an early stage in the evolution of writing. The Rebus method is essentially the use of the sound of known pictures or symbols to construct longer sequences. In this kind of eye dialect therefore the author relies on the known sound of simple words or word parts to identify dialectal pronunciation, but even if the comic and simplistic side-effects are disregarded, it is obvious that not all pronunciations are amenable to this kind of representation.

5   Attempting to give an accurate representation especially of vowels by double or triple vowel symbols, or by adding *h, w* or *y* to the vowel symbol.

The use of double and triple vowel symbols is of course based on standard spelling in which *oo* and *ee* occur normally and frequently to represent long vowel sounds, more so when a consonant ends the syllable, e.g *feet, pool*. This doubling is extended to *a, i* and even *u*, which are not usually doubled in standard English spelling. Note however that in

- ooo you?   - Mi.   - Mi ooo?

the author uses repetition of symbol as a consequence of having removed the initial consonant sound (wh) in *who*, because the remnant *o* by itself would be misinterpreted. In most cases of doubling, the reader is expected to understand whether the repetition represents a lengthened sound or a different sound. For example, *waan* may represent a lengthening of its standard vowel, or a different vowel sound.

In eye dialect the use of *h, w, y* after vowel symbols to identify vowel sounds more accurately is based on standard English spelling. The combinations *ah, eh, uh, aw* are the most frequently seen, occurring in such words as *dah* (that), *deh* (there), *duh* (the), *yah* (you hear), *yeah* (yes), *Lawd* (Lord), *mawnin'* (morning), *awright* (alright). The symbol *y* is used in some cases as a consequence of a prior change, as for example in *here > he > hey*; *y* is also used after *c* and *g* to indicate the characteristic West Indian pronunciation of words like *cyar* (car), *gyarden* (garden).

The major problem with the use of *h, w, y* in such combinations is that they have almost become 'standard' for eye dialect and are used almost automatically to replace English spelling, without regard to the great deal of variation which takes place in actual speech. As was pointed out in an earlier chapter, there is a tendency on the part of those trying to represent regional and non-standard speech to compress too many non-standard features in too small a space, which results in distortion of normal everyday speech patterns.

Generally the major difficulty or shortcoming of eye dialect is inconsistency. Eye dialect finds itself halfway between standard spelling and phonetic spelling, both of which are consistent. Standard spelling's consistency is a product of convention; phonetic spelling's consistency is based on a one symbol-one sound correspondence; eye dialect's inconsistency is a consequence of trying to achieve too many goals. Eye dialect tries to represent sound more accurately, to use the conventions of standard spelling, and to preserve intelligibility for the normal reader. In view of the fact that there is no consensus representation for eye dialect and that standard spelling is dominant actually and psychologically in the mind of the normal reader, the attempt to preserve intelligibility makes authors move back and forth in the use of eye dialect and standard spelling. The overall effect of this shifting is that representation is suggestive rather than clear or accurate. Suggestivity is normal for most writers of fiction and regarded as part of their craft, but for those who require greater accuracy it is unsatisfactory. Those who are unaware of its shortcomings are apt to believe in it very strongly and become embroiled in empty arguments as a result.

Choice of orthography for the West Indian writer

The practical problems of representing West Indian language variation are not easily solved, whether or not one is conscious of the shortcomings of eye dialect. Choice of orthography in itself is not the most difficult problem for many authors. Morality and the moral responsibility of the writer have always been perceived by society to be of paramount importance, giving rise to the basic question whether the writer should be allowed to record whatever reality or fiction he chooses to or be bound by codes of conduct. In terms of language this may be seen as a choice between standard or 'exemplary' language, non-standard, obscene, and whatever other forms there may be. In the West Indies where language is inseparable from perception of morals and standards of behaviour, representation of non-standard in print is viewed by some as highly undesirable, supportive of backwardness, and an obstruction to proficiency in standard English. So although today in the West Indies official policy allows for native expression as a healthy part of cultural and psychological development, the writer is aware that there is a substantial part of his potential readership that will be turned away by language and characters of the lower social class. Such readership, which often includes civic leaders, teachers and parents, is influential in the economic and literary success of writings.

Economic success for the West Indian writer – the novelist especially – is substantially hampered by the relatively small reader public who can afford to buy books easily and frequently. The novelist therefore either has to look to a regional and an international readership, which by its very nature will require generally intelligible language with a minimum of specialised dialect, or on the other hand he has to give priority to his language and material and let his readership choose itself. This of course is partly dictated by the level of economic independence of the writer himself. This choice is often seen as resulting in 'authentic' representation for personal and national satisfaction, or 'watering down' to achieve economic success. It is a choice which also affects other language-based aspects of culture – music, drama, jokes, etc.

Choice of dialect for the West Indian writer

Along with such practical difficulties goes that which is the most difficult for the artist as a writer – the understanding and mastery of one's own language and that of the society as a whole. The various forms of language in any West Indian society are not simply alternative ways of saying the same thing, but they are forms provoking unusually strong emotional reactions when compared with variant language forms in other societies. West Indian literature, reflecting as it does the life of West Indian classes, colonialism and racial conflicts, has language in primary focus. Language is both the artistic medium and part of the subject matter. The writer, therefore, has to manage language in such a way as to show distinctions between generations, racial groups, social groups, religious groups, the educated, the uneducated and the pretentious parvenus.

The charge that great literature does not require regional or dialectal language is misleading in the context of the West Indies and in the context of modern literature. Whereas much of pre-20th-century literature was courtly and upper-class in origin, sponsored and fostered by royalty and rich patrons and directed towards them, recent literature caters to a wider cross-section of the community. Courtly and upper-class literature was directed towards a readership which used and expected to be addressed in the standard language. For that reason it can be said to be in the dialect of its readers, which is essentially the case for modern literature. In like manner earlier colonial literature was meant for a sophisticated part of the reading public in the 'mother' country as well as for educated colonials in a context of colonialism, whereas more recent West Indian literature reaches a wider public and is often today selected for a diverse school age and university readership born in a post-colonial era.

The charge that great literature is written in the standard language is related to the earlier-mentioned distinction between refined or 'serious' culture and all other forms of culture, and the belief that the 'serious' requires a sophisticated medium. In essence, the argument is that 'serious' and 'refined' concepts can be handled only by the standard language, or alternatively that they are sullied and degraded by non-standard language. In the West Indies this is not only a general belief but is reinforced by practice daily in the newspapers, which have a general and unsuspected influence in this regard. Newspapers daily carry sections written in non-standard English and specifically in eye dialect. These sections are invariably comic in nature, deriding customs, behaviour or politics and also giving the latest gossip. These sections are in the form of cartoons (sketched drawings with words), loose or rhyming verse or a local gossip column. The sections contrast sharply in language form with the rest of the newspaper except for the comics and the occasional West Indian short story or verse carried in some newspapers. The inescapable conclusion from this – that the serious news must be written in the standard and the comic and local may be given in non-standard – is tempered by the fact that much of what appears in West Indian newspapers is received in a set form from international wire services, that much of the locally written sections are characterised by West Indian English and journalese, and that the newspaper itself does have a readership beyond the shores where it is published. However, the tendency of newspaper dialect use to exaggerate eye dialect for comic purposes causes newspaper dialect and the newspaper itself to be lightly regarded by 'serious' writers, who deal with dialect as a syntactic and semantic challenge. So phonology and orthography which can easily be manipulated to amuse the uninitiated general public give way, for the 'serious' writer, in favour of word structure, sentence structure and meanings, which require better understanding of language and language function, elements of style, a traditional and genuine preoccupation of the artistic writer.

The mastery of phonology, however, remains an essential element in the armoury of the West Indian poet and dramatist, as well as the singer and story-teller, whose works all deal with actual performance. The West Indian short story, which is often written to be read aloud, depends to a large extent on local dialects and sounds, principally because it has developed out of a tradition of oral literature which has storytelling with well-known characters speaking in a characteristic way. On the other hand, the West Indian novel, although it is not totally separable from traditional oral literature, is essentially a modern development closely linked to educated elements in the society. It is a well-set genre, requiring the West Indian novelist to conform to known ideas about style, theme, plot, character development, dialogue and social mores. The fact too that publishing of West Indian novels is often done by agencies partially or totally outside the West Indies is not an inconsiderable factor in the limitations placed on the novelist. However, the use of eye dialect is general among West Indian novelists and is seen as complementary to the morphological, syntactic, lexical and semantic features of West Indian English. In fact, the combination of consistently standard spelling with West Indian syntax, words and meanings is not only rare but becomes virtually impossible to maintain because of the interdependence of phonology and morphology.

The easily perceived characteristics of West Indian English, general or territory-specific, are those that occur most frequently in eye dialect, but such representation is not predictable because most authors use a contrastive or 'highlighting' style, within sentences, across sentences and from paragraph to paragraph. For example, the word 'you' may vary not only in spelling in a single work, but within a sentence of dialogue, with the first occurrence given in eye dialect and subsequent occurrences in standard spelling. This is done mainly to avoid dulling by consistent use and partly to allow reading to proceed more easily. This contrastive representation is also characteristic for morphology and syntax, so that the speech of lower-class characters is often in standard spelling, with occasional reminders to let the reader keep on mentally interpreting the dialogue as dialectal and non-standard. Contrastive representation is to a certain extent an effective method of countering the normal tendency of readers to transform the language being read into native patterns. This is of course a tendency encouraged by standard spelling, which allows the reader a measure of freedom in pronunciation. Such transformation proceeds unconsciously unless the reader is strikingly and periodically jarred out of it by the writer. In addition, in the case of those West Indian readers whose customary language diverges greatly from standard English, contrastive representation is an effective way of making them aware not so much of the non-standard, into which in any case they transform everything while reading, but more so of the standard.

The reason a novelist uses non-standard dialect varies considerably, whether it is used as an element of style or as a theme. As a result of its social markedness in the West Indies, language itself is often a subject of conversation in novels, among characters who give varying explanations for social differences and for the present structure of West Indian language. In addition, novelists, besides trying to reflect actual language variation, put dialectal forms into the mouths of their characters for a greater philosophical or thematic purpose: for example, to demonstrate the acceptance or rejection of colonialism, or to present the West Indian as a product of African and European elements. Some novelists also experiment with dialectal forms as a part of literary style. For instance, the 'stream of consciousness' technique in Samuel Selvon's *The Lonely Londoners* is relatable to the technique of James Joyce's *Ulysses*, but it assumes some importance in West Indian literature because it does not conform to the general practice of making a distinction between dialogue (to which dialectal non-standard forms are often restricted) and other parts of the text, e.g. reported speech, omniscient narrator, character-narrator (which are usually given in standard English). When the non-dialogue parts are given in non-standard English, it creates the effect of a narrator (and consequently the author) operating from a special social and philosophical level, and giving a different perspective on life.

West Indian literary dialect differs from West Indian speech in the same measure that writing in general differs from speech. The ellipsis, mazes and shortness of speech segments are matched by explicitness, balance and contrast of literary dialect. Real speech, therefore, is only the raw material which the author uses to create his language. Speech, in real life, is a complement to events; it draws most of its significance and meaning from the events, and so is only a part of reality. For the writer, on the other hand, language is virtually total reality, and so it has a much greater role to play in the creation of events and in the stimulation of emotions. West Indian literary dialect therefore serves as both event and medium of communication. West Indian literary dialect also differs from real life speech in the way that different language-based varieties are represented. For example, French Creole may be used by a writer, but only as isolated words or in short stretches – for practical reasons it cannot dominate the text and cause unintelligibility for the reader unfamiliar with it. Or alternatively, it has to be accompanied by explanatory glosses or comments, which themselves tend to hold back the progress of the action. In addition, the writer has to resolve the problem of spelling words from a non-English source, either by presenting them as they occur in the standard orthography of the source language (e.g. *jour ouvert*) or as they have evolved in West Indian speech (e.g. *jouvet*). This is especially a problem for names of people, events and places, and for flora and fauna generally.

The short history of the West Indian novel reveals a change from an early stage when the author had to consider the inclusion of non-standard dialect in an essential and substantial way as a potential hazard, to the present stage when it is commonplace. However, there has been little change in the extent to which non-standard dialect is used or in the variety of spellings used to represent it, principally because writers think these are liberties essential to their art. On the other hand, it can be claimed that the time-period for the development of the West Indian novel has been too short, the writers too varied and the readership too disparate for a consensus which normally results from interaction and feedback – to have developed. It may be said then that the language of the West Indian novel is developing apace with the societies which produce it.

The short story, drama and poetry are related to the novel in that they are all genres in 'refined' literature, but they differ from the novel in that essentially they belong to both media of language – the written and the spoken. For the play, the spoken is primary, but the playwright in a certain sense has a less difficult task from the point of view of language because actors have liberties in converting the text to speech. The West Indian playwright then does not necessarily have to be fastidious in his orthographic representation, except to the extent that he is aware that plays are also treated as books to be read.

For the poet, whether the written or the spoken is primary varies in the West Indies principally according to the form of language used. Generally, the poetry which is 'performed' is that which is written in the vernacular, whereas that which is written in standard English tends to be treated as cerebral. Performative recitation in standard English as a part of a church or other social function is declining and poetry reading in standard English as a social intellectual exercise does not have a strong history in the West Indies.

The short story in the West Indies has a history of being read aloud, and this is mainly because it has historical connections with the folk tale. It is also closely linked to the newspaper and radio, which have always treated the short story as 'literary', interesting, and a necessary feature of their cultural responsibility. West Indian short stories have also been encouraged by British colonial policy as part of their programming for the BBC. West Indian short stories therefore have to be geared for mass appeal and as such even if written predominantly in standard form, are read on the radio and interpreted in the newspaper in the vernacular. Of course, writers of longer and more 'serious' short stories face the same linguistic problems as novelists.

West Indian folklore – the folk tale

Folk tales are characteristic of all human societies, and their form, function and meanings have been studied and analysed extensively. Folklore generally, being oral, is characterised by constant change in linguistic and other detail across both social and geographical space, as well as historically. Such change has also been the subject of many studies, but it must be noted that the modern development, which again is a generally characteristic one, of transcribing folk tales, editing them and presenting them as reading and educational material, modifies substantially their function and highly variable character. There are however some general aspects of West Indian folk tales in form and type. In the West Indies the most prevalent types have been animal tales, duppy tales, lying tales, fool tales and obscene tales, the last of which have never waned in popularity. Overall, the tales best known as West Indian feature an animal as the main character or trickster-hero.

In Jamaica, Antigua, St Vincent, Guyana and Nevis the main character is in most cases *Anancy/Nancy*. In Grenada (and occasionally Trinidad) the name given to the character is *Zayen* [zaē], from the

147

French word *araignée*, and when the tales are told in English this is translated as *Spider*. In St Kitts, Dominica, Trinidad, St Lucia, Montserrat and Barbados the trickster-hero is in most cases *Rabbit*. In most of the territories *Monkey* occurs sometimes as the trickster-hero, and in no territory is it considered unusual or contradictory when any two of Anancy, Rabbit, Monkey occur in one tale with either one outsmarting the other.

When the names *Rabbit*, *Monkey* and *Spider* occur, they are never used exclusively as human characters. However, *Jack* is used instead of *Rabbit* with the result that it sometimes loses its animal associations. The same thing happens (this is noted from as early as the 1920s) with the name *Nancy*, which not only occurs as *Mr Nancy* and *Mrs Nancy* but also *Miss Nancy* or simply *Nancy*, all referring to human characters, with the last one especially not being distinguishable from its use as a normal name for a girl.

Although many different animals occur in the tales, there is only one other with an African-derived name and that is *Tacuma*. This name is said to be derived from the West African name for the son of Anancy, *Intikuma*, and in the West Indian tales it varies from story to story, with the most noticeable variations in Montserrat, where the name *Terracooma* sometimes occurs and in Nevis *Chickerber*. In West Indian tales Tacuma is not necessarily dependent on or a relative of Anancy, and in fact it is not often clear what animal Tacuma is supposed to be.

Although it is claimed that there is a close historical connection between the name *Anancy* and the Upper Guinea Coast of West Africa on the one hand, and *Rabbit* and the Lower Guinea Coast or Bantu tradition on the other, it is clear that the name used in the Caribbean is also directly related to the specific European power that was dominant and the extent of this dominance. It is also well known that the term *Nancy story* is used throughout the West Indies to refer to all kinds of tales, whether they contain Anancy or not. It is generally believed that *Nancy* is a shortened form of *Anancy* and that because of the prevalence of Anancy in the tales that word became generalised to apply to all tales. It should be noted however that in the earliest full tales, given by Matthew Lewis in 1816, the tales are called 'Nancy stories', with no occurrence or hint whatsoever of Anancy or a spider character. A better explanation of *Nancy* and *Anancy* is that whereas *Anancy* derives from the Twi *ananse* ('spider'), *Nancy* derives from *nansi* in Bambara meaning 'chameleon', and that the chameleon or anthropomorphic nature of the characters is the main feature of the tales. The two words *nansi* and *ananse* in the course of time became confused and inseparable in the West Indies.

Another etymological misinterpretation which plagues the tales is the word *Brer*, which sometimes occurs before names. The traditional explanation of this is that it derives from and means *brother*. Such an interpretation is incorrect because it is not justified by evidence of either phonology or meaning. In spite of the many spellings used in texts, there is little doubt that the general basic pronunciation of the word is [bər] (like the English word *burr*) or a pronunciation without the *r* with variations in the vowel sound (e.g. *bo, bə, bu*). Neither *Brer* nor any of its variations is used as a normal word for 'brother' – it is always used as a familiar form of address. For such a clear and contrastive bifurcation of the form and meaning of the single English word *brother* to have occurred in West Indian speech would have been quite extraordinary. The word *Brer*, the spelling of which was an attempt from the earliest authors on to relate the word which they heard to a known English word, is historically related to *borh, bour, boa*, a common non-standard (British) English dialectal form widely used as a familiar form of address, and is etymologically the last part of the word *neighbour*. The English dialectal form also survives in Barbados additionally up to today as *bo* (e.g. 'I don't know, *bo*'), and is used normally and naturally as a familiar form of address. However, because of the dominance and widespread acceptance of the false etymology of *brer*, that is from *brother*, many folk tales told or written today have *brother* or some non-standard pronunciation of it preceding the names in the tales.

In format West Indian folk tales are characterised by optional opening and closing formulas. Again there is a difference between French Creole influenced territories and the others. In the former, the storyteller may start off by saying 'Cric' to which the audience replies 'Crac', or by saying the more French Creole 'Tim Tim' with the response 'Bois seche'. In the latter territories there is no such introduction and the storyteller starts into the tale with the traditional English-type opening *Once, One time, There was*, etc. The word *Oncet* is also used. Occasionally a more elaborate rhyme occurs, some variation of

Once upon a time
The thing was fine
Plant some vine
And it come white lime.

The verb used in the introductory clause is usually *(there) was . . .*, but the phrase *it had . . .* occurs normally in the French Creole influenced territories and very occasionally in Jamaica.

There is no specific formula for ending the tales in the French Creole influenced territories and for the others there is a clear difference between Jamaica and the rest. In the case of Jamaica the following variant endings occur (this is how they are actually transcribed):

Jack man dora
Jack man dory

Jack man dory fe dat
Jack man dory, me story done

Jack man dory, choose none/now/one
Jack Mantora me no choose any/none

Jack Mandora, me no waan' no more
Jack Mandora, I don't wan' none.

The name *Jack* occurring in the formulaic ending of Jamaican tales also occurs as the name of the main character in St Kitts, Nevis, Montserrat and the Bahamas, where it alternates with *Rabbit* and *Anancy*. The same word occurs in parts of Barbados as an alternative form of address for *man* as in

But, jack, you didn't tell me so

which is closely related to the English *every man jack*. Notice also that the name *Jackman* occurs in English. The relationship between *Jack* and *Rabbit* already exists in *jackrabbit*, which derives from *jackass* + *rabbit* (i.e. a rabbit with long ears and long legs 'a hare'), but it can also mean a male rabbit. The connection between the words can therefore be illustrated thus:

anancy – rabbit – jackrabbit – jack – man (– Jackman)

In Antigua, St Kitts, Montserrat, Nevis, Anguilla, St Vincent and Barbados, the ending formula is some variation of

I step on a piece of lead and the lead bend, and my story end

In Barbados *wire* often replaces *lead*, but in this Nevisian ending both are included:

As I went over de wiah, My shirt ketch fiah
And as de lead bend, My story end.

This Eastern Caribbean ending has parallels in English folklore. Compare the following English formula given by Northall (1892:339):

> 'My story's ended, my spoon is bended
> If you don't like it, go to the next door, and get it mended.'

The use of formulas at the beginning and end of tales has always been optional and on the whole most stories occur without such formulas. No current and essential meaning need be given for the formulas where they are used, and most known explanations tend to be anecdotal. The great variation of the Jamaican ending formula without constant or identifiable theme shows that meaning is not paramount. Explanation of folklore origins and meanings is fraught with difficulty, is usually contentious, and not based on verifiable evidence because of the very nature of the history of transmission of oral literature. In any case, the formulas are better explained in terms of their function, which is to delineate entities or stages in a context which is fluid and informal. The same is true of songs and rhymes which occur within the tales, without giving any specific new information and without having to be an essential element for the meaning or advancement of the plot of the tale. In a broader context, formulas, songs and rhymes constituted an integral part of a situation which demanded spoken communication or interaction at set stages between performer and audience. In fact, the call *Cric* with response *Crac* is not only an opening formula but a method of catching and maintaining the attention of listeners at any point during the story, and is used by the skilful storyteller to heighten excitement within the tale. The words themselves derive from a traditional French tale opening formula

Cric Crac
Cuiller à pot

but the call and response re-interpretation is West African influenced. This kind of language therefore provided a socially integrative function rather than a directive or informative one. The many unintelligible sounds and words occurring in folk tales and mentioned by commentators also perform this function.

Most of the vast number of West Indian folk tales recorded in writing have been produced out of what may be considered their normal context. In the analysis of the language of West Indian folk tales, therefore, one has to deal with both 'performed' tales and 'genuine' tales. Tales produced directly for recording by an isolated storyteller have in most cases been stripped of songs, rhymes, special voices and nonsense sounds, which characterise communal performance. The language generally is made intelligible for the listener, if that listener is perceived as a standard English speaker, by reducing the occurrences of non-standard items. At the same time the temptation to be exotic in such a situation and appease the listener is very real. In a more genuine setting the tales require dramatic vocal skills, especially the Anancy and duppy tales, which are usually directed towards children to amuse and scare them in a mischievous way. Note, for example, the following extract from Keens-Douglas (1975):

'Yu change yu mind 'bout going out?
Don't let me stop yu nah.
Is only leaf dat falling on de roof,
Or den it could be Loupgarou or Socouyant
Yu hear 'bout dem? . . .
Chile yu in plenty trouble.
Dey does have plenty Dwen,
An' Baccoo man from Guyana
An' sometimes dey say
Even Steel Donkey from Barbados

>   An' Rolling Calf from Jamaica.
>   Is alright yu could go if yu want,
>   Don't let me stop yu . . .'

In fact, tales could be considered the earliest and most crucial initiation for some into the supernatural and transcendental. The voices and sounds from tales told in the darkness of night with its own surrounding tropical sounds remain etched in the minds and imagination of people from childhood to old age.

The dramatic presentation of the tales in a genuine context is characterised by general as well as special language features. The call-and-response technique which is known to be characteristic of Afro-American (including Caribbean) singing and religious practice is also typical of storytelling. The audience joins in at appropriate times (e.g. singing) and also optionally comments on the action or repeats words or the last word or phrase when the storyteller pauses. The usual vocal reactions of fear, amusement and surprise of course vary depending on the skill of the storyteller, and characters are given speech which is deemed to be typical of their nature or of their part in the specific story. In fact, the storyteller becomes an actor, making full use of intonation, special effects (vocal and other) including ideophones, kinesics (hand, arm, face and body movements) and whatever else he thinks necessary to impress the audience. However, Anancy specifically and duppies generally have been traditionally given special ways of talking, although there is no clear distinction between the two.

Anancy's speech has four elements: it is an old-fashioned and rural dialect, with a lisp, nasality and rapidity. Walter Jekyll writing in 1907 says:

> 'Annancy has a defect of speech owing to a cleft palate, and pronounces his words badly. He speaks somewhat like Punch, through his nose very rapidly, and uses the most countrified form of dialect.'

Whereas such 'qualities' may have been partly inherited from African sources, it is clear that firstly they try to capture the identity of an animal-man character (i.e. the way a spider would talk if it could), secondly they provoke amusement, fear or whatever emotion the context suggests, and thirdly they give the tales authenticity by locating the main character in a historical and geographical context.

Duppies are also supposed to talk with a nasal quality and, in addition, as Leach (1961:214) explains:

> 'The duppy folk have a language of their own. Various informants told stories in duppy talk – a distortion of Jamaican English made by pursing the lips into a whistling position and then trying to talk . . .

songs [are] sung in the duppy manner; that is, with exaggerated phrasing and intonation.'

Here again such portrayal of duppy vocal behaviour is optional and not necessarily uniform, and is easily explained by the belief that a duppy would speak in a funny way, appropriate to its unreal and changeable nature.

It is, then, the requirements of dramatic presentation and the skill of the storyteller that determine the general language of the tales and that of specific characters rather than faithfulness to a putative source, which in any case is nebulous. Linguistic analysis of the structure of the tales shows elements typical of action and narrative style – short sentences with the verb carrying most of the force, direct speech or dialogue, verb tense corresponding to the time of action in the story rather than to the time of speech (usually called the narrative or historic present), ellipsis, and heavy reliance on context to complement speech. In the context of these tales, in which trickery is usually one of the main elements, word and sentence ambiguity is extensively exploited. In addition, onomatopoeia and other sound-meaning correspondences feature for example in etiological tales when the origin of the noises characteristic of different animals is explained. Extended meaning and ambiguity also come into play when the storyteller deliberately uses his tales, in whole or in part, to refer indirectly to a person in the audience, within earshot, or who has some friend or relative in the audience. Such a practice of 'dropping remarks' is of course not restricted to the context of storytelling.

Lexical references in the tales betray their social level and varied origins, but at the same time show an unlimited world of fantasy and belief. The tales contain (in the context of the West Indies) familiar and unfamiliar beings, animals and places, e.g. men and soucouyants, dogs and tigers, backyards and kingdoms. Names vary from the impossible – i.e. very long nonsense names made up to satisfy some requirement in the story (e.g. Yung-Kyum-Pyung) through the ordinary or the stylised (e.g. Wise-Wisey, Little Foot), to the modified (e.g. Open *Caesar* for Open *Sesame*). Some tales are told using only common nouns, highlighting the actions or results rather than the characters.

Animal tales and duppy tales have gradually decreased in popularity and changed in presentation as a result of social and economic changes in West Indian society. It is quite normal now for such tales to be presented as part of stage, television or radio, either for a general audience or for children specifically. For such prepared and time-controlled contexts there is less variation in the actual words and presentation of the performer, as well as use of what have come to be considered true elements of folk tales, e.g. non-standard dialect, formulas and songs. In effect, just as the actor's lines are the same as those of the text in performance after performance, the same is the case of the storyteller of today, who, in addition, may have his stories on wax or tape. Storytelling therefore has changed to suit the demands of modern Western entertainment in Caribbean society.

Other tales

In contrast, obscene tales, by their very nature, fool tales (called 'noodle' tales by Elsie Clews Parsons) and lying tales have retained their local and informal character. However, there is no sharp distinction between the types themselves or between traditional tales and simple jokes, except that traditions in some cases have familiar characters. In Jamaica obscene tales among children are dominated by a character called *Big Boy*; in Barbados fool tales feature the character *Ossie Moore*; in Guyana there are tales about *Sensible Bill* and *Stupidey Bill*. In Trinidad there is the traditional teasing or insulting joke called *picong* or *fatigue*, which does not have specific form or characters but is typified by its intent and nature. Picong may involve half-truths or outright lies geared to provoke a reaction from the person who is the object of such, and amusement from those listening. The crucial element in picong, one that is fully exploited, is that the tone of the remarks may be indeed understood as that of picong, evoking repartee in kind, or may be misunderstood thus causing greater amusement and more teasing. Although such language behaviour is general in the West Indies and not unlike *the dozens* of Black Americans, in the West Indies it is given a special name traditionally only in Trinidad. General storytelling is not restricted to any context, formal or informal, and as such varies in language. This is not really a recent development, for storytelling has always been a factor in general education, a way of passing on and reinforcing knowledge and values in children as well as adults and so must occur in all contexts. Distinctiveness results from the fact that folklorists, after making academic distinctions in types and motifs, have tended to select some and given them unusual prominence.

An important link between the telling of traditional tales, of everyday jokes, and the reporting of recent incidents is in the use of exaggerated language. Although such exaggeration is in no way exclusively West Indian, the use of graphic concrete images, claims of personal involvement or testimony, and a wide range of linguistic techniques tend to make the non-West Indian listener especially overestimate the truth of the situation or dismiss most of what is said as fiction. In other words, clear separation of truth from fiction and the serious from the comic, in commenting, for example, on the slave master or boss, in 'dropping remarks' about acquaintances, in teasing friends or neighbours, in telling Anancy stories, and in duppy tales, is deliberately or unwittingly obscured by West Indians in their use of language. The right to claim innocence of deliberate wrong-doing is always reserved.

Riddles

Riddles are also a favourite subject of folklorists, but there is little that essentially distinguishes West Indian riddles from others. A riddle is basically a linguistic puzzle with an unusual solution which hinges on a special interpretation of the sound or meaning of words which is initially misleading. Riddles in the West Indies in most cases have answers which refer to known or familiar local phenomena (e.g. coconut, sugar cane, ackee) and vary in language to suit the context, which is unrestricted. In forms the riddle may have alliteration or rhyme, or when written may be set out like verse, but these elements are optional and varied. Also optional are the beginning and ending formulas. In Jamaica the introductory formula is some variation of

Riddle me this, riddle me that
Guess me this riddle and perhaps not

In most of the other islands it is a variant of

A riddle, a riddle, a ree
No man can tell this riddle to me/
Perhaps you could clear this riddle for me

After the riddle is posed, the usual question is

What is that?

to be followed almost immediately (especially when children are telling the riddles) by the answer. The question 'What is that?' is required because the riddle is most often posed with the structure of a statement, e.g.

My mother has a pepper tree. In the night it has plenty peppers, in the day it has none.
[What is that?] (Stars)

Riddles with a question structure, e.g.

What has two ears and one foot and can't use them?
(A coal pot)

or with a command structure, e.g.

Spell dry grass in three letters.
(Hay)

are normal, but much less frequent than those with a statement structure.

The West Indian riddle, then, is distinct only because of its introductory formula and localised answer. The introductory formula is well known and adaptable, but in situations where, for example, children are exchanging riddles, to produce the formula at the beginning of each one is unnecessary. Just as is the case in the tales, the introductory formula is merely a method of 'getting the floor' or of informing listeners that you are going to tell a riddle when these things are not already evident. The words of the opening formula in West Indian riddles have parallels in English rhyming riddles. Note, for example, the following riddles in Opie and Opie (1959:77):

'Riddle me, riddle me
riddle me ree
I saw a nutcracker
up in a tree. (A squirrel)

Riddle me, riddle me, what is that,
Over the head and under the hat? (Hair)

Patch upon patch
Without any stitches
If you tell me this riddle
I'll buy you some breeches. (A cabbage)'

It is quite evident that the words that occur in West Indian riddles as a separable opening formula are incorporated into the riddle itself, even if repeated across many riddles, in the English ones. In African riddles, in contrast, opening formulas are not only universal but almost obligatory. In fact, in Yoruba and Anang (Nigeria), in Gio, Mamo and Sapa (Liberia), in Nandi (Congo), and in several other African languages, the riddler starts by giving a known formula to which the audience responds, in exactly the same way that the call *Cric* and response *Crac* are used to open West Indian folk tales. The opening formula in riddles, however, can be said to have a more crucial additional function than it does in tales. Because of the linguistic semantic nature of the riddle, because it is short and has key words, the listener has to be forewarned or prepared to unravel words. The formula therefore establishes a break or distinction in oral intercourse between normal language and figurative language. The optional opening formula of the West Indian riddle is therefore a blend of two traditions.

Proverbs

The form and prevalence of proverbs in West Indian society have been commented on in an earlier chapter, but from a social and cultural point of view there is an overriding feature of West Indian proverbs which must be pointed out. When compared with the full range of proverbs in other societies West Indian proverbs are seen to have a very strong negative element – they are negative either in form, meaning, implication or context. In any random selection of West Indian proverbs it is quite normal for over 75 percent of them to contain at least one negative word (e.g. *no, never, nothing*). Of the remainder more than half will have a word which incorporates a negative meaning (e.g. *lose, break, burst, kill*), and of the others most are warnings or advice exhorting against something. In effect, although in all the proverbs the wisdom contained therein is unquestionably sound and reflective of experience, it is seldom presented in a positive form as for example in the popular English proverbs

A friend in need is a friend indeed.
Many hands make light work.
A stitch in time saves nine.

West Indian proverbs directly reflect on personal relationships and experience in a social situation historically dominated by negative factors. That the negative aspect of proverbs still features prominently in West Indian language up to today indicates that the level of negativity in social behaviour and outlook is still significant.

The linguistic structure of proverbs, like that of other areas of folklore, shows significant variation and evolution, and this is so especially in those proverbs with a two-clause structure – dependent and main. In older versions of some of these proverbs the dependent clause occurred without an introductory subordinate conjunction, e.g.

Crab walk too much, im lose im claw.
Spit in the sky, it fall in your face.
Bull old, you tek wis' wis' tie him.

In more recent versions of these proverbs, a conjunction (*when* or *if*) is used before the dependent clause. It is clear however in the older proverbs that *if*, *when* and *zero* (i.e. no conjunction) represented three levels of reality. In other words, events that were inevitable or common were introduced by zero (examples just given). Events which were probable were introduced by *when*, e.g.

When cow-tail cut off, God-Almighty brush fly fe' him.
When towel turn tablecloth, there's no bearin with it.
When puss live well, im say rat meat bitter.

The effect of *if*, as it is generally in English, is to give the impression that the event is not probable, or that it may or may not happen, e.g.

If ears grow ever so big, they can't pass head.
If you miss Harry, catch his frock.

The strong presence of proverbs in West Indian society is a direct legacy of their great importance in African societies. In fact, it is said

157

that proverbs are more popular in Africa than anywhere else in the world and that there is a great love for speaking in symbolic terms. Proverbs make use of well-known techniques of persuasion – they appeal to the authority of collective wisdom and tradition and, as happens with the Bible, they are meant to be accepted without question. All this is guaranteed by their familiarity through repetition, their set form, and in many cases their internal structural balance or symmetry, as for example in

When blackman thief, he thief half-a-bit;
When bukra man thief, he thief whole estate.
Dog dont eat dog.
Coward man keep whole bones.

Proverbs are also said to be well suited to small communities in which problems in interpersonal relationships are better resolved by indirect language than by direct confrontation, which causes embarrassment, anger and non-compliance. It is doubtful, however, whether in the West Indies proverbs actually do diffuse tension. For although they do discourage open confrontation, they certainly fan the flames of smouldering tensions. Proverbs, like 'dropping remarks', and like indirect allusions in tales, are barbs or bait to the victim, whom the context discourages from responding, because such would be a major concession in the typical situation epitomised in the proverb

Who the cap fit wear it.

Proverbs are to some extent like riddles in that both contain figurative language which has to be interpreted. Although the proverb is simpler to interpret than the riddle and its significance is usually understood, occasionally part of the force of the proverb in the West Indian context is not only to warn about unwise and unacceptable behaviour, but to give oneself a smug feeling of superiority by believing that the target is not only less sensible than oneself to contemplate a certain line of action, but also so foolish in any case as not to be able to understand the proverb and follow the advice therein. A slightly different situation is the case of a parent who uses the proverb

A hard head makes a sore bottom
or
If you don't hear, you will feel

both as a warning and at the time of punishment which results from disregard of the warning, a situational relationship which carried with it an in-built 'I told you so'.

In contrast to 'Nancy' stories and riddles, no (special) name is given to proverbs by West Indians. To the non-literate West Indian the term *proverbs* has no great meaning or significance, except in its reference to a book in the Bible, but even then the pronunciation of the word is slightly different. Part of the reason for this absence of a term is that, again unlike tales and riddles, proverbs are not distinguished or set apart by opening or closing formulas in West Indian speech; in fact, West Indians are generally not conscious of the extent to which they use proverbs because they fit so smoothly into the progress of normal speech.

Language of children's games

The lore of children, over and above folk tales and riddles, is quite extensive in all societies and reveals quite graphically the importance of language in the maturational stages of man. The pleasure that isolated sounds of language give to the babbling baby increases a hundredfold as the child progresses to adulthood. Babbling is predictable as a stage of development but unpredictable in detail. Likewise, much of language lore of children, while being unpredictable in detail, maintains a basic consistency in function and pattern. The language lore of children is divided into two types: firstly songs and rhymes used meaningfully to establish and control relationships among the children, and secondly language used in the pure artistic sense simply to give pleasure. The latter type includes jingles, nonsense rhymes, tongue twisters and word play, all of which, when successful, produce amusement and satisfaction. In both types, although initially it appears contradictory in the latter, there is a body of material already existing in the community which is altered in detail to suit context and individual, but which is not significantly increased by totally new creations. In other words, children alter the songs and rhymes of their predecessors but do not substantially create totally new ones which are then passed down to their successors. In other words, traditional material remains even though names, places and facts are freshened by topical and local allusions.

Rhymes and songs may occur in isolation or they may be a part of children's games. Children's games in the West Indies (e.g. ring, clapping and skipping games) tend to be played by girls, but all children produce rhymes as well as sing songs as a part of general amusement. In games where players have to decide who is 'it', many different rhymes and formulas are used. Consider the following as an example of such a formula:

Huvana, buvana, baby sneeze
Host, toast, sugar and tea
Potato roast and English toast
Out goes you.

Such a formula survives for many different reasons: there is rhyme; there is contrast between normal and abnormal words in a whole that is semantically nonsensical; there is suitability to purpose in that each word (except *and*) is used to move from one person to the next, without there being a simple list of like elements (e.g. nouns) which would be difficult to remember; there is variation in word length, the contrastiveness of which prevents monotony; the whole formula seems innocent and fair and is long enough that it does not normally give rise to the reaction that it is being manipulated to predetermine 'it'. However, one must not get the impression that it is simple in many cases to account for the popularity and survival of rhymes and songs. On the contrary, this is one of the most baffling features of nonsense rhymes and songs.

In many West Indian children's songs and rhymes, words have evolved to become nonsense words because older versions of these songs and rhymes are from a dialect or language no longer in current usage, or refer to items or events which have become obscure. West African and French Creole words especially generally lost their significance and were re-interpreted to suit Creole English pronunciation. In many cases in Grenada and Trinidad, French Creole and English words exist side by side, understood in entirety by some speakers and not by others. In fact, this kind of mixing heightens the appeal of the songs and rhymes, which do not require simultaneous and complete interpretation of their meaning. A consequence of this which has to be considered is that as a result of the crucial place that the songs and rhymes of childhood have in the linguistic evolution of the individual, freedom to treat language as sounds without meaning may have a spill-over effect on the communicative language of the individual. The assessment of such a consequence however is not easy to measure unequivocally.

Another major element of songs and rhymes is repetition. Repetition is a feature of both structure and usage. Rhymes by their very nature involve repetition of endings, of words, or alliteratively of syllables and sounds. Songs are characterised by choruses. From the point of view of usage, production (aloud and silent) and listening constitute repetition, the effect of which is increased in the very positive context of play and amusement. The effect of repetition is to reinforce, thus ensuring familiarity and survival in basic form and structure. Where the meaning of the words is not paramount, survival is dominated by sound and function. So effective is this repetition that the songs and rhymes of childhood remain with the individual for life. The familiarity created by repetition causes changes in detail to be acutely perceived by children in opposite ways – on the one hand it takes only a few minor changes to provoke the proud belief by a child that she has made up a new song or rhyme, and on the other hand any slight change that a child makes when repeating a song or rhyme will immediately draw the charge 'you saying it wrong'. The countless arguments, fights and breaks in friendship among children resulting from this and other similar charges attest to the importance of detail among them. Repetition is also analysed as provocative of the drum effect, and bearing in mind that clapping or movement normally accompanies rhymes and songs, repetition acts as a method of keeping time or rhythm.

The language of West Indian rhymes and songs is largely determined by their historical source, which in the majority of cases is traceable to European, and specifically British, patterns and words. West Indian rhymes and songs reflect two responses to the European original – adaptation and parody. Parody is universal in children's rhymes and is exhibited in mocking of the known, respected and sacred of adult society both native and non-native. For instance, the religious song 'Trust and obey' of English tradition is common all over the West Indies with a transformed first line 'Trust and don't pay' with following lines in similar vein. Parody of European and American national colours occurs in

Red, white and blue
The monkey married to you

In many cases, the parody already exists in the British tradition and is merely continued and diversified in West Indian tradition. For example, the following English children's rhyme occurs in many different pieces and variations in the West Indies:

'The higher up the mountain
The greener the grass
The higher up the monkey climbs
The more he shows his arse
Ask no questions
Hear no lies
Shut your mouth
And you'll catch no flies.' (Opie and Opie, 1959:97)

Parody often is little more than word substitution, which means that the syntax of the original is not substantially altered. Much of what is parodied is the rhymes and songs that have been presented to the child as religious, artistic or mnemonic material in the formal school setting (i.e. nursery rhymes, prayers, poems, anthems, songs occurring as part of organised recreation), but the child also parodies that which occurs in the general society (i.e. commercials, popular songs, church songs). Although such parody occurs in societies with varying kinds of linguistic situations and although parody is a source of satisfaction because rebellion and creativity give pleasure in the tightly controlled structure of the child's world, there is no doubt that in the West Indies many of the rhymes and songs presented to the child in their 'correct' form contain words and structures unintelligible to the child. The Lord's Prayer, in its older forms, with words such as *hallowed*, *which* ('who'), *trespass*, and clauses such as *thy kingdom come*, *thy will be done*, *for thine is the kingdom*, is a classic example of language far beyond the level of children when it is first presented to them. In fact, because most rhymes and songs are so old or have syntactic licence because of their verse form, their meaning is seldom understood by children. From a linguistic point of view therefore parody is less functional but more meaningful to children.

Adaptation of original material is also an attempt to make it more meaningful, especially in the context of game songs. The following extract from Jacob Elder (1965:37) explains some of the textual adaptation which has taken place in West Indian game songs:

> 'Words that are similar in sound get easily interchanged, e.g., in "Gipsy in da moonlight", many versions have been reported with "Dulcie", "Dootsy", "Tootsy" or even "Wootsie" as the name for the player with the dramatic role. Children find it necessary to interchange "black boy", "brown boy", and "brown haired girl" in the song-game "There's a brown gal in da ring". In one locality in British Guiana, a school-teacher who collected song-games for me found a version of "Lost my glove" with a chorus which runs "Drop, Peter, drop/Drip, drop, drip, drop". The Tobago version of this song-game has no "drip". From the same collector comes a version of "Miss Lucy" with the first line beginning "Miss Lucy has some dry-head daughters" while in the Trinidad version the stanza begins "Miss Lucy has some fine young daughters". From village to village in Trinidad and Tobago the song-game "Diamon' in the ring a'ready" may begin with "Dina", "Diana" or "Ziana" although it has not been ascertained how the line began in the original version.
>
> Textual change is not restricted to words alone. Often a whole phrase or even a whole verse gets substituted for another when new users adopt a song-game. Meaningless expressions are usually the first to be dropped. Many of the French Creole words have been dropped from song-games reaching Trinidad and Tobago English-speaking children from islands like Dominica, Grenada and Martinique. Sometimes the Creole words may be translated into English words that are meaningful to the local singers.
>
> Variation in text has been noted by both Beckwith and Jekyll in the Jamaican song-games which they collected. "Sally Water" seems to be the classic example of textual variation in a song-game common not only in the Caribbean song tradition, but also in those of the United States and Great Britian. Lady Gomme* reported a large number of versions of this game, while in the islands of Trinidad and Tobago the song has been split into two independent tunes one of which, called "Rise Sally Rise", has a new verse added to it which runs: "If it's a white man/ Put him outside/ If it's a black man/ let him come in".'

* Gomme, Alice *The Traditional Games of England, Scotland and Ireland*

Adaptation has proceeded in accordance with evolution of the society so that today in the West Indies not only are digging songs and adult game songs given respectively by Jekyll (1907) and Elder (1965) rare, but also many of the children's songs are no longer heard. In addition, the language has changed because much of ring-game playing and skipping takes place at school during break or lunch period, in a context, especially in urban schools, where the children are from more varied backgrounds, causing the language to be less non-standard. Changes in language and subject matter can be seen in the following given by Dance (1985) for Jamaica:

> 'Room for rent
> Apply within
> When I run out
> Then you run in'

and also in the jingle (taken from a radio commercial) sung by girls in Barbados:

Glow Spread Margarine
Spreading over the Caribbean

both of which are used by the children in games.

Language of folk-songs

Allied historically to game songs and sometimes indistinguishable from them are today's folk-songs, which are usually sung by groups for public performance. Such songs are many and varied, and are usually associated with adults, who not only show less creativity than children but also tend to regard folklore generally with nostalgia and therefore are deliberately conservative towards it. Conservatism in language is aided by the fact that singing and presentation are usually more important in folk-singing than semantics, and also that extreme non-standard language adds an exotic element, thus enhancing the whole performance. On the other hand, folk-singing throughout the West Indies is becoming a highly specialised genre, a normal part of formal music in which groups must have a varied repertoire of songs local, foreign, traditional and modern, sung in different languages. There is no clear distinction any longer between the sophisticated kind of singing and less formal singing of 'the folk'. In other words, folk-singing today reflects a society which has virtually externalised the folk-song into an art form, as opposed to its earlier status when it was an integral part of games and social life. The language of the folk-song today is therefore as varied in structure as that of most other singing in the West Indies.

Locally produced popular music in the West Indies is dominated by calypso and reggae, the former traditional and now respectable, the latter more recent and still predominantly revolutionary in language. It is probably this revolutionary flavour and tone of social protest which have caused reggae music to become more dominant throughout the West Indies at the expense of calypso, which has lost much of its linguistic sting to become party music predominantly. It is interesting to note that Theodore Van Dam, writing in 1954 about the development of calypso, claims that whilst calypsos in Trinidad were mainly satirical, 'Jamaican Calypsos are often more folk type and less satirical than the others . . . while in Barbados many calypso songs are of the English Music Hall type . . .' and in Antigua they were really 'house-moving songs' which were either praising or deriding in nature. Van Dam also cites the following from Courlander (1952) which pinpoints calypso's uniqueness as being linguistic:

> '. . . it is in the particular style of delivery that calypso singing is unique. The use of archaic and synthetic words, the cramming of many syllables into small space, the importance of rhyming and the free conception of rhyme, all these are characteristic.'

Calypsos are said to be historically related to West African songs of derision, exemplified in the 'practice of Halo among the Ewes of the Gold Coast [modern Ghana]', which Gbeho (1954:62) explains as follows: 'With them, when two villages have fallen out, they compose abusive songs against each other.' Calypso in its early years in the West Indies was like other folklore genres, varying from occasion to occasion and dominated in its lyrics by the creativity of the calypsonian. However, calypso has moved from the picong type with impromptu lines to elaborate set pieces. The impromptu teasing type still features, ironically, in live performances in hotels and other such venues where North American tourists have their fantasies about calypso (based on early calypso) satisfied. This type of calypso therefore has been affected by social evolution and gone the way of much of folklore – it is anachronistic, exotic and the subject of academic study.

The language and development of calypso have been commented on extensively on the street corner and in academic circles and will not be dealt with in any detail here. It is clear, however, that contrasts in language between calypso and reggae are conditioned not only by the greater age of the one as opposed to the other, but also by the differences in the societies from which they spring. Trinidad is ethnically and historically a diverse society with many linguistic influences, and calypso reflects French Creole, ornate English, vernacular English, Creole English, Spanish, Hindi, and Eastern Caribbean varieties of English. Jamaica on the other hand is more homogeneous and more resistant to outside influences in the language of its locally produced popular music. Reggae music not only embodies the language of social protest but is specifically identified with Rastafarianism and its violent apocalyptic images. In actual fact, however, just as it is extremely difficult to identify any one element common to all reggae music, it is equally difficult to characterise the language of reggae, varying as it does from internationally known songs in standard English re-set to a reggae beat through 'dub' music to what those uninitiated in 'roots' reggae regard as unintelligible sounds and language. Such variation is neither new nor necessarily Rastafarian in nature nor a reflection of social contrasts in Jamaica and is epitomised in the singing in the 1960s and 1970s of 'Toots' Hibbert, which ranged from 'normal' songs to 'unique' songs containing long stretches of made-up sounds defying mimicry.

Singers of calypso and reggae share with novelists a problem previously pointed out, which is that in order to capture an international audience, they have to change their language in the direction of standard English. The task of the singer is somewhat easier than the writer's because song and verse allow more freedom in syntax in the use of non-standard language and also the singer does not have the problem of orthography. In addition, the singer is aided by repetition, a normal element in singing, which gives the listener more than one chance to catch the meaning.

The diversity of language in West Indian traditional song and music is not as obvious today as before because social changes and creativity have obscured many distinctions in types which existed up to the 1950s and later. There has been cross-fertilisation between types and loss of distinctiveness in each type as ethnic and social groups within territories participated in each other's celebrations and festivities. This has also been inter-territorial as a result of constant migration, especially in the Eastern Caribbean (English and non-English). It is interesting also to notice the post-slavery element from West Africa in the Belmont area of Port of Spain. When one looks at Andrew Pearse's presentation of 1955 (Table 6.1) and realises that he was dealing only with Trinidad, Tobago, Grenada and Carriacou ('whose populations are in frequent interaction') and also that he did not include the East Indian contribution, one can see how much more complex a total West Indian analysis would be and also what West Indians have fashioned to produce their modern folk music and language.

Language of other games

There is one other major area of culture in which language is virtually inseparable from activity and that is sports and games. The terminology of socially restricted or specialised games has little impact on the general public, especially women, who are traditionally excluded from, restricted or segregated in many games in the West

Table 6.1   Aspects of change in Caribbean folk music.

Music	Country	Language
Congo	Trinidad	'Congo', Patois[1]
Rada	Trinidad	African
Shango	Trinidad	African patois
Yarraba	Trinidad	Fon, Patois[1]
Kalenda	Trinidad, Grenada	Patois English
Belè	Trinidad	Patois[1]
Belè	Grenada	Patois[1]
Belè	Tobago	English
Big drum	Carriacou	'African' patois, English
Bongo	Tobago	English
Bongo	Trinidad	Patois[1], English
Sings	Trinidad, Grenada, Tobago, Carriacou	Patois[1], English, nonsense
Pass-play	Trinidad, Grenada, Tobago, Carriacou	English, Patois[1]
Work-songs	Trinidad, Grenada, Tobago, Carriacou	English, Patois[1]
Chanties	Carriacou, Grenada, Tobago	English
Reel dance	Tobago	English
Quesh	Trinidad	French
Sankeys and trumpets	Trinidad, Grenada, Tobago, Carriacou	English
Veiquoix (*veille croix*)	Trinidad	Spanish
Fandang	Trinidad	Spanish
Road march	Trinidad, Grenada	English
Reel engagé	Carriacou	Patois[1], English
Parange	Trinidad	Spanish

[1]   Patois = French Creole

Nature of language (where indicated)

Hymns, chants, songs
(of Yoruba origin)

Words boast prowess of champions and bands, throw challenging insults

Occasional social commentary

Carries derisive comment on behaviour

Verbal context largely about magical power and dead magicians

Sexual burlesque in word and mime and verbal parody of hymns

Carries social commentary

Tale-telling at wakes. Used to maintain audience participation

Games of children's playgroups. Adults passing time at wakes

The words are printed in a book

From Hymnody of Protestant churches or of local formation

Competitive, recitative-style singing of traditional folk Catholic hymns, quizzing on Biblical and school knowledge and 'picong' or ribbing

Serenades and Christmas carols

Source: adapted from *Pearse (1955)*

Indies. However, the language of boys' pastimes such as kite-flying and pitching marbles has extended into the general language of the society in some cases, even if not outside the specific territory. In contrast, the language of cricket pervades the whole of the West Indies and is used by both men and women as metaphorical language in their everyday activities. Two factors of cricket must be noted – firstly the extent to which cricket commentaries dominate the airwaves and the lives of West Indians during cricket competitions, and secondly the amount of time men and boys especially spend arguing about cricket at the game and elsewhere.

The effect of the first has been to familiarise West Indians with the speech of other West Indians, Englishmen, Australians, Indians and New Zealanders as well as to cause West Indians to copy their 'accents', terminology and phraseology. The language of English commentators for a long time in particular reinforced in West Indians an admiration for British speech. Many a West Indian imitated John Arlott describing the English scenery and found great pleasure in doing so. During that time cricket in England was regarded as a 'gentleman's game' and Arlott maintained this tradition in his descriptions of the game with the result that West Indians were significantly influenced by the language of upper-class England as a standard of achievement.

The language of cricket commentaries, other than the specialised terminology, fits into and reinforces common perceptions about West Indians. The West Indian player has always been likened to an animal, a fact that is glossed over because it is presented in the guise of praise. Such metaphorical language has been used to describe West Indians from the early days up to the present. From the West Indian point of view it is quite normal and fits into the imagery of West Indian life; from an English point of view it is difficult to see how the same claim can be made. When Michael Holding is described as 'running like a gazelle' and Clive Lloyd as 'a big cat lurking in the covers ready to pounce', the association with animals from Africa is undeniable. Animal images change to images of violence when West Indian batting is described. For instance, many a stroke by Gordon Greenidge has been said to be 'brutal' or 'savage' as have been those of most of his predecessors. This kind of imagery is quite consistent with the (once held) belief by opponents of the West Indies that even if they had more 'natural talent', they could be undone by their very enthusiasm or defeated because they had less (of the human qualities of) intelligence, courage and persistence.

The narrative style of cricket commentaries is similar to that of most sports, in that events are described in the present tense, even though they have already happened, to give a sense of immediacy, and within short, simple sentences joined primarily by *and* and *but*. Both forms of

the present are used (e.g. *runs* and *is running*), in many cases
interchangeably. The effect of this on normal West Indian speech may
be insignificant, but it is interesting to note that except for the third
person singular ending (-s) and the auxiliary (*is/are*), normal West
Indian description of events is rendered in a comparable way, thus
making the grammar of cricket description compatible with West
Indian speech.

Cricket, like other aspects of West Indian folk life, has language and
activity inseparable – spectator participation in cricket is as normal as
audience participation in folk tales. Many spectators return home
hoarse after a hard day at cricket and the collective volume of talking
among spectators and shouting to the players, which so disturbs
non-West Indians, passes unnoticed by West Indians. The outpouring
of advice, abuse and hilarity at a high level of intensity has a cathartic
effect on West Indians and has often been blamed for a reduced level
of output in other areas. In Trinidad, picong is just as much a part of
cricket as it is of calypso tents. In short, all the pent-up emotions on
the one hand and on the other all kinds of 'smartness' are given free
rein. Nowhere is this more noticeable than in England where a cricket
match provides one of the few opportunities for West Indians to
express themselves publicly and freely as a social group. Cricket,
therefore, provides an arena for linguistic performance, to supplement
and replace those which characterised earlier stages of social
development and it allows individuals at all levels of society to perform
publicly to a whole stand or to varying groups within a stand.

In this presentation of language in culture in the West Indies we have
looked at developmental and current linguistic factors of a distinctive
or decisive nature. We have also stressed the close connection between
language behaviour and social activity. There are four elements that
run through language use in the West Indies and characterise its
culture: creativity, ambiguity, negativity and pseudolanguage.

The very nature of the start and evolution of West Indian
communities required creativity in language and culture – peoples from
diverse origins were brought together to form communities for which
languages and cultures had to be adapted and created out of source
materials as well as by human ingenuity.

Ambiguity is a conscious and unconscious consequence of creativity
in a tightly structured hierarchical society in which oral elliptical
language is dominant, and explicit formal language, characteristically
West Indian but generally acceptable, is still evolving. Linguistic
ambiguity results quite normally from adaptations or transformations
in a language and from overlapping of languages. Ambiguity is also
used deliberately as a safe method of protest and challenge in societies

in which insubordination, once treated as tantamount to treason in the public sphere, is still considered in private relations between individuals as a lack of training, manners and common decency. Correct social behaviour is quite a strong theme in the proverbs of the West Indies.

Negativity in language reflects the harshness of the social and economic history of the West Indies. The processes of de-culturation and enslavement produced a people who, not being able to strike out against and remove their oppressors, struck out against themselves. Denigration and self-destruction are found in eye dialect, picong, 'dropping remarks', proverbs, folk tales, 'fool' jokes, calypsos, and 'cuss-cuss'. Whereas there has been much physical violence among the poor in the West Indies, tensions and violence in general have been diffused into negativity in language.

Negativity is also found in casual West Indian greetings, indicating a certain defensiveness as a first reaction. The West Indian's response to a neighbourly *How are you?* (varying in form according to context) is *Not too bad, So-so, Abiding in the name of the Lord*, or an expression of resignation, or a listing of a number of complaints. Although greetings and responses are in many languages stylised, in the West Indies there is a clear difference in disposition between a neighbourly response and a formal response (e.g. *Quite well; Fine, thank you*). The neighbourly response always has the implication that there could be improvement in the situation. Negativity in language therefore has a worthwhile function.

Pseudolanguage takes many forms. It ranges from 'pig Latin' and nonsense rhymes among children, through playing with the words and sounds of language in song, to glossolalia in religious practice, all of which are characteristic of most human societies. In the West Indies, however, there is a noticeable connection between pseudolanguage, word play of the type exhibited in Rasta language, ambiguity and misinterpretation, and illiteracy. There is no necessary basic connection between glossolalia (speaking in tongues) and illiteracy, but in the West Indies the Pentecostal-type church, in which glossolalia is most likely to occur for cultural and social reasons, has attracted more poor and illiterate people than those from the middle and upper classes. As a result glossolalia, although supported by biblical reference, is regarded as unsophisticated behaviour and is parodied extensively in the West Indies. In like fashion, Rasta language, although meaningful and creative in itself, is regarded by many educators and others as an escape into easy, undisciplined language behaviour. Even the lyrics of today's popular West Indian music – reggae especially – which depend heavily on sound effects, are often assessed in terms of intelligibility in formal sentence structure and the level of education of the singer. Most pseudolanguage is deliberate or context-defined, but the volume of it, the attractiveness of it, its association with certain classes in the society together with the strength of orality in West Indian culture diffuse the perception of a need for explicitness and clarity in communication in modern West Indian society.

7 · *Language in formal education*

Standard English has been regarded by all West Indian governments from the beginning of the 20th century and before as the optimum form of language for conducting business and for instruction in public schools and (more recently) the University of the West Indies and the University of Guyana. For at least the first half of the century the non-standard English vernaculars and French Creole were believed to be a real impediment to the acquisition of standard English and so teachers were charged with the task of discouraging or eradicating them. The third quarter of the century, in which the University of the West Indies began to take over the leadership role in education and in which the More Developed Countries (i.e. Jamaica, Trinidad and Tobago, Guyana, Barbados) became independent, witnessed a gradual change in official policy towards the non-standard vernaculars and French Creole. In the last quarter of the century the governments have set out a language policy in accordance with the English syllabus of the Caribbean Examinations Council which recognises the rights of the people to use their native speech, encourages artistic expression especially in the vernaculars while at the same time stressing the appropriateness of different varieties and the unchallengeable role of standard English as the language of formal instruction, public business and international communication.

The change in policy reflects three facts: that West Indians are increasingly deciding their own fate; that they are becoming more positive about themselves and their heritage; and that they have discounted the belief that one (form of a) language prevents a person from learning another. In short, emphasis has shifted towards the teaching and learning of language as wholesome, functional and cultural and away from teaching standard English as an absolute to the exclusion of all else.

Policies in general are in part leadership, in part a recognition of reality, and changes in policy are usually met with varying intensities of opposition and support. This is no less so in language, a subject which always provokes more emotion than understanding. Surprisingly, however, the present language policy is understood and supported by most teachers, especially the younger ones. Women, who constitute the greater percentage of teachers in early education, are in most societies more conservative in language use and more standard in language forms and structures, but in this case have shown no great opposition to policy change. The official recognition of the use of non-standard dialect in schools became a public issue only in Trinidad and Tobago, where there was loud and negative reaction for some time in 1975 when the new Language Arts syllabus for primary schools recognised the real nature of and the cultural and psychological value of the native language of the child entering school. Such negative reaction was in part a result of ignorance of the extent to which teachers have always used non-standard language for purposes of comprehension in primary education and ignorance of the difficulties of teaching the skills of reading and writing in non-native language. In other West Indian territories the change in language policy has been more a conservative evolution than a sudden revolution.

There is little doubt that the change in the political and social situation in the West Indies which brought about the change in language policy has made the tasks of teaching and learning language more complex and so more difficult. A teacher today is not simply instructing children to form grammatical standard English sentences, but teaching standard English without deliberately alienating the child from his own speech, teaching the child to appreciate literature (including West Indian literature) and preparing the child for exams which include West Indian literature. In other words, the syllabus is broader, less foreign, less dictatorial and requiring a better and more sensitive teacher. The older vision of a clear target in a homogeneous and tightly disciplined classroom with an exemplary teacher is no more than an illusion or self-delusion on the part of those who so romanticise their own education. On the other hand, the modern teacher in a hard-pressed economy may be mentally distracted by the conviction that his task could be aided by modern technology and better pay.

The learning situation for the West Indian child today must be examined against the background of evolution of West Indian societies from colonial plantation type, in which oral culture was dominant and written literature elitist, to societies with intermediate and modern technology with diversifying economies that have tourism as a dominant force and in which audio-visual culture is dominant. We will now look at the area of linguistic meaning and learning in the classroom situation against such a background.

Communication by language

There are many ways in which human beings communicate with each other, but the major linguistic (including paralinguistic) means are as displayed in Fig 7.1. In this schema it is seen that meaning is rendered with and without the use of sound. However, whereas the non-sound element is always present, the use of sound is not; a simple illustration of this is the nodding or shaking of the head to give a positive

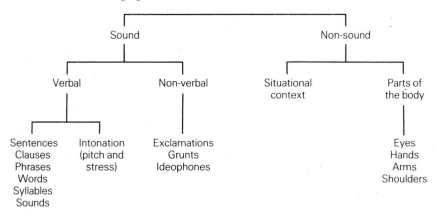

Fig. 7.1   A schema for rendering linguistic meaning.

or negative answer. In most cases of face-to-face communication, all of the sound and non-sound elements accompany each other in a complementary way, but in the majority of cases the non-sound elements contribute more than half of the meaning in this kind of communication.

In the classroom situation in the Caribbean where the use of the body parts for rendering meaning is discouraged, the sound elements increase in importance because they have to assume most of the role of the non-sound elements. In writing, specifically, the verbal elements, as opposed to the non-verbal, are almost exclusively used, with stress and intonation only partially represented by punctuation. Whereas for the pre-school child successful acquisition of language involves learning to use all the sound and non-sound elements, for the older child in school success requires expertise in only some of these elements. The importance of each element varies according to the nature of the situation or the expectations of society, and usually lack of expertise in one area will cause a compensatory dependence on another. In cases where the society's expectations are fairly rigid, severe negative consequences are the result of lack of expertise. For example, a lower-working-class child going into an unfamiliar secondary school may be categorised by the teachers as unintelligent, not because the child does not demonstrate adequate verbal skills but because he does not 'look bright' or is awkward. The disastrous effects of such an early categorisation by teachers on the subsequent academic performance is well documented in studies on teachers' expectations. It is nowhere better illustrated than in Britain where many immigrant children and also black children born in Britain have been characterised as 'educationally sub-normal' because they did not behave according to the society's expectations.

Use of parts of the body in communication

Parts of the body, as a paralinguistic element of rendering meaning, are involved only in face-to-face communication, but situational context – a term which is very general in reference – is a part of all communication. It is quite clear that the more shared knowledge there is between participants in communication – that is, the better they know each other – the more they will depend on context and the less on overt verbal precision. It is equally true that the more general and distant the communication, the greater is the dependence on verbal skills. The extent to which parts of the body are used to precede, accompany, follow, supplement and replace actual verbal communication varies from society to society. Even though societies like those in the West Indies may generally be described as demonstrative, in certain contexts within the society the use of some body parts is discouraged, while the use of others is encouraged.

The parts of the body which are prominent in the rendering of meaning are the hands, arms, shoulders, the eyes, eyebrows, eyelids, the mouth and lower jaw and the head as a whole. The use of the hands, arms or shoulders is discouraged where polite and sophisticated behaviour is required, so that pointing (especially at people) in public and shrugging of shoulders are disapproved of by middle-class parents. In the classroom situation in the West Indies, proper posture has traditionally been stressed and the use of hands and arms discouraged as supplements or replacements for speech. In the case of the head, nodding and shaking of the head are not disapproved of generally in the society, but in child-adult interaction and in the classroom situation as replacements for speech they are discouraged.

The eyes and area surrounding are the most sensitive parts of the body used in face-to-face communications since they can quite easily reflect or mask the intentions and knowledge of the speaker. For example, not looking the teacher in the eye may be interpreted as an evasive tactic, a lack of interest, lack of intelligence or plain ignorance. Quite often children are deemed to be 'not trying' because they do not consistently look at the teacher with knitted brows or look where the teacher instructs them to. Occasionally this has regrettable consequences, as is evidenced by the case of a child who was severely and repeatedly beaten by a teacher for not looking at the book while another child was reading. In actual fact, the child was looking at the book, but was cross-eyed, a condition the teacher was unaware of and in his zeal for compliance did not suspect.

On the other hand, to look straight into a person's eyes, if that person is socially superior or (in the case of a child) an adult, can be interpreted as a show of insubordination. In other words, a social inferior or suppliant is supposed to be 'cap-in-hand' with 'head bowed' and 'eyes lowered'. There is also a clear difference between middle-class and lower-class behaviour in child-adult interaction, which has consequences in the classroom. In the lower class specifically, the child is treated as an inferior and so is not supposed to look the adult in the eye. When the lower-class child goes to school into a situation which is more authoritarian in nature, in order to succeed the child has to learn when, and when not, to look the teacher in the eye. Teachers very often castigate, compliment, reject and accept the responses and lack of responses according to the non-sound elements of rendering meaning used by their pupils. In more recent times, it is evident that the school is assigning an increasing role to the correct use and exploitation of the visual elements of communication to match the growing role of television in modern technological societies.

Use of intonation and 'accents' in communication

The learning of significant intonation and stress patterns, after the early acquisition of basic patterns, depends outside the classroom on peer group patterns and in the classroom on the models for reading and spelling presented to the child. Traditional reading exercises in the classroom have been dominated by correct and careful enunciation rather than natural flow and intonation of material. The school has tended to cultivate a stilted and unnatural reading style in which words are broken down into syllables and given a spelling pronunciation (e.g. *often* read as [of-ten] rather than as [of-n]). This style is reinforced by repetitions and drills produced by the class in unison and for older children in the reading of plays from earlier. periods performed in accordance with the tone and structure of the English in which the plays are written. At the same time constant negative correction by teachers encourages in pupils a strategy which soon becomes pervasive: namely, change whatever is natural because most likely it is wrong.

In the general society where intonation and stress patterns vary greatly in educated speech, foreign speech, varieties of West Indian speech and varieties of local speech, the child seldom has a single strong model to follow that is acceptable as the society's 'best' speech. The variety of social 'accents' in the West Indies and the varying and strong reactions to them make the choice of speech patterns after those of early childhood acquisition a very difficult matter and one full of contradictions, opening the child to accusations from peers of being 'stuck-up' or the opposite, from adults and parents of feeling oneself better than one's family, or of having no ambition, or on the other hand of being a good example or of being well-spoken and 'bright'.

Choice therefore becomes a personal and sensitive matter in which the individual's speech always seems to be a compromise.

Since the school concerns itself with clear articulation, reading style, recitation of poetry and dramatic presentations – all as academic pursuits in which the pronunciation patterns do not blend happily into normal West Indian speech – development of intonation and stress patterns for the educated West Indian is not a gradual filling-out of a homogeneous system but an increase in repertoire with a varying mastery in most cases of the later acquired patterns and a selective and contrastive use of these patterns.

Development of words and meanings in communication

Vocabulary development, embracing in the narrowest sense words, syllables and sounds, follows a fairly precise path. The young child initially associates a sound (e.g. [bus]) with one specific entity or action, then as a first stage of abstraction associates the name with all similar actions or entities. At the first stage of abstraction the child's idea of the meaning is vague and suffers from over-inclusion, e.g. the sound [bus] may refer to all vehicles or all moving things of a certain size. Progressively, however, the meaning becomes clearer in the child's mind. Early over-specification – that is, too narrow a definition of an entity or action – may persist for a long period in the child's mind, especially with words which are not actively used.

From the very start, development in vocabulary is dependent not on simple numerical growth of items but on the awareness of the abstract relationships of composition, complementarity, contrast and deixis. Composition deals with the relationship of part to whole and consequently the notions of unity, order and number (singular: plural). Complementarity is a relationship in which one thing implies another, e.g. *parent : child*; *husband : wife*; *aunt/uncle : nephew/niece*. Contrasts refer to opposites generally, e.g. *young : old*, and also includes gender opposites, e.g. *father : mother*; *cow : bull*. Deixis is illustrated by words such as *I : you*; *here : there*; *now : then* whose meaning is identified according to speaker, place and time, all of which constantly vary. Development in vocabulary therefore follows inquiringly and naturally along the paths of these relationships, bringing to life more and more words in the mind of the individual.

Further development of vocabulary in the individual is dependent on actual experience, but the interrelationship between abstraction and specificity remains as basic. Abstraction refers to cases where a word represents a class of object or a generalisation of process rather than a single specific object or process. Specificity is the opposite. In standard

English abstractness is in many cases rendered by suffixes (e.g. *-ity, -ness, -cy, -ment*) to root words (e.g. *pure, abstract, normal, develop*), and specificity by borrowing of roots from classical languages and converting them into synthetic units (e.g. *telephone, atom, isotope*). In West Indian non-standard English, abstractness, when it is rendered without simply adopting standard English words, is dependent on basic words and involves the following:

i   The use of the concrete for the abstract. For example, in the saying *greedy kill puppy*, the adjective *greedy* is used for the more abstract noun *greed*, and *puppy* for the more abstract *youth*.

ii Constructions with basic root words (e.g. *hard ears, big eye*).

The meanings of terms can be narrowed down and made more specific, as is the case also in standard English, by qualifiers and modifiers (e.g. *neck back, yard fowl*). When abstractness and specificity are looked at directly in word formation, in order to master them the West Indian child has to shift from a basic and analytical type of structure to a synthetic structure, the meaning of which is not self-evident.

In contrast to the above, in some areas of the vocabulary there are no major structural contrasts between standard English and West Indian non-standard English. In both, prepositions and prepositional constructions, for example, are used according to the level of specificity required in the context. However, in standard English one can distinguish between the hardworking simple prepositions (*in, on, by, from*, etc.) whose meaning is aided by contextual clues, and the less frequently used prepositions and prepositional constructions (e.g. *underneath, in spite of, despite, with regard to*) which occur in more educated usage.

Development of non-basic vocabulary depends on your experience. If in your experience as a social inferior or as a child you are seldom required to articulate your points carefully because hearers are always ready to interpret whatever you say, then it limits your active vocabulary. To change this is a radical and difficult step in a situation where the communicative context shows no change. In other words, if a pupil thinks that he will be understood, without being expressly told or convinced that 'the onus is on you to make yourself clear, not on the hearer to decipher what you say' in a situation where

– the opposite has always been true,
– where there is little change in situation,
– he is convinced either that the hearer understands him or that the hearer will come to his own conclusion in any case, or both,

the degree of compliance will be low. Failure to appreciate this problem provokes the traditional charge of 'laziness' levelled at children by teachers. In other words, the habits and expectations of the general society do not disappear and cannot be summarily dismissed in the classroom learning context.

From a psychological point of view, the West Indian preference for word formation using basic words rests on the need for direct, clear and overtly ambiguous communication. Transparency in West Indian speech clearly does not mean communication with a single level of interpretation, and ambiguity, figurative and creative use of language have been clearly illustrated in the previous chapter. However, ambiguity and metaphorical language are clearly indicated to the hearer either by the form, a formula, the context or nature of the language. For instance, even if a riddle is not introduced by a formula, the form of it, the question at the end and curiosity awakened by a puzzle lead the hearer to search for hidden meaning. The same is true of the proverb, whether or not the hearer interprets correctly. The calypso by context, form and history is sung to an audience expecting allusion to sex, scandal or some other emotionally provocative area. Figurative language that is produced with such subtlety that only a few realise there are hidden meanings and successfully interpret them would in fact be functionally ineffective.

Understanding the speech of the educated

Levels of interpretation in educated language have all degrees of subtlety and are not necessarily marked contextually or formally. In addition, the allusions may be cerebral, academic, non-salacious and non-sensuous. They may also be allusions from different cultures and different historical periods, using unfamiliar imagery. Getting acquainted with such unclear and unappealing use of language will not always be stimulating or satisfying. Unlike oral literature where marking has to be clear because language is impermanent, written literature is less obvious in order to provoke reflection, re-reading and further discovery. It is perhaps well-intentioned but misguided to adapt all materials to suit West Indian children. To make material culturally relevant, clearer and more immediate is reasonable as a first step, but its danger is that it may be doing no more than reinforcing limiting cultural habits. It is equally or more important to get the child to understand the requirements of written literature. In other words, learning to read involves acquiring patience to concentrate, the habit of actively looking for hidden meanings and retracing one's steps to find anything missed in the first attempt. Children cannot be tricked into reading, because their whole experience of learning to spell words, learning to use them in sentences and understanding their different meanings is a practical and ever-present testimony of its difficulty.

Formal language learning is generally thought to have as its aim the mastery of the correct forms and meanings of words, clauses and sentences. However, much of the social decorum that is learnt after early language acquisition necessitates language use for the purpose of dissembling. The naivety or directness of the child, which is often the cause of embarrassment, is seen as inappropriate and has to be replaced by correct social language behaviour. At the same time, in a social situation arising out of slavery and domination, the dominated have to learn early on the art of dissembling. Part of the problem of measuring development in West Indian children is assessing the extent of learning of socially sanctioned dissembling; that is, the level of acquisition of socially decorous and appropriate language, as distinct from dissembling by the socially oppressed. The poverty of language of working-class children in formal situations as opposed to volubility and colour of language of the same children in peer group unrestricted situations is well documented. Learning of correct forms and meanings therefore does not guarantee successful use of language, for the strategies of dissembling used by the lower class in dealing with the upper class are not the same as those used by 'educated' upper- and middle-class speakers.

Formal language learning assumes that children have already mastered the pragmatics of language; that is, they know how to make statements and requests, to ask questions, to deny, etc., and that there is a logical relationship between linguistic construction and pragmatic function. There is an assumption, for example, that a question form is a request for information or that a statement is a relating of information, but this is quite far from what obtains in educated speech. The rhetorical question is a favourite method of making a statement in educated speech, and a simple statement may be intended as an order. For example, the statement 'The door is closed', said by one speaker to another, both of whom can see clearly that the door is closed, is effectively a polite version of 'Open the door'. Munby (1978:50–51) gives a list of twenty possible 'verbal realisations for suggestion', some of which are as follows:

May I suggest (that you try) the . . .
If I may make the suggestion, the . . . is popular here
Would you care to try the . . .
Another possibility would be the . . .
I wonder if you fancy . . .
Perhaps the . . . appeals to you

Because the form and appropriateness of such educated rhetoric is not formally taught, the pupil may end up like the learner of Spanish (or any other foreign language) who goes to a country where the language is native and finds out that his own speech is correct but not real.

There is no question that all normal individuals learn to make statements, to deny, to request, to command, to curse and that West

Indians are familiar with the rhetoric of educated English, whether or not for psychological reasons or as a result of peer group pressure they come to use it extensively. In any case, it is clear that there is a difference between general communicative ability in a direct face-to-face situation and purely verbal competence in the restricted contexts of writing and speech in the classroom. The difference is fostered by the assumption that learning is meant to proceed from the acquisition of fundamentals (i.e. correct forms and structures) to facility in manipulating social and educated language. The former is regarded as the business of the classroom and the latter as the individual's own business.

Of the average sixteen hours that an individual is awake, less than one-third is spent, in the case of a child, in the classroom. It is evident then that although the classroom provides training and guidance, the peer group and family, because of their nature and because of the time factor, are much greater influences on language learning and use. To measure language learning as if it were a purely classroom activity dealing with forms and meanings is analogous to identifying the size of an iceberg as what you see above the surface. A better representation of the proportionate influence of the classroom in language learning is given in Fig. 7.2. The social, the psychological, the pragmatic and the element of time make classroom learning a square peg in a round hole.

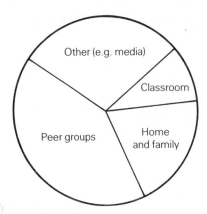

Fig. 7.2   Influences in language learning.

The relationship between the standard and non-standard in communication

A most vexatious point in discussions about language learning is the influence of the non-standard on the standard. To achieve better understanding of the possible effect, the role of classroom learning as a part of general learning must be kept in correct perspective. First of all, the successful acquisition of standard English is virtually inseparable, under normal circumstances, from availability of opportunity for appropriate use in actual real-life situations – standard English is not learnt in a vacuum or simply in the classroom. Secondly, the native competence of an individual normally changes in accordance with his active social usage – active and extensive use of educated speech causes modifications in the individual's non-standard speech as a result of loss of practice in the latter. Notice that concomitant changes of this kind also occur when St Lucians and Dominicans today – as was the case with Grenadians and Trinidadians earlier – change from (non-standard) French Creole to non-standard English. Such changes therefore are not restricted to upward social change but are typical of horizontal social change.

Thirdly, native language or dialect remains actively or passively a part of the individual for life – elements of the native language (the actual language learnt as a child) remain inextricably tied to the thought process, the constant verbal activity of the brain. It should be quite clear therefore that perfect mastery of standard English through deliberate instruction only is impossible, because the native language can never be completely shifted to one side, but surfaces periodically in a contrastive way in the production of standard English.

Fourthly, since in West Indian English standard and non-standard items are not necessarily always in contrast but in many ways complement each other, not only is the distinction between the two often vague, but the non-standard is not easily, effectively, expressively or satisfactorily replaced in the mind of the West Indian. For example, a known non-standard word such as *juck/jook* is not satisfactorily replaced. In the speech of educated West Indians talking among themselves, standard and non-standard occur together integrally as discourse contrasts in style. Consider the very simple illustration

The letter came yesterday.
You joking!
No. I'm serious.

The absence of *are* (or a shortened version) in the second line is not stigmatised and hardly noticed by educated West Indians. Consistent and unnoticed use of non-standard items by teachers in the classroom situation is quite normal, not because the teacher has lapses of concentration or is ignorant of 'correct' English, but because such items form an integral part of West Indian discourse in formal settings. Deliberate interjection of non-standard English is also a part of the repertoire of skilful and learned West Indian speakers when they want to make a point more graphically. To remove or replace this part of an educated West Indian's style range is to make him a less influential and competent speaker.

Failure of earlier attempts to eradicate non-standard English are easily explained by the fact that non-standard English is native and so virtually unremovable and by the fact that non-standard English is a part of educated speech, part of the model presented in the classroom. However, there has to be, from a formal pedagogical point of view, a dividing line between non-stigmatised Creole English and acceptable West Indian English, one that is determined by conscious rather than unconscious acceptance. Divergences from the basic grammatical structure of English (e.g. absence of auxiliary) cannot be accepted as standard West Indian literate English, even though they are unconsciously accepted in discourse in a formal context. Divergences in idiom and meanings (e.g. *tea*) can be accepted, for standard West Indian literate English is meant to be that variety of English acceptable to West Indians as the medium of expression in literary works, newspapers, magazines and other writings in which there is an assumption that educated usage is intended.

To claim that standard West Indian English is nebulous is little different from claiming that standard English is nebulous. When a West Indian teacher falls back on a British or American dictionary or grammar book to resolve the language problems of his pupils, he is both putting his pupils at an unnecessary disadvantage and refusing to use his own training and judgement. The uniformity which characterises the teaching of basic grammatical structures leads many people to believe that literate English in its totality is uniform and solely concerned with spelling, agreements in tense and between subject and verb. These, on the contrary, were always meant to be the base on which literate English flourished, evolved and diversified. Literate English, West Indian or other, is not something written in a bible to be constantly consulted to see whether actual usage conforms or not. Newspaper journalists in the West Indies, in this respect, must be credited with having creatively developed their own West Indian journalese to satisfy their public.

Deductive and inductive procedures in teaching language

Today, both basic grammar and creative writing are seen as important in teaching English, but time is spent on basic grammar because it is an impediment to the progress of many. Theory and practice of the teaching of basic grammar have evolved over the years, spurred on by unsatisfactory achievement in examinations and by research work. There are two fundamental procedures in teaching languages, the one a reverse of the other – one is called inductive, the other deductive. The deductive method is to teach a principle or rule first and follow it with practice in examples. The inductive method is to present examples (sentences of the language) from which a principle or rule later emerges.

Older tradition promoted the deductive procedure, but misused it by treating rule learning as an end in itself, as if the transition from rule to correct language was automatic. Pupils knew the rules (e.g. the verb must agree in number with the subject; *i* before *e* except after *c*), but the habitual implementation of them was not achieved. As a result many educators expressed dissatisfaction with the deductive method. For example, Cecil Gray, writing in 1971, says:

> 'Unless we put correct and automatic responses as our first aim, and analysis after, we will continue to plod the way of frustration and wastage. If we admit, however, that it is more important for our pupils to be right than to know about being right, then we should be prepared to consider a change of approach since there are so many complaints about the results of the old one.'

Methods have changed, but results do not show improvement. Failure results from factors which are in part specifically West Indian and in part germane to the learning process. West Indian children find the repetition of standard English sentences pointless because they do not understand what they are supposed to be learning since they believe they already know the sentences they are repeating. Even in genuine foreign language learning, imitation and repetition are less than successful unless the pupil believes he is learning something new, something that could really be useful were the occasion to arise. In addition, imitation and repetition are extremely boring and require extraordinary motivation when prolonged over twenty or thirty minutes and over a certain number of days.

Learning proceeds better when the learner perceives principles. Language learning research shows quite clearly that learners, children and adults, employ strategies for learning. In normal first-language learning, the appearance of forms such as *cutted* used as a past form and *mans* as a plural testifies to the perception of a rule and the use of analogy in learning.

The relative importance of rule and practice in language learning cannot be definitely determined. It is more important to realise that they are two sides of the same coin and that the learning process needs both for success. It is also important to realise that language learning has to be directly related to social reality and language function. Many West Indians who have achieved a high level of competence in English and who have witnessed changes in teaching methods have come to the conclusion that learning takes place in spite of method used, especially if there is a high level of motivation. However, since motivation is idiosyncratic and public schooling is today universalist in intent, teaching policy has to place emphasis on methods and procedures instead of relying in a crucial way on the motivation of the learner.

Problem areas for the West Indian learning English

One of the greatest frustrations in teaching English is that the problem areas are well known and have become so dominant and persistent that they dwarf whatever other achievements are made, so that English teaching has become synonymous with identifying and correcting grammatical mistakes. The elevated importance of grammar and the problem areas therein generally constitute the major day-to-day task of today's English teacher in the West Indies.

The major areas of difficulty in English grammar for the West Indian are as follows:

i   Use and forms of the verbs *be, have* and *do* as verbs as well as auxiliary verbs.
ii   Subject-verb concord.
iii Inflections in verbs, nouns and pronouns.
iv   Negation.
v   Use of prepositions.
vi   Use of subordinating conjunctions.
vii Differences between *there, they* (and *their*).
viii Mazes.
ix   Pronunciation- and structure-influenced spelling.

These areas are problematic generally and not only for West Indians. West Indians, however, have special problems arising out of their own non-standard English and the effect it has on perception of words, their spelling and function. For instance, (vii) presents problems for learners. It requires discrimination between at least three different structures, because some West Indians pronounce *there* and *they* almost identically, because the *there is/are* construction is not the preferred one, and because [də] at the head of the sentence in some constructions in non-standard West Indian English has a vague and indefinite reference, thus relating to both *they* and *there*, e.g.

də kill im	'they (someone) killed him'
də have a man	'there is a man'

The problem of discriminating between *they* and *there* is therefore greatly increased. Note that this is not a difficulty that can be remedied by imitation and repetition alone.

The difficulty with '-ed' forms used as past participles or in adjectival constructions is also directly related to non-standard West Indian

English. The general absence of emphasis in structure and vocal articulation of this suffix in non-standard West Indian English results in passive as well as active error, the former being a carry-over from non-standard, the latter being hypercorrection. Examples of the latter are as follows:

I agree that the educated should use*d* standard English
One must also realise*d* that in St Lucia one must be able . . .
. . . or people might be planning to victimise*d* him
In this state it is easy to overlook*ed* the possibility

Prepositional use is an iceberg or underlying problem rather than an easily spotted red-ink type of problem, and it is one that affects choice of structure. If part of prepositional usage is divided into locative (place), instrumental, and dative (indirect object or recipient), it is in the locative that one sees most clearly that the use of the preposition is not compulsory, as it is in standard English, but is left out when 'the place' itself is being highlighted and the word order is changed. Note the following examples:

He gone in/to town	→	*Is town he gone*
He living in Belmont now	→	*Is Belmont he living now*
He get it from out of there	→	*Is out of there he get it*

Although initially these sentences do not seem to produce problems in written exercises, one soon realises that this is because the type of sentence shown in the second column does not usually occur in written exercises. This, however, is a case of eliminating without replacement – the contrast in speech, which shows exactly what the speaker is focusing on, is not paralleled in writing.

In the case of instrumental and dative prepositional usage there is a relationship between non-use of these structures, preference for verb-oriented sentences, and the use of short simple sentences joined by *and*. Compare

He take a stick and hit the dog
with
He hit the dog with a stick

and compare

He bring it and give me
with
He brought it for me

Close examination of usage shows that although both types of structure occur in non-standard West Indian English, the more the context is one of action and narration of events, the more the simple *verb* + *and* + *verb* structure occurs. In addition, it is heavily reinforced by teaching practice, which unavoidably introduces the very simple sentence first and uses it extensively as a basis for illustrating noun-verb concord.

The preference for simple sentences joined by *and* and other co-ordinating conjunctions is therefore not a matter of childish segmentation but one that arises out of oral, non-standard preferences. In addition, when attempts are made to counterbalance this, it is oral literature, specifically ornate English, which leads to the preference for the less obvious, less hardworking subordinating conjunctions of English together with other decorative words and unnecessary punctuation marks. Errors therefore may be direct or they may result from strategies of avoidance and compensation, in which case seemingly different problem areas stem from the same source.

The many factors involved in learning and the rendering of meaning, in non-standard and oral West Indian English, and in the problem areas of standard English, mean that the teacher of English in the West Indies must be aware of the following:

i   Native language does not disappear completely.

ii   Native speaker competence in standard English is not achieved by formal instruction alone.

iii   Language is social and functional.

iv   Standard English and non-standard English often utilise different strategies for rendering meaning.

v   Inductive and deductive methods are both required in teaching and learning.

vi   What are the indicators of learning and achievement in the case of language learning.

vii Analogy, hypercorrection, avoidance and compensation are fundamental elements of language learning.

viii Ambivalence and ambiguity form an integral part of the West Indian social system.

ix   Most learners, after the first steps of primary level, are quite convinced that they already know what they are being taught.

x   The structures of standard English are psychologically unreal or unsatisfactory for some learners.

xi   Ornate English is greatly admired.

Practical aims and objectives in English language teaching

Realistic objectives in teaching standard English in the West Indies have to take all the points listed above into account. This does not imply that the target itself should be limited, but that the teacher should encourage self-attainment just as actively as he pursues instruction in the facts of language. Dennis Craig, writing in 1976, sums up the objectives and attainment as follows:

> '... on the way towards achievement of proficiency, many compromises are inevitable: some learners might persist in retaining certain of their original speech characteristics in the most nearly Standard language they learn to produce, others might achieve good native proficiency in reading and writing the Standard language but at the same time persist in their original non-standard speech even on the most formal occasions, and so on. It does not seem that bidialectal education ought to expect more than this.'

Recognition of the social and psychological conflicts in learning standard English is not equivalent to resolution of these conflicts. One may ask though whether it is practicable or even morally right to attempt to resolve conflicts which have become an integral part of the learner's make-up. It can be argued, for instance, that ambivalence and ambiguity are good strategies for survival if you are an underdog. One can answer this by saying that in giving the individual additional skills, the individual has more options and so is better equipped not just for survival or maintenance but also for progress. Standard English has to be viewed as a useful instrument, giving access to internal and external communication, to information, technology, artistic and spiritual expression.

In spite of the lack of clear separation between standard and non-standard English in the West Indies, a model for teaching (and learning) has to make quite clear the differences between native dialect and target dialect. The initial concern must be a knowledge of the linguistic facts of native and target; then the identification of learning strategies used to move from one to the other and the results of these strategies; then an appreciation of successful or partially successful achievements; and finally the encouragement of different techniques for dealing with varying degrees of success and failure.

The objectives of a model for teaching and learning standard English in the West Indies may be summarised as follows:

i   The exposure of the learner to all (or as many as possible) of the strategies/devices of the standard.
ii The achievement of proficiency in the standard for effective communication.
iii An analytical knowledge of the native dialect/language and the social and linguistic interaction between this and the standard.
iv The resolution of psychological conflicts created by language awareness.

Few educators in the West Indies would agree with Jack Richards who, writing in 1978 about ex-British colonial society in the Eastern world, says:

> 'The goals of English teaching in such settings is not to improve

proficiency or to eradicate errors, but to develop fluency in the
different lectal norms of the community according to rules for their
sociolinguistic appropriateness.'

What Richards' suggestion does show, however, is that models vary
from place to place and that each country and region has to work out
its own objectives rather than adopt models from elsewhere or depend
on some putative universal model. Of course a proposed model must
be informed by general theory and practice.

A model for English language teaching

There is a degree of variability in language teaching simply because the
four factors involved – the learners, the teacher, the materials and the
context – can all vary. Paradoxically, language teaching is seen as and
to a great extent has to be a well-structured and prescribed operation
with clear-cut, detailed goals. This kind of contradiction is unavoidable
in choice of model and syllabus construction because of the demands
of time, space and money on teacher and learner. The model is more
complicated in the case of the West Indies because whereas models
elsewhere are identified, developed and used either for foreign
language learning or native language learning, here it embraces in two
ways elements of both. Firstly, as stated in objective (iii) on p. 188,
there must be analytical knowledge of the native language, and
secondly, standard English for most West Indians is neither foreign nor
native.

The objectives and syllabus in the learning of a foreign language are
different from those for native language. Simply put, the difference
between the two is that in the latter you are learning about a language
and in the former you are learning a language. One of the implications
of this is that the pedagogic grammar for native language is
preoccupied with structures and forms because the relationship
between form and meaning is implicit. On the other hand, in
pedagogic grammars for foreign language learners the relationship
between form and meaning must be explicit. In other words, the
learner always has to establish a logical link between foreign noises
and familiar meanings. The history and practice of English language
teaching in the West Indies of course evolved from an imported British
native language model into many different paths because of differences
in public and private as well as religious and secular education.

In the kind of situation which obtains in Trinidad and Tobago –
public and private education, church and state control of schools,
different racial groupings, varying attitudes to languages/dialects other
than standard English – policy and practice remain far apart. The
Carrington-Borely Project in Trinidad noted, among other things, a

wide variety of textbooks and some incompetence among teachers in the Language Arts programme in schools in Trinidad and Tobago. The situation in Guyana, a country of similar ethnic and religious composition, geographically bigger and more disparate, is equally variable, although the Government has a tighter control over policy.

The cosmopolitan nature of the socieites in Trinidad and Guyana is not characteristic of all the territories, but the differences between the territories, for example between Jamaica, St Lucia and Barbados, necessitates in most cases different techniques in each territory. Our intention here is neither to specify a model for all territories nor a model for each territory, but to comment on and suggest techniques within a broad framework, which does not in a detailed manner specifically address the problems of St Lucia and Dominica where both bidialectal and bilingual models are required.

Teaching of West Indian children should proceed with the following immediate aims: encouragement, intelligibility, appropriate formal correctness – in that order. This is partially explained by Walter Edwards (1978:56) in the following proposals:

> '1. Allowing free discussion in class of topics of interest to the students and allowing pupils to use their natural speech behaviour without inhibition
>
> 2. The use of language output from these discussions "as a basis of systematic quasi-foreign language practice" involving substitution and transformational practices, controlled dialogue and dramas where only standard language is used.'

Psychology and actual practice clearly indicate that early and consistent attack on (correction of) the language forms of the child in an already authoritarian situation causes children to adopt defensive and negative tactics to escape from the teacher and from learning. In other words, many children are stopped cold right at the start without ever really recovering. There can be little argument then with the idea that the child must be encouraged to proceed confidently, after which restricting guidance can take place. Preoccupation with correction is infinitely simpler and so more popular among teachers than inspiring confidence and giving guidance. Preoccupation with correction also quickly leads to a loss of perspective of the aims of teaching. It is well known that teaching of the early steps of English so concerns itself with correctness of pronunciation, spelling and concord that little attention is paid to comprehension, except as a separate, specific exercise.

Although standard English is not a foreign language in the West Indies and the teaching of meaning need not be explicit in all cases, written words and sentences must be related to natural language, principally by giving them the right intonation, to make them intelligible. In the same way the child is taught to move from writing individual symbols to cursive handwriting, the child has to be taught to move from word-calling to 'cursive' or meaningful reading – it will not happen automatically as is assumed by many. In addition, there are many cases when the meaning of standard English must be explicitly made clear. The same perception of difference which causes teachers to insist on a difference between *can* and *may* should also lead them to explain the difference between standard and non-standard *does*, *did*, *had* and to explain how *have* is used in standard English.

When, with encouragement, intelligibility has begun to be realised, correctness must be pursued within reason. A student whose work is covered from top to bottom in red ink knows at once that the form of his writing is bad, but gets no sign of the validity of his thoughts. Some years ago 'contrastive analysis' was popular as a basis for teaching languages, and it supported the apparently logical tendency to concentrate on difference and especially areas of constant error. This procedure, however, instead of leading to positive and effective use of all the strategies of the language, encourages the negative strategy of avoidance or the sterile love of correctness. Correctness is ostensibly demanded by the wider society as a symbolic standard, but effective usage is a much better guarantee of success.

A good syllabus is based on a proper selection, presentation and gradation of materials. Gradation is for the most part a response to normal maturation or in other words increase in difficulty corresponding to increase in age. Maturation itself is cognitive (thinking processes and the brain), psychological and social in nature. The stages and limits of learning and attention-span are not agreed on by all psychologists, neither are those of language learning (which is regarded as a special kind of learning) by psycholinguists. Tradition, experience and the need to deal with average rather than special learners have shaped gradation in the school syllabus. Gradation is also acceptance of the belief in movement from simple to complex or in other words the notion of building blocks – from unit to composite (e.g. *will eat* is regarded as simpler than and presented before *will have eaten*).

Socially adapted, rather than cognitively based, patterns of language behaviour illustrate differences and gradation between upper- and middle-class children on the one hand and lower-class children on the other. Poor children living in close quarters with adults become familiar from very early with the language of sex, obscenity and adult business, which very often startles young female teachers from a middle-class, protected upbringing who are put to teach these children. The naive preoccupations of middle-class children and the traditionally innocent school language does not appeal to these children and causes them to lose interest very easily. Children who are forced to operate in the immediacy and reality of the adult world show less patience in and understanding of the classroom situation, which is a restrictive and protracted preparation for the adult world in which paradoxically they already find themselves. Materials and language presented to West Indian children therefore have to relate to normal human development as well as to varying experiences of children from different social classes.

Exercises used in teaching and their effectiveness

Over the years a number of types of presentation have become traditional in the teaching/learning situation. Most textbooks contain a variety of types in order to maintain interest and to illustrate reality. Although no one type is eminently superior to all others, there is no doubt that each type has its own level of effectiveness and provokes different skills in learners. The primary and secondary levels of education are structured on the belief that learning is best achieved by practice in the classroom. At university level, on the contrary, except in the case of foreign language learning and some other disciplines, learning is regarded as the understanding of principles primarily and so greater emphasis is put on listening in the classroom.

Practice is realised in exercises, which can be either written or oral in nature or both, as is the case especially in early language learning when sound is being related to writing. Table 7.1 sets out the major exercises used in language, their nature and effect. Each exercise identified is manifested in different ways. For instance, repetition for a beginner learning the alphabet may be copying the letter A several times; or for any learner it may be repeating after the teacher; or it may be reading aloud, which in some cases is simply oral copying of written material. A transformation exercise may involve simply changing present tense to past tense or it may be more elaborate, e.g. changing a passage of reported speech to direct speech. In addition, exercises overlap and complement each other because ideally they should be invisible in the learning process. Unfortunately, however, an exercise sometimes becomes a hindrance to learning because by its format it runs counter to normal discourse. Take for example the question-answer drill, a suggested format for which is given by Craig (1969:22):

> 'The one essential is that the teacher must, when she is doing a pattern practice, get the pupils to give full statements as replies. If for example, the teacher asks "Where's the book?", she must get back the full answer "It's on the table", instead of the usual "On the table".

Most West Indian teachers would agree with this recommendation, but researchers in discourse analysis point out that this kind of prescription

Table 7.1 Types of presentation and their effectiveness.

Type of exercise	Nature	Effect
Repetition	Passive	Short-term memory Little permanence
Multiple choice	Suggestive	Encourages guessing and other strategies for getting correct answer, without necessarily learning target
Transformation	Mostly suggestive	Familiar classroom types, basic and varying in appeal; usually result in familiarity with isolated targets, but not guaranteeing combined, appropriate or effective use
Completion	Suggestive-creative	
Substitution	Mostly creative	
Expansion	Creative	
Identification (question and answer)	Creative	Natural, but often not interesting; provokes all types of answers, including evasive and ambiguous ones
Summaries	Passive and creative	Encourages re-statement of given material
Controlled conversation (and role-playing)	Creative	Provokes interest, encourages social appropriateness in use
Composition	Creative	The most difficult type, because it is based on the ability to think of ideas and then to translate them into written language

is contrary to the rules of discourse, that it creates a more unreal situation and produces stilted language, both of which militate against successful acquisition. Furthermore, if one of the objectives of learning standard English is proficiency in appropriate speech, then this kind of prescription puts undue emphasis on grammatical well-formedness at the expense of functional language.

In transformation, completion, substitution and expansion exercises the attention of the learner is focused on a specific grammatical point. For example, to teach forms of the verb *to be* a drill of the following type is often used:

I   – here
The girl – here
The boys– here
You   – at home
They   – at the back

Conscientious learners can achieve a high degree of success in this type of substitution when they concentrate on specific points being tested and when they have ample time to do it, but as soon as attention is shifted elsewhere and thinking time is reduced, the rate of error increases. Consequently, in some substitution drills, especially in areas like subject-verb concord, which is not totally strange to learners in the West Indies, the objective is more like that of some foreign language drills; that is, to get the pattern internalised and habitual by constant practice rather than by deliberate and conscious choice. In fact, better drills, based on the one given above, will occasionally focus attention away from the verb and to the adverb (phrase) by making the adverb (phrase) part of the substitution. This can be achieved by using props in the real-life classroom situation to make the substitution of adverbs a challenge to the pupil, who at the same time is required to give the correct verb form in the answer.

Transformation drills have been traditionally used for negation and tense-form practice. In the case of the latter, one of the more popular exercises is changing present tense to past or converting direct speech to reported speech. The concentration on form in this kind of exercise presumes that basic meanings and relationships remain the same and that 'sequence of tenses' is an operation primarily of form. However, there are in this kind of exercise different types of change, some of which involve a modification in the meaning of the verb. Compare the following, for example:

(a) He says that he is coming
(b) He said that he was coming
(c) He said that he is coming

If one deems (c) to be incorrect, one must realise that it is produced as a clarification of the ambiguous (b), seeing that in (b) it is not clear whether the person is or is not still coming. Strict grammaticality is therefore in a trade-off with precision in meaning.

The polite social use of *might, could, should, would* and also the inherent ambiguity of them are not paralleled in their supposed present tense forms *may, can, shall, will* in standard English itself. Any transformation exercise which suggests an automatic replacement in these forms is disregarding meaning and social practices. For West Indian learners specifically, drills which match *does* to *did* and *have* to *had* without regard to the differing meanings of *does* and *did* and also without regard to the general absence of *have* in non-standard West Indian speech and the increased reference of *had*, and lack of parallel between the two pairs in most West Indian territories, are encouraging a frustrating exercise.

Combination drills that are essentially completion drills have been used traditionally for conjunction practice. The learner is called on to provide a logical link between clauses as in

The child broke the toy ... his mother told him not to
The man put on the coat ... it was raining

This kind of drill is effective for young learners, but it develops passive recognition of the linkages rather than encourages active production of them. In some older learners who believe that longer sentences are indicative of erudition, there is a practice of decorating sentences with link words (conjunctions and adverbs) without paying careful attention to the meaning of these words. Words like *whereby, since, but, therefore* occur frequently with little attention paid to the relationship these words establish between following and preceding clauses. Learning of conjunctions from drills in which more than one conjunction is often logical may in itself encourage some negative aspects of verbosity. The drill has no way of guaranteeing cause and effect, sequence or contrast relationship in adjoining clauses. Supplementary exercises dealing with the most common link words in English and presented like vocabulary exercises, comparing and contrasting meanings, help in the correct use of conjunctions.

Designing a syllabus for practical purposes

Selection of areas to be taught in English classes has been historically dominated by the link between language and literature. In earlier centuries in Europe language teaching was incidental to literature teaching and essentially arose out of it. Literature teaching has as its target the aesthetic, moral and spiritual appreciation of language in culture. Within the 20th century, however, language teaching has acquired the additional task of establishing and maintaining communication within and across countries. The earlier goal has affected the later goal in that the prejudices and judgements which aesthetic appreciation requires continued to be applied in the choice of materials and areas selected for teaching the language for communicative purposes. For instance, the notion of a 'sentence' with specified and necessary constituents was shaped by written literature and different styles of it illustrated in the classroom traditionally by selections from famous novelists and other literary figures. Increasingly language teaching today is being disconnected from the influence of literature teaching, and the practice of teaching English for Special Purposes (see p. 197) is becoming more popular, even if still regarded as principally for adults rather than for general primary and secondary teaching.

Selection of areas to be taught in English classes in the West Indies has to be based on linguistic as well as functional criteria: correct and appropriate English. In addition to the already known and discussed features of standard English, which differ from Creole English and which have always been stressed in West Indian classrooms, there are others, especially areas of pronunciation, that can usefully be taught. For instance, since changes in pitch of voice are responsible for distinctions in meaning in some Creole English words, these can form the basis of exercises for learners. Ironically some of these distinctions remain in fairly formal uses of English in the West Indies without any generally predictable reaction to them. For example, the sentence

He is a [mesən] or [bekə]

with either of the two articulations of the last word corresponding to *Mason/Baker* and *mason/baker* respectively, is acceptable at all levels in the West Indies. This non-negative reaction may indeed be helpful in introducing the devices of Creole English into the classroom in a positive way. These pitch distinctions could then lead on to exercises on stress distinction as for example between

(Creole) he does 'come   Standard English   he 'does come
         he did 'come   Standard English   he 'did come

and the corresponding meanings.

There are several other meaningful distinctions between Creole English and standard English in pronunciation which can be worked into exercises to make the learning process more varied and interesting. This is definitely an area that has been underused in English language teaching in the West Indies, principally because of the declamatory and stilted styles favoured by teachers. The importance in native language teaching of intonation has been pointed out by Currie (1973:49) who says:

> 'Points of prominence in language help us identify what Halliday has described as information units . . ., or more informally "message blocks". This organization of messages is not effectively described by syntax, but needs a sensitive intonation system to describe it effectively.'

Preference for certain types of exercises today is being determined by economic rather than academic factors. In the first place, authors and publishers find it more profitable to produce write-in workbooks, because these books can be used only once. So whereas previously a textbook was passed down through many generations without profit to author or publisher, this is not encouraged today. Of course the reasons given for write-in workbooks are stated in functional and academic terms – for example, that the exercises in workbooks are more appealing to the pupil and easier on the teacher. It is not pointed out that they are easier because they require less thought and less initiative – finishing a sentence is much simpler than writing a whole sentence. It is especially in mass exams – those determining movement to and placement in secondary schools, and secondary terminal ones (e.g. Caribbean Examinations Council exams) – in which ease and speed of correction and the need to maintain parity in marking are of the greatest importance, that format becomes crucial. Computer and automatic marking, which are faster and less costly, are possible in the slot-filler format, but virtually impossible when whole sentences and essays are written. It is always tempting therefore to try to keep costs down and also avoid challenges to the judgement of examiners by opting for a format which is predominantly of the slot-filler type.

The choice of exam format of course directly determines what is done in the classroom, since success in teaching is measured by performance in exams. Pupils who are being prepared for general examinations concentrate almost exclusively on the format and content of the prescribed exams, for which nowadays textbooks are specifically written. This relationship between examination and teaching is pointed out by Drayton (1986):

> 'With the "nationalisation" of English and of the school systems a number of English language textbook series have been produced for the Caribbean. Some of these take account of new ideas about the teaching of English to creole speakers but most are written to support an examination syllabus.'

Unfortunately, the skills developed in slot-filler type tests, for example, are not always very useful in university and other post-secondary work which require production and control of whole sentences and paragraphs.

Gradation and presentation are of course inseparable, relating type of exercise not only to level of maturity but also to immediate objective. The movement from encouragement to intelligibility to appropriateness must be exhibited at every level and across levels. Amusement and reward may be good motivators at the early stages of primary education, but are less productive at the later stages of secondary education. The necessity for such change, especially in the context of the West Indies today, is stressed by Pollard (1984:15) who says:

> 'Classroom strategies at the earlier stages of the teaching of English suggest processes which emphasize repetition of the correct English forms within activities that are enjoyable to the child. At the school leaving levels however where the population is more sophisticated and can be motivated towards accurate English expression at least by the prospect of a job which might require it, more obvious and more radical intervention is not only possible but necessary.'

Gradation and presentation also are determined by differences in social and linguistic realities in each territory.

Appropriate English, otherwise referred to as *English for Special Purposes* or the more restricted *Kinds of Writing*, is practical in intent because it looks at the types of language used in the society, contexts to which they correspond, the projected needs of the individual and then selects and concentrates on a restricted number of specific types. The teaching of letter writing as a part of traditional English teaching is an example of this. Current jargon which talks about 'effective communication' is the same as what is here called 'Appropriate English'. The shift to Appropriate English is based on the observation that each discipline, each area develops its own jargon and that with increasing specialisation, learning of jargon will not occur accidentally or incidentally. It is also based on the observation that the notion of 'plain' English for all purposes may be desirable, but in reality is becoming more and more an illusion and cannot be retained as a practicable comprehensive goal.

Some of the practical, everyday uses of English which individuals are expected to understand but which differ in form of English are as follows:

Letters (official and personal; application and other forms)
Newspaper headlines
Newspaper classified advertisements
Advertising (newspaper, radio and television commercials)
Labels (giving names, composition and warnings about products)
Directions (for use and assembly of products; recipes in cooking)
Medical language (from doctors and the news media)
Legal language (laws generally; 'fine print', wills and other documents)
Highway signs, warnings and maps
Weather reports (daily; warnings about the extent of natural disasters)
General (political, economic, social, literary, sports)

In many parts of the world individuals, including very literate adults, forfeit their rights to benefits and relief because of their inability or unwillingness to confront and complete application forms successfully. In the West Indies, in addition to suspicions about the motives of those requiring information and other social and psychological problems, questions on application forms, because they involve words which can be ambiguous, create frustration very easily. For example, a form with the question *Colour* . . . creates a number of problems for most West Indians. The same may occur if the form has the option *Married/Unmarried*. Whereas income tax forms and other such detailed and complex forms may always require unusual competence, there is no question that teaching the skills needed for the completion of common forms and the understanding of official and Civil Service language should form a part of secondary education rather than be left to incidental learning.

Most people quickly realise that newspaper headlines are designed to boost sales of the newspaper and are not always a good reflection of the contents. As such they fall into the category of general advertising. Newspaper headlines, relying as they often do on a play on words, are deliberately provocative or ambiguous, but at times they are difficult to understand because of compressed syntax and so are lost on many readers. Compressed syntax and 'shorthand' conventions are also characteristic of the classified advertisements, but more important in this section is adequate interpretation based on what is actually said and what is not said. On the whole, the relationship between suggestion, ellipsis and actual statement, which is normal in all newspapers, could better be appreciated by inspection and analysis rather than simply by experience.

The relationship between language and other disciplines

Whereas competence in language does not guarantee academic success, it is evident that language failure causes general failure. There are not many, if any, disciplines outside the fine arts in which excellence can be achieved without the medium of language. There are of course a number of practices which can be lucrative (e.g. gambling, stealing, speculation) and need no linguistic skills, but these are outside the ambit of general formal education. The relationship between competence in language and success/failure in other subjects can be demonstrated quite easily be examining materials presented to children in the early years of learning mathematics.

Note firstly the comment made by Phillips (1974):

> 'It was found that pupils who possessed computational skills which were applicable to certain classes of computational exercises were unable to apply them to the same problems stated verbally. For example, a pupil who knew that $11 + 9 = 20$ could not get the following two problems correct:
> 1. Find the sum of 11 and 9
> 2. I had 11 nuts, my mother gave me 9 more. How many do I have now?'

Now consider the following problems taken from *New Capital Arithmetic for the Caribbean, Bk. 2:*

> (a) 'Each day a shopkeeper took a quarter more money than he took the day before. If he took $5 on Monday, how much did he take on Wednesday?' (p. 48 no. 5)
> (b) 'Dick has twice as many marbles as Tom, and Harry has three times as many as Tom. If Tom has 12 marbles, how many have they altogether?' (p. 25 no. 3)

First of all, it is quite evident that if one were to set out these problems – especially (b) – using only numbers, they would be infinitely simpler than they are when stated in words. Part of the function of basic arithmetic in school is to combine calculation with English, obviously because that is the way it occurs in the real world. Secondly, it must be noted that ambiguity can at times deceive some pupils. For example, in (a) the word *quarter* may be interpreted by some pupils as 'twenty-five cents' rather than as 'one-fourth of'; and in

> (c) 'How many glasses holding ½ litre could be filled from a jug which holds 7½ litres?' (*Bond, Second year papers in mathematics for the Caribbean* p. 23 no. 10)

a 'smart aleck' may suggest that the glasses are full and the jug is empty.

Traditionally, in the early years of mathematics pupils are required to use 'statements' to solve problems. In many cases it is the formulation of the statement that gives more trouble than the calculation itself, which means that it is language that is at the root of the difficulty. To produce a good syllogism or sequence of statements out of the information given in a mathematical problem is clearly more an exercise in logic and language than in arithmetic. The relationship between language, symbolism, logic and calculation becomes more intricate as one progresses through algebra, geometry and calculus. It is therefore quite an erroneous belief that mathematics and English are two separate and distinct disciplines. This is not to say that one needs great linguistic skills to calculate well, but that calculation in a vacuum falls short of its objective. Indeed, many a student at the higher levels of secondary school and university has gone through the rigours of 'integration and differentiation' without really understanding how these calculations are used in real-life problems. In addition, many people stand in awe of higher levels of mathematics and physics because they envision them as totally abstract; that is, without a medium or language to link the signs, symbols and numbers to meaning and everyday life.

Language in written literature

In the selection of areas for the English syllabus in schools, from the beginning of the elementary stage to the end of the secondary stage, pride of place has traditionally been given to literature (poetry, short stories, novel, drama). Looked at in a historical perspective, the study of literature was assumed to be so basic and necessary that there was no overt need for its justification. In today's world, however, where business and technology are dominant, literature teachers constantly find themselves having to justify the need for the study of literature. The situation is made even more difficult for them within English teaching itself firstly by attempts to separate language teaching from literature teaching and secondly with the growing emphasis on Appropriate and Effective English at the expense of literature.

The study of written literature as a fundamental and necessary part of school education is based on the belief that understanding human nature and cultural values is indispensable for enlightened existence. Very few, if any, educators would disagree with the notion that the inculcation and preservation of spiritual values is an integral part of basic formal education. They would however disagree about the extent of the role of literature study in achieving this. In a narrower sense the argument is put forward that the introduction to literature at the school level provides the individual with a boundless arena of spiritual and aesthetic pleasure for the rest of his life. The individual is thus able to participate actively or passively in the cultural life of his community or read for his own personal pleasure, but with a keener sense of art and beauty which is captured in the term 'critical appreciation'. Another more global argument put forward is that civilisations are judged by their artistic achievements, so that when one cites Aztec or Ancient Chinese civilisations, it is the artistic and aesthetic elements which dominate. The very word 'civilisation' has strong connotations of culture.

The written word, however, is only one avenue to art and culture; it is only one way of fashioning and preserving the spiritual values of a community. It is neither the most natural nor the most powerful medium, and in the West Indies specifically it is not the most traditional one. The weakness of the written word is that it is passive – it has to be sought after and unravelled; the oral and the visual are more striking and inevitable. Unravelling of the written word requires time, concentration and effort, all of which are at a premium in the modern world. The simple argument therefore is: If there are other more powerful, in some cases more traditional, and less difficult ways of determining the spiritual values and culture of West Indian societies, why is it necessary for children to spend so much time on written literature?

One answer to this argument is that in the teaching of Appropriate and Effective English, because people have always drawn on the techniques of persuasion inherent in the language of written literature, the study of written literature is the most fertile ground for understanding language use. In other words, the traditional categories of literature study – theme, structure/plot, style, content, purpose – are the very same factors that govern Effective English. Therefore, where once literature was an objective in itself, whose appreciation was aided by knowledge of its constituent factors, it can now also be treated as general exemplification of factors which are used in specialised forms of persuasion (i.e. in advertising, labels, newspaper articles, etc.). The use of the 'beautiful' to teach the 'mundane' may seem to some to be a travesty of culture, but it is certainly justified if it raises the level of the mundane. The teaching of literature can then be seen partially as a general preparation for the more specialised uses of the language.

Literature study in the early years of secondary education is an ideal way of encouraging serious reading. Critical reading is a necessary habit for a major part of the population in a country, if it is to develop meaningfully in the areas of life. It is unlikely that serious reading, involving research and inquiry in libraries and other storehouses of information, can be better cultivated for any area of human endeavour than by using literature as the base for the development of the reading habit. A small entrepreneur may decide to set up a business and think that his only concerns are getting money from the bank and producing a reasonable service or product. He will soon find out however that there are other human concerns as well as areas of information needed for success, and that he could have saved himself a lot by reading available relevant material. Mistakes are made because of inadequate research and planning, which in turn result from a lack of appreciation of reading or ignorance of the importance of written information. The ability to read, peruse and assess information with a view to planning at any level is dependent on the early, seemingly unrelated habit of literature study.

Literacy and illiteracy

Although the importance of being able to read and write is generally recognised in the West Indies, it is probably the social importance of this ability that has the greatest impact on individuals. Individuals make use of all kinds of subterfuges to conceal inability to read and write, while on the other hand some who are barely literate triumphantly point out those who try to conceal it, or harbour feelings of superiority over illiterate friends and acquaintances. It is obvious from the history of the West Indies that there is widespread expertise in coping with life, either subsisting or succeeding, in spite of illiteracy. For some individuals, therefore, aside from the shame of being illiterate, there is little disadvantage, and some even have the strong belief that education is not necessary for success. This kind of belief, together with a more genuine ignorance of the benefits of education, causes many parents not to make sure their children attend school or to take the more extreme and unfortunate step of stopping them from going to school.

Of course economic factors at the household level and at the national level determine the extent of literacy in a country, but since these are outside the control of the school and other educational institutions, one has to deal more directly with those factors relating to the teaching-learning situation. Overcrowding in classrooms and inadequate facilities are not going to disappear overnight, but in themselves they do not cause illiteracy – many lowly schools have a relatively good record of scholarship and many better-provided modern facilities seem to be floundering in problems and minimal success. The temptation to blame economic factors for lack of success is a strong one but very often only a convenient scapegoat.

Illiteracy caused by non-attendance of school is a deep-seated, historical, economic and circular problem in the West Indies. Illiteracy, or unsatisfactory level of literacy, in spite of attendance at school, is a teaching-learning problem caused by bad attitudes and policies as well as inadequate teaching and studying techniques. Adult illiteracy, by which individuals are identified as totally illiterate or functionally illiterate, varies from territory to territory. For instance, in St Lucia, Dominica, Grenada and Jamaica, at least 40 percent of the adult population is functionally illiterate, whereas in Barbados the figure is much smaller. Where adult illiteracy is high there is an accompanying dropout rate and absenteeism among school-age children, which itself breeds illiteracy and reduces the percentage of those who go on to higher levels of education and eventually return to primary and secondary schools as teachers. Even in Trinidad and Tobago, where illiteracy and availability of funds are not crippling problems, the educational system is not satisfying itself by producing an adequate number of trained teachers to man all of the schools at all levels. In Grenada not much more than one-third of the secondary school teachers are university-trained, and in Jamaica the majority of primary school teachers still do not have adequate secondary school education. An overall view of the level of teacher education in the West Indies shows that it is unsatisfactory.

In all territories a number of older teachers without formal teacher training but with years of experience have moved into administrative and policymaking positions, where they are confronted by formally trained administrators with varying experience. Such a situation, tailor-made for contention and in-fighting, does little to help in the enunciation and execution of a clear and meaningful school policy. It very often produces a laissez-faire working policy by which an unsatisfactory situation perpetuates itself to the detriment of pupils. Formerly, school policy tacitly relied on high social motivation among teachers as an incentive for success. Nowadays, teachers do not see themselves as any more noble than other workers; they belong to unions and behave as most other workers do in their society. In such a situation of controversy and routine, the teacher has to be a professional in the sense that he or she must go to work every day and effectively carry out school duties without undue pressure. For this to be done, policy, techniques and goals must be clearly stated, generally adhered to and be within the competence of the average teacher. It makes no sense to expect the teacher to perform beyond his competence or inclination. At the same time, and again as in the case with other workers, the teacher must be trained to perform his job in accordance with stated policy and objectives, but in circumstances in which job satisfaction and success will remain for some time nebulous and low for many. Success must be secured by efficiency in the system, and not necessarily by extraordinary staff.

BIBLIOGRAPHY

IRAL = *International Review of Applied Linguistics in Language Teaching*
JAFL = *Journal of American Folk-Lore*
SCL = Society for Caribbean Linguistics

Abrahams, Roger   1970 'Patterns of performance in the British West Indies'
In Whitten, N. and Szwed, J. (eds.) *Afro-American Anthropology* Free Press.
    1975 'Folklore and communication on St Vincent' In Ben-Amos, D. and
Goldstein, K. S. (eds.) *Folklore: Performance and Communication* Mouton.
Abrahams, Roger and Szwed, J.   1983 *After Africa* Yale University Press.
Alexander, L.-A.   1981 *Patois Influence in St Lucian English Speech*
Caribbean Study UWI, Barbados.
Alleyne, M. C.   1961 'Language and Society in St. Lucia' *Caribbean Studies*
1 pp. 1–11.
    1980 *Comparative Afro-American* Karoma.
Allsopp, S. R. R.   1972a 'Some suprasegmental features of Caribbean
English and their relevance in the classroom' Paper presented at
UWI/UNESCO Conference, UWI, Trinidad.
    1972b 'The problem of acceptability in Caribbean creolized English' Paper
presented at UWI/UNESCO Conference, UWI, Trinidad.
    1980 'How does the Creole lexicon expand?' In Valdman, A. and
Highfield, A. (eds.) *Theoretical Orientations in Creole Studies* Academic Press.
Andrews, J. B.   1880 'Ananci stories' *Folklore Record* vol. 3 pt. 1 pp. 53–55.
Bailey, Beryl   1962 'Language studies in the independent university'
Caribbean Quarterly vol. 3 no. 1 pp. 38–42.
    1963 'Teaching of English noun-verb concord in primary schools in
Jamaica' *Caribbean Quarterly* vol. 9 no. 4 pp. 10–14.
    1966 *Jamaican Creole Syntax: a transformational approach* Cambridge
University Press.
    1971 'Can dialect boundaries be defined?' In Hymes, D. H. (ed.) 1971.
Bailey, R. W. and Robinson, J. (eds.)   1973 *Varieties of Present-Day English*
Macmillan, New York.
Barrett, L. E.   1976 *The Sun and the Drum* Sangster, Jamaica.
Bascom, William   1949 'Literary style in Yoruba riddles' *JAFL* 62 pp. 1–16.
Bates, William C.   1896 'Creole folk-lore from Jamaica *JAFL* 9–10
pp. 38–42, 121–128.
Beckwith, Martha   1924 *Jamaica Anansi Stories* American Folklore Society,
Stechert, New York.
    1928 *Jamaica Folk-lore* Memoirs of the American Folklore Society vol. 17,
Stechert, New York.
Beier, U.   1954 'The talking drums of the Yoruba' *African Music Society
Journal* vol. 1 no. 1 pp. 29–31.

1956   'Yoruba vocal music' *African Music Society Journal* vol. 1 no. 3 pp. 23–28.

Bennett, Louise   1966   *Jamaica Labrish* Sangster, Jamaica.

Bickerton, Derek   1972   *Guyanese Speech* Mimeo, Guyana.

Blacking, John   1960   Review of *The Drum and the Hoe* by Harold Courlander in *African Music Society Journal* vol. 2 no. 3 pp. 78–79.

Blackman, Margot   1982   *Bajan Proverbs*, Cedar Press.

Bond, J. M.   1974   *Second year papers in mathematics for the Caribbean*

Borely, C. and Carrington, L. D.   1977   *The Language Arts Syllabus, 1975. Comment and Counter Comment* School of Education, UWI, Trinidad.

Brewster, Paul G.   1976   *Children's Games and Rhymes* Arno, New York.

Brook, G. L.   1963   *English Dialects* Andre Deutsch, London.

Burchfield, R. W. (ed.)   1972   *A Supplement to the Oxford English Dictionary* Oxford University Press, England.

Burrowes, Audrey   1983   'Barbadian Creole: A note on its social history and structure' In Carrington, L. D. (ed.) 1983.

Carr, Andrew T.   1952   'A Rada community in Trinidad *Caribbean Quarterly* vol. 3 no. 1 pp. 36–54.
   1956   'Pierrot grenade' *Caribbean Quarterly* vol. 4 no. 3/4 pp. 281–314.

Carrington, L. D.   1969   'Deviations from Standard English in the speech of primary school English in St. Lucia and Dominica' *IRAL* vol. 7 (3) pp. 165–184.
   (ed.) 1983   *Studies in Caribbean Language* SCL, Trinidad.

Carrington, L. D. and Borely, C.   1969   'An investigation into English language learning problems in Trinidad and Tobago' Project 15.

Cassidy, F. G.   1952   'Language and folklore' *Caribbean Quarterly* vol. 3 no. 1 pp. 4–12.
   1961   *Jamaica Talk* Macmillan, London.
   1980   'The place of Gullah' *American Speech* 55 (1) pp. 3–16.

Cassidy, F. G. and LePage, R.   1967   *Dictionary of Jamaican English*, Cambridge University Press, England.

Christie, Pauline   1983   'In search of the boundaries of Caribbean Creoles' In Carrington, L. D. (ed.) 1983.

Collymore, Frank   1970   *Barbadian Dialect* The Barbados National Trust, Barbados.

Cooper, Vincent   1978   'Aspects of St. Kitts–Nevis tense-aspect semantic feature system' Paper presented at 2nd Biennial Conference of the SCL, Barbados.
   1984   'The St. Kitts Angolares: a closer look at current theories of language development in the Caribbean' Paper presented at the 5th Biennial Conference of the SCL, Jamaica.

Courlander, Harold   1952   'Many islands, much music' *Saturday Review* 18 October 1952 pp. 58–60.

Cox, Edward L.   1984   *Free coloreds in the slave societies of St. Kitts and Grenada* University of Tennessee Press, Knoxville.

Craig, D. R.   1969   *An Experiment in Teaching English* Caribbean University Press.
   1971   'Education and Creole English' In Hymes, D. H. (ed.) 1971.
   1976   'Bidialectal education: creole and standard in the West Indies *Linguistics* 175 pp. 93–134.

Crowley, Daniel J.   1954   'Form and style in a Bahamian folktale' *Caribbean Quarterly* vol. 3 no. 4 pp. 218–234.

Cundall, Frank   1904   'Folklore of the negroes of Jamaica' *Folklore* 15 pp. 87–94, 206–214, 450–456.

Currie, William, B.   1973   *New Directions in Teaching English Language* Longman, London.

Dance, Daryl C.   1985   *Folklore from Contemporary Jamaicans*, University of Tennessee Press, Knoxville.

D'Costa, Jean   1983   'The West Indian novelist and language: a search for a literary medium' In Carrington, L. D. (ed.) 1983.

Drayton, Kathleen   1986   *The most important agent of civilisation, Teaching English in the West Indies, 1838–1986*, Mimeo, UWI, Cave Hill, Barbados.

Edwards, Walter F.   1978   'Linguistic, cultural and social considerations in the preparation of English language teaching programmes in Guyana' Paper presented at the 5th International Congress of Applied Linguistics, Montreal.
1983   'Code selection and shifting in Guyana' *Language in Society* 12 pp. 295–311.

Elder, Jacob D.   1965/73   *Song games from Trinidad and Tobago* Trinidad.

Elphinston, James   1787   *Propriety ascertained in her picture; on Inglish speech and spelling rendered mutual guides* Vol. 2 Jon Walter, Blackfriars.

Evelyn, Veronica   1982   'Varieties of English in Antigua and their usage' Seminar paper, UWI, Barbados.

Farquhar, B.   1974   *A grammar of Antigua Creole* Ph.D dissertation, Cornell University.
1984   'Some observations on the use of Creole in Guadeloupe and Antigua' Paper presented at the 5th Biennial Conference of the SCL, Jamaica.

Finnegan, Ruth   1970   *Oral Literature in Africa* Oxford University Press.

Fisher, L.   1976   'Dropping remarks and the Barbadian audience' *American Ethnologist* vol. 3 no. 2 pp. 227–242.

Fredrickson, T. L. and Wedel, P. F.   1984   *English by Newspaper: How to read and understand an English language newspaper* Newbury House, Rowley, Massachusetts.

Gbeho, Philip   1954   'Music of the Gold Coast' *African Music Society Journal* vol. 1 no. 1 pp. 62–64.

Georges, R. A. and Dundes, A.   1963   'Toward a structural definition of the riddle' *JAFL* 76 pp. 111–118.

Gray, Cecil   1971   'Teaching English in the West Indies' *Caribbean Quarterly* vol. 9 nos. 1, 2 pp. 67–77.

Halliday, M. A. K.   1967   *Intonation and Grammar in British English* Mouton, The Hague.

Hancock, I. F.   1980   'Gullah and Barbadian – origins and relationships' *American Speech* 55 (1) pp. 17–35.

Harries, Lyndon   1971   'The riddle in Africa' *JAFL* 84 pp. 377–393.

Haynes, L.   1978   'Words and meanings in Guyanese classrooms' Paper presented at the 2nd Biennial Conference of the SCL, Barbados.
1984   'The Caribbean short-story in diachronic perspective' Paper presented at the 5th Biennial Conference of the SCL, Jamaica.

Hughes, Alister   1966   'Non-standard English of Grenada *Caribbean Quarterly* vol. 12 no. 4 pp. 47–54.

Hymes, D. H. (ed.)   1971   *Pidginization and creolization of languages* Cambridge University Press, England.

Irish, J. A. G.   1985   *Alliougana Folk* Jagpi, Montserrat.

Isaac, Martha   1982   'Prepositional usage in the written work of St. Lucian students' Seminar paper, UWI, Barbados.

James, Sybil   1972   'Teaching literature in a dialect/standard situation *Caribbean Quarterly* vol. 18 no. 3 pp. 73–76.

Jekyll, Walter   1907   *Jamaica Song and Story* Publication of the Folklore Society, vol. 55.

Johnson, J. H.   1921   'Folk-lore from Antigua, British West Indies' *JAFL* 34 pp. 40–88.

Jourdain, Elodie   1952   'Creole – a folk language' *Caribbean Quarterly* vol. 3 no. 1 pp. 24–30.

Joyce, James   1914–1966   *Ulysses* Vintage (Random House), New York.

Keane, Yvette   1978   'A cross-reference of Vincentian idioms with those of other Anglophone Caribbean territories' Paper presented at the 2nd Biennial Conference of the SCL, Barbados.

Keens-Douglas, Paul   1975   *When Moon Shine* Scope Publishing Caribbean, Trinidad.

Knight, H. E., Carrington, L. and Borely, C.   1974   'Preliminary comments on language arts textbooks in use in the primary schools of Trinidad and Tobago' *Caribbean Journal of Education* vol. 1 no. 2 pp. 24–47.

Laurence, Kemlin   1971   'Trinidad English – "mamaguy" and "picong"' *Caribbean Quarterly* vol. 17 no. 2 pp. 36–39.

Leach, MacEdward   1961   'Jamaican duppy lore' *JAFL* 74 pp. 207–215.

LePage, Robert   1950   'The English language' *Caribbean Quarterly* vol. 2 no. 2 pp. 4–11.

     1951   'A survey of dialects in the British Caribbean' *Caribbean Quarterly* vol. 2 no. 3 pp. 49–50.

     1957–58   'General outlines of Creole English dialects in the British Caribbean' *Orbis* 6 pp. 373–391; 7 pp. 54–64.

     1969   'Dialect in West Indian literature *Journal of Commonwealth Literature* 7 p. 17.

LePage, Robert and DeCamp D. (eds.)   1960   *Creole Language Studies I* Macmillan, London.

     (eds.) 1961 *Creole Language Studies II* Macmillan, London.

LePage, Robert and Tabouret-Keller, A.   1985   *Acts of Identity: Creole-based approaches to language and ethnicity* Cambridge University Press, England.

Lewis, Matthew G.   1834   *Journal of a West Indian planter in Jamaica* John Murray, London.

Lynch, Louis   1964   *The Barbados Book* Andre Deutsch, London.

Marckwardt, Albert   1962   'Applied linguistics' *Caribbean Quarterly* vol. 8 no. 2 pp. 111–120.

Martin, Lelia   1982   *A Description of Kittitian Dialect* Caribbean Study, UWI, Barbados.

Merriam, Alan P.   1956   'Songs of the Ketu cult of Bahia, Brazil' *African Music Society Journal* vol. 1 no. 3 pp. 53–67.

Mieder, Wolfgang and Dundes, Alan (eds.)   1981   *The Wisdom of Many – essays on the proverb* Garland Publishing Inc., New York and London.

Munby, J.   1978   *Communicative Syllabus Design* Cambridge University Press, England.

Murray, J., Bradley, H., Craige, W. and Onions, C. (eds.)   1933   *The Oxford English Dictionary* Oxford University Press, England.

Naipaul, V. S. 1967 *The Mimic Men* Penguin, England.

Newall, Venetia 1978 'Aspects of the folklore of the Jamaican ethnic minority in Britain: a preliminary consideration' In Dorson, Richard M. (ed.) *Folklore in the modern world* Mouton, The Hague pp. 103–108.

Nketia, J. H. 1958 'Traditional music of the Ga people' *African Music Society Journal* vol. 2 no. 1 pp. 21–27.

Northall, G. F. 1892 *English Folk Rhymes* Kegan Paul, Tranch and Trubner.

Ong, Walter J. 1982 *Orality and Literacy* Methuen.

Opie, Iona and Opie, Peter 1959 *The Lore and Language of Schoolchildren* Oxford University Press, England.

Ortiz Oderigo, N. R. 1956 'Negro rhythm in the Americas *African Music Society Journal* vol. 1 no. 3 pp. 65–69.

Parsons, E. C. 1919 'A West Indian tale' *JAFL* 32 pp. 442–443.
    1925 'Barbados folk-lore' *JAFL* 38 pp. 267–292.
    1930 'Ring games and jingles in Barbados' *JAFL* 43 pp. 326–329.
    1933 *Folklore of the Antilles, French and English* Memoirs of the American Folklore Society vol. xxvi part 1.
    1936 Ibid. vol. xxvi part 2.
    1943 Ibid. vol. xxvi part 3.

Pearse, Andrew 1955 'Aspects of change in Caribbean folk music' *Journal of the International Folk Music Council* UNESCO vol. vii pp. 29–36.

Pepicello, W. A. and Green, Thomas A. 1984 *The Language of Riddles* Ohio State University Press, Columbus.

Phillips, W. 1974 'The cognitive processes underlying certain classes of mathematical problems' *Caribbean Journal of Education* no. 1 pp. 66–72.

Piersen, William D. 1971 'An African background for American Negro folktales' *JAFL* 84 pp. 204–214.

Pollard, Velma 1983a 'The social history of dread talk' In Carrington, L. D. (ed.) 1983.
    1983b 'Figurative language in Jamaica Creole' *Carib* 3 pp. 24–36.
    1984 'Word sounds: the language of Rastafari in Barbados and St. Lucia' *Jamaica Journal* vol. 17 no. 1 p. 15.

Ramchand, Kenneth 1970 *The West Indian Novel and its Background* Faber and Faber, London.

Ramdat, Kuntie 1978 'Some areas of Indic influence in the creolized English of East Indians in Guyana' Paper presented at the 2nd Biennial Conference of the SCL, Barbados.

Reaver, J. Russell 1972 'From reality to fantasy: opening and closing formulas in the structure of American tall tales' *Southern Folklore Quarterly* 36 pp. 369–382.

Reisman, L. 1970 'Cultural and linguistic ambiguity in a West Indian village' In Whitten, N. and Szwed, J. (eds.) *Afro-American Anthropology* Free Press, New York.

Richards, Jack 1978 'Models of language use and language learning' In Richards, J. (ed.) *Understanding Second and Foreign Language Learning: Issues and Approaches* Newbury House; Massachusetts.

Richardson, Bonham 1983 *Caribbean Migrants: Environment and human survival on St. Kitts and Nevis* University of Tennessee Press, Knoxville.

Rickford, John R. (ed.) 1978 *A Festival of Guyanese Words* University of Guyana, Georgetown.

Roberts, Helen H. 1926 'Possible survivals of African song in Jamaica' *Musical Quarterly* July 1926.

Rodman, Selden 1952 'Palette under the palms' *Saturday Review* 18 October 1952, pp. 54–56.

Ryan, Patricia 1985 *Macafouchette*, Trinidad.

Selinker, L. 1972 'Interlanguage' *IRAL* vol. x (3) pp. 209–231.

Selvon, Samuel 1957 *The Lonely Londoners* St Martin's Press, New York.

Sharp, S. 1949 'Dialect' *Caribbean Quarterly* vol. 1 no. 2 pp. 16–20.

Sherlock, Philip 1966 *West Indian Folk-tales* Oxford University Press, England.

Shields, Kathryn 1984 'Jamaican Creole or Standard Jamaican English? Teaching Language in the Jamaican Context' *York Papers in Linguistics* II pp. 279–290.

Smith, Pamela C. 1896 'Two Negro stories from Jamaica' *JAFL* 9–10 p. 278.

Springer, H. W. 1953 'On being a West Indian' *Caribbean Quarterly* vol. 3 no. 3 pp. 181–183.

Swanzy, H. L. V. 1949 'Caribbean voices: prolegomena to a West Indian culture' *Caribbean Quarterly* vol. 1 no. 2 pp. 21–28.

Tanna, Laura 1983 'Anansi – Jamaica's trickster hero' *Jamaica Journal* vol. 16 no. 2. pp. 21–30.

Taylor, Archer 1951 *English Riddles from Oral Tradition* University of California Press.

Thieme, Darius L. 1960 'Negro folksong scholarship in the United States' *African Music Society Journal* vol. 2 no. 3 pp. 67–72.

Trowbridge, A. W. 1896 'Negro customs and folk-stories of Jamaica' *JAFL* 9 pp. 279–287.

Turner, L. D. 1949 *Africanisms in the Gullah Dialect* University of Michigan Press, Ann Arbor.

Van Dam, Theodore 1954 'Influence of West African songs of derision in the New World' *African Music Society Journal* vol. 1 no. 1 pp. 53–56.

Wake, C. Staniland 1883 'Ananci stories' *Folklore Journal* vol. 1 pp. 280–292.

Warner, Maureen 1971 'Trinidad Yoruba – Notes on survivals' *Caribbean Quarterly* vol. 17 no. 2 pp. 40–49.

Wells, John 1982 *Accents of English 3: Beyond the British Isles* Cambridge University Press.
       1983 'The Irish element in Montserrat Creole' In Carrington, L. D. (ed.) 1983.

Werner, A. 1907 'Introduction' In Jekyll, Walter 1907.

Winford, Donald 1979 'Grammatical hypercorrection and the notion of "system" in Creole language studies' *Carib* 1 pp. 67–83.

Wona 1899 *A selection of Anancy stories* Aston Gardner, Jamaica.

Wright, Joseph 1898 *The English Dialect Dictionary* vol. 1, Oxford University Press.

Wyld, Henry Cecil 1920 *History of Modern Colloquial English* T. Fisher Unwin, London.

Zachrisson, R. E. 1927 *English Pronunciation at Shakespeare's Time as taught by William Bullokar* Uppsala, Leipzig.

1982 *New Capital Arithmetic for the Caribbean* Bk. 2.

1983 *Caribbean Dialogue* vol. 1 no. 1 Journal of the Caribbean Association for the Teaching of English.

INDEX